R

TEACHING THE RESEARCH PAPER
From Theory to Practice, From Research to Writing

Edited by
JAMES E. FORD

The Scarecrow Press, Inc.
Metuchen, N.J., & London
1995

British Library Cataloguing-in-Publication data available

Library of Congress Cataloging-in-Publication Data

Teaching the research paper : from theory to practice, from research to writing /
edited by James E. Ford.
    p.   cm.
Includes bibliographical references.
ISBN 0-8108-2910-X (acid-free paper)
    1. English language—Rhetoric—Study and teaching. 2. Research—
Methodology—Study and teaching. 3. Report writing—Study and teach-
ing. I. Ford, James E., 1943– .
PE1404.T397   1995
808'.042—dc20   94-17407

CONTENTS

Contents

INTRODUCTION: THE NEED FOR *TRP*

This is the first book ever published on research paper instruction. What I mean by such a bald, categorical claim is that, although there are guides and manuals aplenty for students to consult as they strive to produce their own research papers, never before has a book addressed itself to those who assign the papers and instruct the students about how to perform their labors. One can begin to appreciate the significance of this general neglect of research paper instruction by focusing a little on the situation in one field, English studies, which by historical accident has inherited the primary responsibility for research paper instruction at both the high school and college levels. (Historians probably come second after English teachers, though teachers in some other disciplines are not far behind; whether they *teach* it or not, almost all academic fields *require* some form of the research paper.)

As everyone knows, the field of English generates numerous volumes dedicated to the most specialized, obscure, and au courant aspects of the pedagogy of writing and literature; therefore, the following anomalies should be especially shocking: First, the previously noted absence of a book-length treatment of research paper instruction has persisted in spite of the fact that the research paper is taught at the college level in 84 percent of all freshman composition courses and in 40 percent of all advanced composition courses (no statistics exist for the elementary and secondary levels). Second, research paper instruction, which has been a common feature of the curriculum for over sixty years and now consumes about a third of the freshman and advanced composition courses in which it is taught, had to wait until 1982 for its first published bibliography, though more than 200 relevant articles had already appeared. Third, research paper instruction has had only two sessions of the Modern Language Association, the largest professional organization of humanists, including English teachers, devoted to it, in spite of the fact that 56 percent of all freshman English teachers dedicate 29 percent of their teaching time to it.

The number of student- and teacher-hours expended on the research paper in other English graduate- and undergraduate-level courses is similarly immense. It just happens that the statistics cited above were drawn from a 1982 survey which focused on research paper instruction in the writing curriculum alone (James E. Ford and Dennis R. Perry, "Research Paper Instruction in Undergraduate Writing Programs: A National Survey," *College English* 44 [December 1982], 72–78). These statistics suggest that research paper instruction may be the most demanding responsibility within the English profession which has yet to be "professionalized." It has been ignored in the periodic overviews of the profession conducted by MLA, NCTE, and CEA, the profession's major organizations. The annual and semiannual bibliographies published in the major writing journals omit it completely. In fact, some of the editors of these publications have admitted to rejecting material addressing research paper instruction issues because, as one of them wrote to me, they have "reservations about the research paper as a concept." (As a *combined* average, *College English* and *College Composition and Communication,* the two most important relevant periodicals, have published fewer than one article on research paper instruction every two years since the first one appeared in 1923.)

As the statistics already quoted show, ignoring research paper instruction has not made it go away. Nor is it likely to. A comparison of these statistics with those gathered by Ambrose Manning in 1961 ("The Present Status of the Research Paper in Freshman English: A National Survey," *College Composition and Communication* 12 [May 1961], 73–78) witnesses to the widespread persistence of the research paper in departments of English. Manning found that in 1961, 83 percent of colleges and universities were requiring a research paper in the freshman course, leading him to conclude that "the research paper has more status presently than any other one thing in the Freshman English Program." Whatever may have been the fortunes of the research paper throughout the intervening twenty-year period—there are indications that it suffered somewhat in the 1960s— the 1982 survey revealed trends toward an *increase* in research paper instruction. The offerings had increased during the preceding five-year period in slightly over 20 percent of both freshman and advanced programs (decreasing in about 7 percent and 4 percent, respectively). In 1982, plans to augment the requirement were reported in 7 percent of the lower-level programs and in almost 8 percent of the advanced. None of the 370 schools responding to the survey had eliminated a research paper requirement in five years and only two were planning to do so.

As in Manning's time and in 1982, the research paper remains today an extremely strong feature of the curriculum (again, not only in English). However, I would not equate strength with "status," in the sense of high position or prestige, as Manning seems to have done. The neglect of—the outright antipathy toward—the subject on the part of many of the profession's leaders, as well as the frequent painful moans one hears from a great number of colleagues, puts me in mind of my four-year-old son's reaction to green beans: "I hate 'em but I eat 'em." (The response of a smaller, though still sizable, proportion of English teachers more closely approximates that of my daughter, two years old at the time, to the same vegetable: "I hate 'em but I *don't* eat 'em!") Surveys of the state of research paper instruction within the other disciplines in which it looms large would surely reveal similar responses.

Teaching the Research Paper is for secondary and college teachers in all academic fields who like to teach the research paper; it is also for those who do not like teaching it but do so anyway, for whatever compelling reasons; and it is for those who neither like nor teach. It is also—especially—for those who have not yet made up their minds. All the above are invited to engage their fellow teachers from a number of fields who herein provide essays which debate the theoretical nature and value—the very existence—of the research paper, and also offer some very practical ideas about how to teach it. The theory section begins with the research paper debate, in which are argued propositions as to whether there is such a thing as the research paper to be taught and, even if it does exist, whether there are any practical benefits to be realized from teaching it. Some of the points raised in the debate are then examined more closely in essays which attempt to understand the research paper as a type of writing, to understand it in its rhetorical context. A fairly general overview of the present and possible future state of the research paper concludes this theoretical division and serves as a bridge to the second major portion of *TRP*, dealing with the practicalities of research paper instruction. Of special note in this practice section are the discussions of the roles of libraries and librarians in the research and writing process. One of the biggest problems in the assigning of research papers, which are usually library papers, is that the assigning teachers have been too little concerned with the library research portion of the task. Next, and perhaps of most interest to classroom teachers who want to know how to design an entire research paper course or a unit within a course next term—if not, indeed, what to do next Monday in a class already underway—a generous selection of essays and notes offers eminently practical suggestions which range from enlightenment on how to create a research paper course for a class of minority students to hints on handling that old bugaboo, plagiarism. (Readers should be open to the possibility that an article in one section may serve a purpose formally assigned to another section. For example, two essays which explore the rhetorical context of the research paper also give the outlines of two quite different research paper courses, and one piece assigned to the libraries and librarians section describes a three- to five-week unit on the research paper.) Each section is followed by a short bibliography listing additional resources on related topics.

The majority of essays which comprise *TRP* were written especially for the collection; others were selected, as were many of the bibliographic items scattered throughout this volume, from "Research Paper Instruction: Comprehensive Bibliography of Periodical Sources" (compiled by James E. Ford, Sharla Rees, and David L. Ward, *The Bulletin of Bibliography* 39 [June 1982], 84–98; the bibliography is available in a preliminary version through the ERIC system [ED 197363]). Additionally, more current items were drawn from a careful search of materials published since the 1982 bibliography appeared. This search revealed a growing interest in research paper instruction: compare the well over 300 items which have appeared during the past ten years with the 200-item total for the fifty-year period preceding 1982. These post-1982 articles reveal that research paper instruction has benefited from current developments in a number of fields, including process-oriented writing theories—even postmodernist critical theories; computerization, both for word processing and on-line data-base searching; and minority and ESL concerns. The reprinted articles were selected primarily because of their high quality, usefulness, and suggestiveness, and because they represent the variety of resources available. Some were also chosen because, even if their existence is known, they are difficult to obtain. The reader will note that most of the essays written especially for *TRP* have notes; that is, they are researched papers. Almost none of the 200-plus articles published up to 1982, and relatively few since then, show any awareness at all that anyone else had ever addressed the topic under discussion. (Too typically, a 1988 article offering a "A New Approach to the Research Assignment in College Composition Classes" through the use of reviews of plays reproduces in its essentials a 1957 description of a unit which employs movie reviews.) Many of the contributors to this volume have recognized previous contributions in order to advance beyond them. This attempt at cumulative growth is a sign of professionalism, as is the concern with both theoretical and rhetorical issues which is apparent in some of the essays. The essays and bibliographies are offered together as a vade mecum for the first stages on the way to a more professional concern in all academic fields with research paper instruction. It is the hope of all the contributors to *TRP* that their readers will use their work to make still further progress. To those who would reject these intellectually and pedagogically nourishing offerings out of hand, I issue the time-honored challenge of a parent to a child frowning over her beans: How do you know you don't like 'em if you don't try 'em?

James E. Ford
University of Nebraska–Lincoln

FROM THEORY . . .

Theoretical Pros and Cons

THE "RESEARCH PAPER" IN THE WRITING COURSE: A NON-FORM OF WRITING

Richard L. Larson

Let me begin by assuring you that I do not oppose the assumption that student writers in academic and professional settings, whether they be freshmen or sophomores or students in secondary school or intend to be journalists or lawyers or scholars or whatever, should engage in research. I think they should engage in research, and that appropriately informed people should help them learn to engage in research in whatever field these writers happen to be studying. Nor do I deny the axiom that writing should incorporate the citation of the writer's sources of information when those sources are not common knowledge. I think that writers must incorporate into their writing the citation of their sources—and they must also incorporate the thoughtful, perceptive evaluation of those sources and of the contribution that those sources might have made to the writer's thinking. Nor do I oppose the assumption that a writer should make the use of appropriate sources a regular activity in the process of composing. I share the assumption that writers should identify, explore, evaluate, and draw upon appropriate sources as an integral step in what today we think of as the composing process.

In fact, let me begin with some positive values. On my campus, the Department of English has just decided to request a change in the description of its second-semester freshman course. The old description read as follows:

> This course emphasizes the writing of formal analytic essays and the basic methods of research common to various academic disciplines. Students will write frequently in and out of class. By the close of the semester, students will demonstrate mastery of the formal expository essay and the research paper. Individual conferences.

11

The department is asking our curriculum committee to have the description read:

> This course emphasizes the writing of analytical essays and the methods of inquiry common to various academic disciplines. Students will write frequently in and out of class. By the close of the semester, students will demonstrate their ability to write essays incorporating references to suitable sources of information and to use appropriate methods of documentation. Individual conferences.

I applauded the department for requesting that change, and I wrote to the college curriculum committee to say so.

While thinking about this paper—to take another positive example—I received from the University of Michigan Press a copy of the proofs of a forthcoming book titled *Researching American Culture: A Guide for Student Anthropologists,* sent to me because members of the English Composition Board of the University of Michigan had decided that the book might be of use as a supplementary text at Michigan in writing courses that emphasize writing in the academic disciplines. Along with essays by professional anthropologists presenting or discussing research in anthropology, the book includes several essays by students. In these essays the students, who had been instructed and guided by faculty in anthropology, report the results of research they have performed on aspects of American culture, from peer groups in high school to connections between consumption of alcohol and tipping in a restaurant, to mortuary customs, to sports in America. If anyone was in doubt about the point, the collection demonstrates that undergraduate students can conduct and report sensible, orderly, clear, and informative research in the discipline of anthropology. I am here to endorse, indeed to applaud, such work, not to question the wisdom of such collections as that from Michigan or to voice reservations about the capacity of undergraduates for research.

Why, then, an essay whose title makes clear a deep skepticism about "research papers"? First, because I believe that the generic "research paper" as a concept, and as a form of writing taught in a department of English, is not defensible. Second, because I believe that by saying that we teach the "research paper"—that is, by acting as if there is a generic concept defensibly entitled the "research paper"—we mislead students about the activities of both research and writing. I take up these propositions in order.

We would all agree to begin with, I think, that "research" is an activity in which one engages. Probably almost everyone reading this paper has engaged, at one time or another, in research. Most graduate seminars require research; most dissertations rely upon research, though of course many dissertations in English may also include analytical interpretation of texts written by one or more authors. Research can take many forms: systematically observing events, finding out what happens when one performs certain procedures in the laboratory, conducting interviews, tape-recording speakers' comments, asking human beings to utter aloud their thoughts while composing in writing or in another medium and noting what emerges, photographing phenomena (such as the light received in a telescope from planets and stars), watching the activities of people in groups, reading a person's letters and notes: all these are research. So, of course, is looking up information in a library or in newspaper files, or reading documents to which one has gained access under the Freedom of Information Act—though reading filed and cataloged documents is in many fields not the most important (it may be the least important) activity in which a "researcher" engages. We could probably define "research" generally as the seeking out of information new to the seeker, for a purpose, and we would probably agree that the researcher usually has to interpret, evaluate, and organize the information before it acquires value. And we would probably agree that the researcher has to present the fruits of his or her research, appropriately ordered and interpreted, in symbols that are intelligible to others, before that research can be evaluated and can have an effect. Most often, outside of mathematics and the sciences (and outside of those branches of philosophy which work with nonverbal symbolic notation), maybe also outside of music, that research is presented to others, orally or in writing, in a verbal language.

But research still is an activity; it furnishes the substance of much discourse and can furnish substance to almost any discourse except, possibly, one's personal reflections on one's own experience. But it is itself the subject—the substance—of no distinctively identifiable kind of writing. Research can inform virtually any writing or speaking if the author wishes it to do so; there is nothing of substance or content that differentiates one paper that draws on data from outside the author's own self from another such paper—nothing that can enable one to say that this paper is a "research paper" and that paper is not. (Indeed even an ordered, interpretive reporting of altogether personal experiences and responses can, if presented purposively, be a reporting of research.) I would assert therefore that the so-called research paper, as a generic, cross-disciplinary term, has no conceptual or substantive identity. If almost any paper is potentially a paper incorporating the fruits of research, the term "research paper" has virtually no value as an identification of a kind of substance in a paper. Conceptually, the generic term "research paper" is for practical purposes meaningless. We cannot usefully distinguish between "research papers" and non–research papers; we can distinguish only between papers that should have incorporated the fruits of research but did not, and those which did incorporate such results, or between those which reflect poor or inadequate research and those which reflect good or sufficient research. I would argue that most undergraduate papers reflect poor or inadequate research, and that our responsibility as instructors should be to assure that each student reflect in each paper the appropriate research, wisely conducted, for his or her subject.

I have already suggested that "research" can take a wide variety of forms, down to and including the ordered presentation of one's personal reflections and the interpretations of one's most direct experiences unmediated by interaction with others or by reference to identifiably external sources. (The form of research on composing known as "protocol analysis," or even the keeping of what some teachers of writing designate as a "process journal," if conducted by the giver of the protocol or by the writer while writing, might be such research.) If research can refer to almost any process by which data outside the immediate and purely personal experiences of the writer are gathered, then I suggest that just as the so-called research paper has no conceptual or substantive identity, neither does it have a procedural identity; the term does not necessarily designate any particular kind of data or any preferred procedure for gathering data. I would argue that the so-called research paper, as ordinarily taught by the kinds of texts I have reviewed, implicitly equates "research" with looking up books in the library and taking down information from those books. Even if there is going on in some departments of English instruction that gets beyond those narrow boundaries, the customary practices that I have observed for guiding the "research paper" assume a procedural identity for that paper that is, I think, nonexistent.

As the activity of research can take a wide variety of forms, so the presentation and use of research within discourse can take a wide variety of forms. Indeed I cannot imagine any identifiable design that any scholar in rhetoric has identified as a recurrent plan for arranging discourse which cannot incorporate the fruits of research, broadly construed. I am not aware of any kind or form of discourse, or any aim, identified by any student of rhetoric or any theorist of language or any investigator of discourse theory, that is distinguished primarily—or to any extent—by the presence of the fruits of "research" in its typical examples. One currently popular theoretical classification of discourse, that by James Kinneavy (*A Theory of Discourse* [Englewood Cliffs, N.J.: Prentice-Hall, 1971]), identifies some "aims" of discourse that might seem to furnish a home for papers based on research: "referential" and "exploratory" discourse. But, as I understand these aims, a piece of discourse does not require the presence of results of ordered "research" in order to fit into either of these classes, even though discourse incorporating the results of ordered research might fit there—as indeed it might under almost any other of Kinneavy's categories, including the category of "expressive" discourse. (All discourse is to a degree "expressive" anyway.) The other currently dominant categorization of examples of discourse— dominant even over Kinneavy's extensively discussed theory—is really a categorization based upon plans that organize discourse: narration (of completed events, of ongoing processes, of possible scenarios), causal analysis, comparison, analogy, and so on. None of these plans is differentiated from other plans by the presence within it of fruits of research; research can be presented, so far as I can see, according to any of these plans. And if one consults Frank J. D'Angelo's *A Conceptual Theory of Rhetoric* (Cambridge, Mass.: Winthrop, 1975), one will not find, if my memory serves me reliably, any category of rhetorical plan or any fundamental human cognitive process—D'Angelo connects all rhetorical plans with human cognitive processes—that is defined by the presence of the fruits of research. If there is a particular rhetorical form that is defined by the presence of results from research, then, I have not seen an effort to define that form and to argue that the results of research are what identify it as a form. I conclude that the "research paper," as now taught, has no formal identity, as it has no substantive identity and no procedural identity.

For me, then, very little is gained by speaking about and teaching, as a generic concept, the so-called research paper. If anything at all is gained, it is only the reminder that responsible writing normally depends on well-planned investigation of data. But much is lost by teaching the research paper in writing courses as a separately designated activity. For by teaching the generic "research paper" as a separate designated activity, instructors in writing signal to their students that there is a kind of writing that incorporates the results of research, and there are (by implication) many kinds of writing that do not and need not do so. "Research," students are allowed to infer, is a specialized activity that one engages in during a special course, or late in a regular semester or year, but that one does not ordinarily need to be concerned about and can indeed, for the most part, forget about. Designating the "research paper" as a separate project therefore seems to me to work against the purposes for which we allegedly teach the research paper: to help students familiarize themselves with ways of gathering, interpreting, drawing upon, and acknowledging data from outside themselves in their writing. By talking of the "research paper," that is, we undermine some of the very goals of our teaching.

We also meet two other, related difficulties. First, when we tend to present the "research paper" as in effect a paper based upon the use of the library, we misrepresent "research." Granted that a good deal of research in the field of literature is conducted in the library among books, much research that is still entitled to be called humanistic takes place outside the library. It can take place, as I mentioned earlier, wherever "protocol" research or writers' analyses of their composing processes take place; it can take place in the living room or study of an author who is being interviewed about his or her habits of working. It can take place in the home of an old farmer or rancher or weaver or potter who is telling a student about the legends or songs of his or her people, or about the historical process by which the speaker came from roots at home or abroad. Much research relies upon books, but books do not constitute the corpus of research data except possibly in one or two fields of study. If we teach the so-called research paper in such a way as to imply that all or almost all research is done in books and in libraries, we show our provincialism and degrade the research of many disciplines.

Second, though we pretend to prepare students to engage in the research appropriate to their chosen disciplines, we do not and cannot do so. Faculty in other fields may wish that we would relieve them of the responsibility of teaching their students to write about the research students do in those other fields, but I don't think that as teachers of English we can relieve them of that responsibility. Looking at the work of the students who contributed to the University of Michigan Press volume on *Researching American Culture,* I can't conceive of myself giving useful direction to those students. I can't conceive of myself showing them how to do the research they did, how to avoid pitfalls, assure representativeness of data, draw permissible inferences, and reach defensible conclusions. And, frankly, I can't conceive of many teachers of English showing these students what they needed to know either. I can't conceive of myself, or of very many colleagues (other than trained teachers of technical writing), guiding a student toward a report of a scientific laboratory experiment that a teacher of science would find exemplary. I can't conceive of myself or many colleagues guiding a student toward a well-designed experiment in psychology, with appropriate safeguards and controls and wise interpretation of quantitative and nonquantitative information. In each of these fields (indeed probably in each academic field) the term "research paper" may have some meaning—quite probably a meaning different from its meaning in other fields. Students in different fields do write papers reporting research. We in English have no business claiming to teach "research" when research in different academic disciplines works from distinctive assumptions and follows distinctive patterns of inquiry. Such distinctions in fact are what differentiate the disciplines. Most of us are trained in one discipline only and should be modest enough to admit it.

But let me repeat what I said when I started: that I don't come before you to urge that students of writing need not engage in "research." I think that they should engage in research. I think that they should understand that in order to function as educated, informed men and women they have to engage in research, from the beginning of and throughout their work as writers. I think that they should know what research can embrace, and I think that they should be encouraged to view research as broadly, and conduct it as imaginatively, as they can. I think that they should be held accountable for their opinions and should be required to say, from evidence, why they believe what they assert. I think that they should be led to recognize that data from "research" will affect their entire lives, and that they should know how to evaluate such data as well as to gather them. And I think that they should know their responsibilities for telling their listeners and readers where their data came from.

What I argue is that the profession of the teaching of English should abandon the concept of generic "research paper"—that form of what a colleague of mine has called "messenger service" in which a student is told that for this one assignment, this one project, he or she has to go somewhere (usually the library), get out some materials, make some notes, and present them to the customer neatly wrapped in footnotes and bibliography tied together according to someone's notion of a style sheet. I argue that the generic "research paper," so far as I am familiar with it, is a concept without an identity, and that to teach it is not only to misrepresent research but also quite often to pander to the wishes of faculty in other disciplines that we spare them a responsibility that they must accept. Teaching the generic "research paper" often represents a misguided notion of "service" to other departments. The best service we can render to those departments and to the students themselves, I would argue, is to insist that students recognize their continuing responsibility for looking attentively at their experiences; for seeking out, wherever it can be found, the information they need for the development of their ideas; and for putting such data at the service of every piece they write. That is one kind of service we can do to advance students' humanistic and liberal education.

This essay was presented as part of a panel of four papers at the MLA meeting in December 1981. It was originally published in *College English* (December 1982). Copyright 1982 by the National Council of Teachers of English. Reprinted with permission.

THE AIMS AND PROCESS OF THE RESEARCH PAPER

Robert A. Schwegler and Linda K. Shamoon

Many members of our department—and yours too, we suspect—have stopped teaching the research paper in composition courses because the papers they receive are so often disappointing and because they believe that freshmen and sophomores may not be sophisticated enough to do the kind of thinking necessary for a worthwhile research paper. These instructors say they view the research paper not simply as a review of information found in secondary sources, but as an argument with sources which expands the student's (and the reader's) view of the subject. But, they complain, students seem overwhelmed by what they find in outside sources and are incapable of weaving the information they have gathered into an argument that presents and defends their point of view.

Composition textbooks and writing teachers have tried to deal with this problem in three ways, each of which has proven inadequate in some respect.

One answer has been to provide better training in gathering and arranging information (that is, library and documentation skills). Though these skills have some value, they still are likely to have little impact on the quality of the papers students write in composition courses or in other courses because academic research is a process of inquiry, problem solving, and argument, not simply an information-gathering process.

A second answer has been to place considerable stress on the argumentative nature of the research paper. But though academic research papers contain arguments, they cannot be called argumentative in aim or structure because they do not focus on altering the values, ideas, or emotional attitudes of an audience or on moving the audience to action of some kind: intellectual, emotional, or physical.

19

The kind of research papers scholars write and reward their students for writing is, instead, what James Kinneavy calls "scientific discourse": writing that makes interpretive statements about some aspect of reality (a poem, a historical event, a social movement, or a chemical reaction) and demonstrates the validity of these statements (*A Theory of Discourse* [Englewood Cliffs, N.J.: Prentice-Hall, 1971], 88–89).

A third answer has been that we should give up teaching the research paper altogether because it bears little relationship to the writing that students are asked to do in other courses. Yet students are often required to write papers based on research, and the strategies appropriate for these papers are easy enough to recognize—and to make part of research paper instruction in composition courses.

As we see it, the first step in a satisfactory answer to the research paper problem is to recognize the considerable difference between the way students view the research paper (and have been taught to view it) and the way most college instructors and other researchers view it. The second step is to begin to base research paper instruction on a sound understanding of the features of academic research writing, features that characterize the professional writing of most college instructors and that form a model that instructors rely on—often unconsciously—to evaluate student papers.

We became acutely aware of differing views of the research paper when we interviewed instructors and students about their views of the research process, the aims of research, the forms of research writing, and the appropriate evaluation standards for academic research papers. The responses revealed not only the differences in outlook of the novice and the professional, but also substantially different attitudes toward the research process and the aim, forms, and audience of the research paper. These contradictory perspectives go a long way toward explaining the dissatisfaction many instructors feel when the have finished grading a set of research papers and the irritation students feel when they receive a poor grade on a paper they were sure did all that a research paper is supposed to do.

When asked why they write research papers and why teachers assign the papers, students responded:

> "to learn more about a topic"
> "to learn how to use the library"
> "to show how much you know"

> "information . . . they want a small topic where you can get just
> about everything on it"
> "they want to see specifics . . . to see how well you can use your
> research skills."

When asked about the process of researching and writing, students
offered the following scenario:

> "You usually don't get around to it for a while, but when you
> do you start out with a little bit of an idea; then you get a lot of
> books and put the information on note cards: you keep the note
> cards and bibliography sorted out: then you put together the
> pieces of information that are related, start on a rough outline,
> and finally write the paper."

When asked what standards they expect instructors to apply, the
students said,

> "The instructor knows about the topic; he knows what you
> should have in that paper; he's going to look for those points in
> the paper."
> "They'll say use Kate Turabian . . . go by the book . . . every
> page is laid out."
> "Depends on the teacher . . . some are too mixed up in
> grammar and punctuation; they'll ignore the content."

These comments show that students generally view the research
paper as informative in aim, not argumentative, much less analytical;
as factual rather than interpretive; designed to show off knowledge of
library skills and documentation procedures. The paper is viewed as
an exercise in information gathering, not an act of discovery; the
audience is assumed to be a professor who already knows about the
subject and is testing the student's knowledge and information-
gathering ability. Thus, according to the students, evaluation is (and
should be) based on the quantity and quality of the information
presented, on correctness of documentation, but not on form and
style (English papers excepted).

When asked about the purpose of research and the research paper,
instructors replied that the aim is to test a theory, to follow up on
previous research, or to explore a problem posed by other research or
by events. For most instructors, however, research is a "continuous
development," a pursuit of an elusive truth:

"What you do in research is to try to throw open a window on the world at a given point; open up the window and see what it looks like *there;* but as soon as that point has been identified it has already moved into the past so that one would not expect it to remain the same."

For most instructors, the research and writing process follows a clear but complex pattern:

"The original focus begins with getting interested in an idea during reading or a review of the literature and getting a sense of where the field stands theoretically and methodologically—and jotting down notes about problems, drawbacks to the research, how theoretical and methodological ideas can be improved. From there I would say, after a considerable amount of reading, how I would do it better, what research approach I would use to fill in a gap, answer a question, compare two theories—to me it's a giant puzzle and I try to assess how well the pieces fit together and then I design a research project to add more pieces to the puzzle or clarify the edges, or build a new puzzle."

"The community of scholars (peers) working in the area and the classroom, too, are sources of ideas . . . there is a certain amount of serendipity involved."

"Studies have shown that virtually the last place you go is the library . . . the first step is to call around to colleagues to identify sources . . . another start is to pick up a bibliography through *Bibliographic Index.*"

"I know the whole strategy. I'll have a couple dozen sentences in my head, particularly introductory sentences, analytic sentences, and conclusion sentences, [and then I'll sit down to write]."

And the instructors also have specific ideas about how research and research papers should be structured—and about how they are usually evaluated by the other scholars that make up the intended audience:

"There is a continuous degree of uncertainty through the process . . . but when you write the paper you really have an obligation to state your views and to state what you have perceived or concluded in strong enough terms so that there is some validity to the statement."

"If you don't follow the appropriate paradigm, then other
scholars will attack your work."
"I look for a formula in every article that comes into our
journal. . . . [An empirical article, for example:] Introduction,
theoretical overview, justification of the issue, literature review,
methods, sample, measurements, design, data, analysis, summary, references, footnotes. . . . The review of research must be
analysis, not just a summary; it must tell me what the scholars
said and what it means in relationship to the whole . . . each
individual analysis is part of the puzzle and I want to know how
much of the puzzle is complete."

Academics view the research paper as analytical and interpretive,
an attempt to explore some aspect of the world and to make verifiable
statements about it. Research generally begins with an observation or
a need for knowledge which is then explored in a systematic manner.
Projects often arise from the concerns of a community of scholars or
in response to the work of a particular scholar. The community also
forms the intended audience for research papers, and its expectations,
as realized for example in the editorial policies of journals, help guide
choice of topics and writing strategies. Though the instructors we
interviewed see the research process as open-ended, often tentative,
they see the research paper as restricted in aim and conventional in
style and structure.

The contrasts between the instructors' view and the students' view
are important. Students view the research paper as a close-ended,
informative, skills-oriented exercise written for an expert audience by
novices pretending to be experts. No wonder then that students'
papers often roam freely over the subject area, are devoid of focus, and
are loaded down with quotes. Academics, on the other hand, view the
research paper as open-ended and interpretive, written for an audience of fellow inquirers who have specific expectations of logic,
structure, and style. Academic research papers reflect this view by
being narrowly focused, aware of the scholarly audience, and frequently tentative in advancing a conclusion.

Our students' view of the research paper is echoed and supported
by the instruction they receive in most composition classes and by
textbooks. Some textbook writers acknowledge the considerable gap
between the kind of research writing scholars do and the kind we
teach, but they argue that informative or argumentative papers are
appropriate work for novices. *The Research Paper Workbook,* by Ellen

Strenski and Madge Manfred (New York: Longman, 1981), is typical:

> At this stage of your career you are an apprentice scholar and will be concerned mostly with secondary research, which means finding out what the recognized authorities on a particular topic have to say about a topic that has caught your interest. (P. 2)

While this "apprenticeship" argument contains a certain amount of truth, it is nonetheless misleading. Instructors in content-area courses do not expect undergraduates to produce fully developed research articles like those which appear in scholarly journals. Yet they do expect students' work to adhere to the aims of academic research writing and to begin to display its stylistic and structural features. In our conversations with instructors and in related studies of instructors' responses to students' research papers (discussed in our unpublished paper, "Teaching the Research Paper: A New Approach to an Old Problem," and in a paper presented by Professor Schwegler at a meeting of the North East MLA in March 1979, "Form and Aim in Analytic Writing"), it became clear that college instructors view the research paper as a means to accomplish one of the primary goals of college instruction: to get students to think in the same critical, analytical, inquiring mode as instructors do—like a literary critic, a sociologist, an art historian, or a chemist. And it was also clear that many teachers draw paper assignments and evaluation standards from their view of what a scholarly research article is and does, adapted of course to an undergraduate level.

Thus while it makes sense to treat the undergraduate research paper as part of an apprenticeship, we need to make sure that the aim, structure, and style of the papers we assign conform to the kinds of papers that content-area instructors will expect from our students. The features of the academic research paper are easy enough to identify and convey to undergraduates. And because the conventions for the most part transcend disciplinary boundaries (except in superficial matters like use of personal pronouns and documentation style), they can be made part of research paper instruction in composition courses and in lower-level, content-area courses.

What, then, are the aims, structures, and stylistic features of the research papers (or articles) college instructors write and also expect their students to write?

The aim of the academic research paper is twofold, reflecting the duality of the research process it aims to represent. The research paper is at once open-ended and limited—exploratory and demonstrative. It begins with the known, as defined by current scholarship, and moves into the unknown, attempting to pursue an admittedly elusive "truth." At the same time the statements it makes about the nature of its subject are generally limited to those whose validity can be demonstrated with a high degree of probability according to the method guiding the inquiry and according to evidence drawn from the subject. This emphasis on method of investigation is one of the distinguishing features of research writing. Reliance on a particular method of inquiry limits the kind of statements that can be made about a subject; as Kinneavy puts it, "scientific discourse consists in a consideration of one facet of an object and the making of certain kinds of assertions . . . about this facet" (p. 88). In addition, since it is generally difficult to make statements of high probability about a broad topic, most academic research papers are severely restricted in scope, dealing for example with a single aspect of a poem, a central chapter in a novel, or a single facet of the structure of DNA. There is usually an attempt, however, to relate the conclusions reached about a single facet to the whole, to treat a single chapter as a key to a whole novel, or the habits of a social subgroup as central to an understanding of the whole culture.

These then are the underlying aims or features of the research paper: awareness of scholarly content: method of investigation; specific subject (data); conclusion abut the nature of the subject; and relationship of specific subject to broader subject area. And these underlying features manifest themselves in research papers as essential textual features, that is, as conventions. They appear at the beginning of a paper as indicators of the range and perspective of the study, in the body as guides to the rhetorical strategies, and in the conclusion as a restatement of the point of view of the study and a statement about its implications. (See Appendix A.)

The opening section of an academic research paper, regardless of field, cites previous research, usually in an attempt to limit the subject or problem and to provide an intellectual context for the study. The introduction also introduces the broad subject area and specifies what limited aspects of it are to be examined and used as evidence for the conclusions. In addition it specifies the method of inquiry and states in some form (as thesis or hypothesis) the conclusions whose validity is to be demonstrated or tested. (A sample is provided in Appendix B.)

These conventions are features of professional research papers regardless of discipline, though the manner in which they are presented may differ somewhat according to field, subject, and the writer's style. We also have found that these features generally are present in those student research papers which are highly rated by content-area instructors and absent, to varying degrees, in lower-ranked papers. It is not entirely clear whether it is the absence of the surface conventions or of the conceptual patterns they represent that affects the graders' response, but these features do appear to be closely linked. What *is* clear is that the conventions and the strategies they represent should be part of research paper instruction, in an elementary form at least. One note of caution: while a few of the conventions appear at the beginning of the kinds of research papers presented in composition handbooks, important ones, like the method marker, usually do not; and those conventions which do appear have rather different functions in an informative or argumentative paper.

The overall rhetorical and conceptual structure of academic research papers reflects the structure of the research process, a process which is not, as most composition texts suggest, a matter of simple information gathering or a search for support for an argumentative thesis. And though it is open-ended, academic research is not formless, as most of us are aware; it begins with a review of current knowledge and then moves through a variation of one of four basic patterns, which in turn influence the organization of the research paper. These patterns can be distinguished by their relationship to previous scholarly discussion and by the roles filled by the other elements of the research process. The patterns are as follows:

1. *Review of research.* This pattern takes as its subject not some external phenomenon, but the process of scholarly debate itself. It reviews the methods, data, and conclusions of prior research, pointing out emerging patterns of agreement and conflict and attempting through critical analysis to shed new light on the development of research in a particular area.

2. *Application or implementation of a theory.* This pattern consists of the application of a generally accepted theory to a new situation or subject; the theory is generally not questioned, and the burden of proof lies in showing that it can be used to explain or understand the new phenomenon. For example, a theory developed to

account for the structure of a specific social group or even a set of poems can often be applied to similar subjects.

3. *Refute, refine, or replicate prior research.* Much research begins when a scholar takes issue with the assertions, data, or methodology of someone else's research. The disagreement leads to a reexamination, a remeasurement, or a reinterpretation, and eventually to a new set of assertions. Other research, related in pattern though not direction, may accept the original research and attempt to corroborate it.

4. *Testing a hypothesis.* This is the classic and in some ways most challenging pattern of research. It begins with the isolation and close observation of a phenomenon, followed by the formulation of tentative assertions about the phenomenon (hypotheses), and concludes with the testing of the assertions through observation and measurement of the phenomenon they purport to describe. Because this language may seem somewhat foreign to our enterprise, let us point out that Cleanth Brooks' classic essay in *The Well-Wrought Urn* (New York: Harcourt Brace and World, 1947), "Keats' Sylvan Historian: History Without Footnotes," fits within it.

Though the first pattern, the review of research, might seem particularly useful for undergraduates, it can be rather tricky, as most of us no doubt are aware. Undergraduate classes at all levels, however, make use of the second pattern, the application of a theory, whether it be in asking students to apply a method of analysis used in class to a novel they have read on their own or in asking them to apply an anthropological theory to an understanding of a culture. And as these examples suggest, the use of this pattern is not limited to research papers: it appears frequently in brief critical papers and examination essays as well. The third pattern, the response to prior research, is also widely used, though most often in upper-level courses; it is particularly useful for research papers, and it appears as well in the classic essay question, "Scholar X says the following about Shakespeare's comedies. . . . Refute, extend, or modify this criticism based on your knowledge of the plays."

In short, these patterns play an important role in the undergraduate research papers assigned in content courses and in other forms of academic writing as well. In an appropriately simplified form they should be made part of instruction in the research paper, both as patterns of thought and patterns of expression. Care should be taken, however, to distinguish between standard exercises in evaluating source material, which are appropriate to argumentative and informative writing, and the development of an awareness of research patterns, which is an exercise in understanding academic discourse.

To sum up, we suggest that the aims of the academic research paper and its conventions are limited, even formulaic, enough to be made part of instruction in the research paper. And we also suggest that it is important to take note of these features because students will find in other courses that the features become the grounds for evaluation. Implementing these recommendations in practical ways is another important matter, of course, but not one we are equipped to deal with here. We would suggest, however, that simply presenting students with a listing of the surface features of the academic research paper is a practice likely to encourage them to produce papers that are sterile exercises. The proper approach is to view the research paper as a process of thought and expression and to recognize its limits as well as its strengths.

Appendix A

1. Indicators of range of study
   a. Statements that identify the phenomenon under study (chunk of reality; subject of paper; source of data)
   b. Statements summarizing other research or professional experience (may serve to indicate areas of current debate among knowledgeable readers; may help limit the aspects of the phenomenon to be investigated)
   c. Statements indicating method of investigation
   d. Statement of hypothesis or thesis
2. Indicators of treatment of research material and pattern of discussion (frequently derived from method of investigation)
   a. Section headings
   b. Topic sentence or boundary sentences
   c. Lexical markers
3. Conclusion
   a. Restatement of thesis or hypothesis
   b. Limitations of study
   c. Indications of validity or reliability of the study's outcome
   d. Paths for future study

Appendix B

The indicators of range are usually found in one form or another in the opening section of a research paper, as in James Kinney's "Classifying Heuristics" (*College Communication and Composition* 30 [1979], 351–356).

Statement #1
(Phenomenon under study)⎯

⎡ Thinking and writing go together, but how?
Interest in invention is widespread; heuristic procedures to
⎣ stimulate thinking proliferate.

Statement #2
(limit phenomenon; cite previous research; cite current
debate)
⎯⎯⎯⎯⎯⎯⎯⎯⎯⎯⎯⎯

⎡ Ann Berthoff has spoken for the
need for "critical inquiry into . . .
the simultaneity of thinking and
writing, of the role of consciousness
in composing." Lee Odell has posed
specific questions about the forms
and functions of heuristics. For a
broader understanding of heuristics, however, and as part of an inquiry into the role of consciousness in the composing process, I
think we must erase the distinction
Odell makes between the Macrorie/
Elbow–style free writing and
heuristics. Odell restricts heuristics to "systematic inquiry procedures" and labels them "process of
⎣ conscious inquiry."

Statement #4 (hypothesis) ⎯⎯
Statement #3 (method marker)

⎡ My intention here is to demonstrate that other classes of heuristics exist besides the systematic
type accepted by Odell and to
show that free writing is also a pro-
⎣ cess of conscious inquiry. (P. 351)

This essay was presented as part of a panel of four papers at the MLA meeting in December 1981. It was originally published in *College English* (December 1982). Copyright 1982 by the National Council of Teachers of English. Reprinted with permission.

Practical Pros and Cons

APOLOGIA PRO PEDAGOGIA MEA: OR, HOW I KICKED THE RESEARCH PAPER HABIT AND LEARNED TO TEACH FRESHMAN ENGLISH

Joseph F. Tuso

In the earlier battles of the American Revolutionary War, British troops, advancing in an open, orderly fashion, were more than once devastated by withering musket fire coming from an enemy concealed behind shrubs, rocks, and trees. When a British company commander was asked at an official inquiry why he had continued to use such a disastrous tactic, the officer replied, "But we have always done it that way."

When we who teach freshman English are called to that great, final teaching evaluation in the sky, and the divine Master Teacher asks us why we taught the research paper in our freshman courses, I suspect that many of us, too, will have to reply in the words of that apocryphal British officer, "But we have always done it that way."

After fifteen years, both as professor and chairman, of observing closely a hundred English professors at three different institutions, I now believe that most faculty teach the research paper because they *like* to. Perhaps they even *need* to. With the research paper thus embedded in our professorial viscera, I have little delusion that I can change your mind on the subject. I intend only to explain why I personally no longer include the paper in my freshman teaching.

To define my terms, by the research paper I mean the usual, formal, written study of 1,500 to 4,000 words with notes, bibliography, and the usual multiple smudges and typos. By the freshman sequence, I mean the equivalent of two three-semester-hour courses enrolling freshmen with English aptitudes ranging from the 20th to 70th percentile, excluding both basic English and honors students.

Let me confess at the outset that I, too, once taught the research paper. I teased my freshmen with topics; I titillated them with tours of the library; I relished each pathetic note card; I had numerous one-on-one conferences; I graded the final product with religious fervor, commenting on almost every jot and tittle. I taught the paper at first because I had to, later because I was accustomed to, all the while thinking very little of *why* I was teaching it. But since, to use a cliché, the unexamined course is not worth teaching, some serious reflection later helped me realize just how much my dogged determination to teach the research paper was costing my students and me.

Historically, the research paper assignment is a Johnny-come-lately to American English departments. America's first colleges and universities were teaching institutions largely patterned after the British model. They prepared people for the ministry or law, as did Yale and Harvard, or for cultured professional living, as did Virginia, or for practical pursuits, as did Ben Franklin's Pennsylvania. Grammar, rhetoric, and philology were the staples of English language study.[1] Students didn't write research papers simply because there was then no research.

The modern approach to research developed first in the universities of nineteenth-century Prussia, then crossed the Atlantic and took root in America just before World War I. We don't know where or when an American student was assigned the first research paper, but by 1929 a number of major American educators held that it "occupied a justified position in the educational process."[2]

Perhaps the first research paper was assigned at Harvard, where students had to draw from the Great Books to support their ideas. Then later perhaps one professor, who either didn't like all of the Great Books or hadn't read all of them himself, one day assigned his students a paper on *the* Great Book he liked the most. And the students could of course quote from secondary materials about *the* Great Book, which by this time were beginning to pile up in the Harvard library. The paper, assigned first to upper-division or graduate students, was later assigned to lower-division and even freshman students, and thus the freshman research paper was born.

Next English literary history replaced grammar, rhetoric, and philology in our departments and held sway until the 1940s, and with American literary history arising in the 1920s, the climate was almost perfect for growing bumper crops of research papers. The later arrival of literary criticism finally institutionalized the paper at all levels at a time when secondary works began to outnumber primary works by ten to one, then a hundred to one. From 1940 to 1960, everyone—professors, graduate students, undergraduates—was busily writing or grading research papers of various sorts, including the macroresearch paper, the doctoral dissertation.

With the 1960s, however, literacy test scores plummeted to record lows as many universities and colleges across the land opened their doors wider. Research began to take new directions to help solve the new problems that accompanied the great influx of poorly prepared students, and rhetoric and composition theory came into their own as disciplines.

But many English departments and many English professors are still teaching in the pre-1960s world. As UCLA's Richard Lanham has said, most English departments today are perfectly well equipped to teach students who no longer exist—white, middle-class, Anglo-Saxon, Protestant eighteen-year-olds.[3] And it was exactly this group who had formerly written all those research papers.

We are now at the point where the composition and rhetoric specialist has the inside track on merit raises, mobility, and promotion while we are still offering the standard English literature courses that fewer and fewer students seem to want. No wonder the mild envy or even downright antagonism which some professors of literature feel toward professors of composition and rhetoric. Now we know how professors of classics, philology, and rhetoric felt sixty years ago as they and their beloved studies were replaced by literary history and literary criticism.

In this historical context, the freshman research paper—which indeed serves a purpose which I promise to discuss later—has become a sticking point in the current battle between the so-called liberal-humanists, on the one side, and the so-called utilitarian-pragmatists, on the other. The latter feel that they *must* teach the paper to be true to their professional values; the former feel the paper *must* be abandoned, and for the same reason. Somewhere in all of this the freshman student is being lost sight of, just as in most battles the innocent bystanders often suffer the most. What we need today in the profession, however, are liberal-utilitarian-humanistic-pragmatists, or (as they used to be called) Renaissance men and women, who will have wisdom to teach in freshman English what is best taught there for the sake of the students.

My own reasons for abandoning the research paper are rather simple. My school, New Mexico State University, has no sequence, but a single four-hour freshman course. I simply cannot waste 20 to 25 percent of this course on an exercise of such dubious value when there is so much else to do. Depending on their major, most of our students do write research papers later in advanced composition, or in business or technical writing courses, which are taught by our English faculty. And we've found that our students are far more ready and motivated in these later courses to do a solid job in researching and writing a report than they were as freshmen.

But even if we had a six-hour, two-course freshman sequence, I still would not teach the paper. My freshman students need to write more than I can grade, at least in the old-fashioned sense of comprehensive marking. They need to lose their writing apprehensions by learning to succeed in and even enjoy numerous writing assignments from sentences, through paragraphs, through essays. They need to read and learn to analyze many samples of excellent writing from literature and from the essay. They need to discover their own voices and to learn how their own writing process works—and doesn't work. All of my experience has shown me that doing one research paper doesn't help much toward any of this, and we needn't feel guilty in the freshman course if we concentrate on developing our students' analytic skills. For most of our students, synthetic skills are better developed when they later have the maturity and motivation required for more complex undertakings, and the research paper is far more complex than we care to admit.

In a hard-nosed, iconoclastic article in the *Association of Departments of English Bulletin,* William Harmon gives us a startlingly simple course sequence:

> Freshman English, a one-year course in reading and writing, to be taken by all freshmen without exception. . . . The writing should not exceed one page per week. Anybody who can write one good page can write two hundred good pages.[4]

Harmon's course obviously excludes the research paper. As for the reading in the course, Harmon holds that

> between the reader and the thing to be read, nothing ought to be allowed to supervene or intervene: no teacher, no introduction, no outline, no summary, no historical or biographical

setting, no annotation, no explanation, nothing . . . The primary job of a teacher is to get the hell out of the way.[5]

Harmon's idea is fascinating, but of course we've never done it that way. If we did, if we took the time to help our freshmen develop their analytical skills with the rigor which that takes, and if our students could then successfully write about what they've learned and how they've learned it, we'd be doing our job in a freshman course that would obviously have no time for the research paper.

A final, hyperbolic statement by Harmon further highlights the value which he places on such rigorous work:

> I am not sure that we shouldn't award the [English] degree cum laude to anyone who can show proof of having thoroughly read *one* good book. Anybody who has mastered *ten* good books has earned a full professorship with permanent tenure.[6]

The level of accomplishment which Harmon postulates is lofty indeed, and is not very often reached in our courses. But if we came even close to Harmon's standard, could we still believe that the time our freshmen spend on the research paper is time well invested? I think not.

Why do we professors depend so heavily on research in our literary work and yet ignore its value so utterly in assisting our teaching? There is no body of convincing evidence that teaching the research paper in the freshman course is worthwhile, yet there is ample evidence that many other kinds of activities are indeed valuable. Our departments must articulate our goals and objectives in the freshman course, and each of us must do the same. And there are experts to whom we can turn—Kenneth Pike, Richard Young, Mina Shaughnessy, Ken Macrorie, Peter Elbow, James Britton, Janet Emig. Even a cursory reading of the major works of these researchers reveals that there is so very much demonstrably good that *can* be done in the freshman sequence that we simply cannot afford to waste time on the research paper any longer.

Historically, just as there was never any significant reason that the teaching of composition should be entrusted to English professors,[7] there is no compelling reason that the teaching of the research paper should be entrusted to us. Might the teaching of writing be better served, in fact, were we as a profession to drop the research paper completely. If we did this, might not departments of psychology, history, or chemistry, as some of them are already doing, teach more formal writing in their disciplines to students who are more prepared and motivated toward the task than are our freshmen?

Textbook publishers seem convinced that we all teach the freshman research paper. A fine composition text which I used in the fall of 1980, *The Practical Writer: Paragraph to Theme,*[8] is devoted 23 percent to the research paper, 27 percent to grammar and punctuation, and only 50 percent to rhetoric and composition. If I had a three-course sequence and could have students do several research papers in the third course, this is the book I would use. But I have never had the luxury of a three-course freshman sequence.

Another popular text, Jim Corder's *Handbook of Current English,* devotes but 12 percent to the research paper.[9] In his introduction to that section, Corder lists the supposed benefits of students' doing such a paper.[10] Since he gives all of the usual reasons I've heard to support the exercise, I will discuss each of his wrongheaded statements in turn.

Corder's first promise to his freshman reader is that, by preparing the paper, he or she will gain practice in exploring the possibilities of a subject and in limiting it satisfactorily to the required length. Balderdash. Not much practice, not much exploration, and generally not much limitation. The student realizes here that he or she must somehow come up with 1,500 to 4,000 words on a subject which he or she would rather not have to write at such length about in the first place.

Corder next promises that, through the research paper, the freshman will gain access to the resources of the library and training in the most efficient ways of locating information. Tommyrot. The student will get an introduction to the library, and a glimpse of the shelves and perhaps the microfilm reader. When did you or I really begin to feel comfortable in the library doing research? When did we first know we were using the library well? Some colleagues I've asked recently tell me that they still don't feel comfortable and confident in the library. I myself didn't know I was using research tools effectively until I had almost completed my master's thesis, and today one can earn a master's at many first-rate schools without even doing a thesis. Use the library? We're kidding ourselves, and cheating our students.

Corder's third promise is the one that we probably cherish most as our major reason for assigning the paper in the first place. After the first two golden promises have been fulfilled, the student will now gain practice in using source material intelligently, in choosing between what is useful and what is not, in evaluating the ideas of others, and in organizing and interpreting the information. However, the student will equally gain practice in using source material foolishly, in choosing what is useless, in confusing the ideas of others, and in misorganizing and misinterpreting the information. And in the freshman course, he or she will do all of this only once. Corder's freshman must be a quick study.

Promise four is far less lofty and is perhaps the silliest one of all. The research paper exercise, says Corder, will acquaint the student with the documentation and manuscript form typically expected in academic work and in reports and papers prepared for publication. But just what is that documentation *typically* expected in academic work? The *MLA Style Sheet?* Turabian? One of dozens of others? What is academic work? The arts? The sciences? Astrology? And is there *a* documentation and manuscript form typical of papers presented for publication, or are there many? I feel a bit guilty for carping at Corder here, since I used a similar ploy with my students in the early days. "If you can master this system," I would tell them, "and are consistent in its use throughout the paper, you'll later have no trouble using whatever system you must use." What a stupid phony I was. Unless we use the documentation system appropriate to our discipline very frequently, we inevitably forget many of the details. I *still* have to refer freely to the *MLA Style Sheet* when I'm preparing a piece, and I use it properly now because I'm motivated to, not because of the research paper I did in freshman English thirty years ago. Just how useful to the student is Corder's nodding acquaintance with all of these complex conventions?

Corder's final promise, his most blatant dishonesty, ranks with Sinon's assuring the Trojans that there was no one in that big wooden horse. The research paper, says Corder, gives the student the opportunity to learn something new about a subject and to gain specialized, thorough knowledge of it. The research paper will certainly force the student to encounter new information about a subject, for example, a critic's view of Raskolnikov's mental state in *Crime and Punishment,* but unless the student has first mastered that novel through tough, probing analysis, the new information most probably will be useless. Moreover, the student's view of the subject will be necessarily restricted by the number and quality of the critics which he or she will have the time to peruse. The complexities of most literary criticism as well as of scientific, historical, or technical authorities may do more harm than good to the novice researcher. Do we really wish to expose freshmen to highly complex ideas at a time when they are simply not yet ready to cope with them, a time when they may find them so incomprehensible as to be even intellectually repellent?

I remember when one of my freshmen was doing a paper on *Beowulf,* for example. I referred him to one of my favorite reference works and could hardly wait to see how pleased he would be with what he would find there. When next I saw him we were both frustrated because, although he was a bright student, he couldn't cope with the reference work, even though the book seemed easy to me. I had found the book useful and relatively clear in my mid-thirties after I had been involved in *Beowulf* studies for quite some time. Could I have handled this secondary work when I was eighteen? I doubt it. A beginning piano student starts off simply and doesn't attempt Beethoven until he or she is ready—the same principle applies.

If in research our freshmen will of necessity use the secondary ideas which they *are* able to assimilate and synthesize, we shouldn't expect much quality, for we surely won't get it. Nor will the students be able to gain thorough, specialized knowledge of the subject, as Corder implies. Does even the A+, one-shot paper on the Crimean War give the freshman a thorough knowledge of the subject? Of course not. And how does the teacher accomplish all of Corder's important objectives—which he cautiously labels "practice," "an introduction," "training," "acquaintance," and an "opportunity"— with a section of thirty-six or more freshmen to teach, or two such sections in a semester, or perhaps even three or four at a junior college?

With the single research paper we keep trying, we keep failing, sometimes not even realizing we're failing. We hold onto the idea that the "good" paper could certainly be written if we used better methods, or if the students were less lazy or wouldn't plagiarize. We'll admit to almost anything except the possibility of the uselessness and inappropriateness of the assignment itself. Why? Because we've always done it that way.

But even with all I've said, the research paper may well be fulfilling a vital function for those who teach it. Teachers have it to look forward to while grading all of those dreadful themes earlier in the course. Once the papers are completed and we can actually hold them in our hands, they are solid evidence of our excellence as English teachers. And don't we all need that kind of self-respect so that we may function as true professionals?

This paper was presented as part of a panel at the December 1981 MLA meeting.

NOTES

1. John Gerber, "Historical Drift," *ADE Bulletin* 67 (Spring 1981), 1–7.
2. Robert W. Frederick, "The Term Paper as a College Teaching Device," *School and Society* (Feb. 23, 1929), 256–257, as described in James E. Ford, Sharla Rees, and David L. Ward, "Research Paper Instruction: Comprehensive Bibliography of Periodical Sources, 1923–1980," *Bulletin of Bibliography* 39 (1982), 84–98.
3. Stated in a panel on "Writing Across the Curriculum" at the ADE Western Summer Seminar, UCLA, June 26, 1981.
4. "So Many Words: An Epistle to the Laodiceans," *ADE Bulletin* 65 (Sept. 1980), 11–14.
5. Harmon, 12.
6. Harmon, 14.
7. William Parker Riley, "Where Do English Departments Come From?" *College English* 28 (1967), 347.
8. Edward Bailey et al. (New York: Holt, 1979).
9. Jim W. Corder, *Handbook of Current English,* 6th ed. (Glenview, Ill.: Scott, Foresman, 1981).
10. Corder, 422.

PRACTICAL ASPECTS OF RESEARCH WRITING

Stephen M. Watt

Most students enrolled in introductory composition courses accrue significant practical benefits from writing research papers. In my attempt to persuade you of the validity of this statement, I should like to define "practical" in two ways: as something concerned with or dealing sensibly with everyday activities or work, and as something obtained through practice. For this latter definition in particular, I might add a brief etymological note; namely, that of the several lexemic ancestors of both "practice" and "practical," the most relevant to this discourse is the Middle French verb *practiser*, which means "to alter." Given these definitions, I should like to pose and answer two questions: Is research writing situated in a freshman composition course integral to a practice which alters for the better our students' writing and thinking processes—presumably the general objectives of most composition courses? And does it contribute to the preparation of students for the writing tasks they are likely to encounter outside of the composition classroom? The answer to each question is yes. And the implications of this answer manifest themselves both on the surface structure of method and in the deeper structure of theory. Further, I might suggest that both our frustration at student failures in writing research papers and the frustration felt more acutely by many students as well, which together have constituted the primary cause for so much dialogue on the issue of research writing, stem from what I perceive to be a wrenching disjunction between theory and method. While this paper will focus first on the *practical* benefits of research writing to be gained by all but perhaps the most ill equipped students with severe fluency and usage problems, it may later find theory lurking somewhere beneath the region of practicality.

The implications of the first sense of "practical" above, the referent of which is the writing our students do outside the composition class, provide, I think, a suitable place to begin the discussion. And this first sense of "practical" leads almost inevitably to a consideration of a practice appropriate to the introductory composition class. What kinds of writing assignments might our students expect in other courses? What skills will they need to respond competently to these assignments? When Laurence Behrens asked his students about their writing for other courses (as I have asked mine), he discovered that most of them were writing essays in which they organized and presented some definable body of information. To succeed in these writing situations, he concluded, students needed to develop strategies which kept "the subject matter, rather than the opinions or the sensibility or the taste of the responder in the foreground."[1] For this reason, Behrens argues that if the composition course is to serve the "practical" needs of both our students and our colleagues in other departments who have valorized the course by requiring their students to take it, then it must part company with most composition readers and provide students with considerable experience in presenting information. In addition, because our colleagues evaluate essay examinations, reports, case studies, and, yes, even research papers on the basis of their clarity in the presentation of information, there is little reason to help students "discover their own voices," their own selves, or the language-constituted world in which they live. These are the goals of the "liberal-humanist," not of the "utilitarian-pragmatist" which Behrens professes to be. And, in one respect, I think Behrens is right: teachers of composition need to recognize the "practical" writing assignments our students will be given and help them prepare for this writing.

However, I am unwilling to accede to the notion that a pragmatic stance necessarily opposes that of the "liberal-humanist." To the contrary, it seems quite reasonable that, after asking students to write several essays from different perspectives of the same body of information, we challenge them to consider not only *how* their ideas have changed (and I think it is likely their ideas *will* change), but *why* they have changed. In short, one need not be pragmatic to the virtual exclusion of humanistic objectives; serving practical needs does not *have* to lead to the overthrow of self-reflexivity, or to the annihilation of ethical views of rhetoric. Nevertheless, Behrens' central question is a good one, one to which I again return: What kinds of writing will our students do when they leave our class? Many of them, if my students are typical of most students, *will* write research papers in psychology, political science, and sociology classes. Many more who may not write a research paper per se will be required in finance and business administration classes to draw upon many of the skills associated with research writing: evaluating sources, making careful decisions about the suitability of quoted passages and paraphrased material, and finally solving problems immanent in the information they are scrutinizing. Most important, upper-division undergraduate courses demand that students "make ideas their own"—articulate original thesis statements—and, as Charles Yarnoff argues, this occurs only after writers examine their own ideas critically "in relation to experience and to alternate ideas."[2] *This is the single, most important practical benefit of research writing.* Because the process of invention for research writing importantly includes the weighing of "alternate ideas," it is especially useful in preparing students to locate their ideas within an ideational context broader than personal experience. All the other putative benefits of research writing—those underscored by Sheridan Baker in *The Complete Stylist* about students making a scholarly "contribution" through their research, and by the omnipresent insistences that students learn valuable things about documentation, the library, and the nature of the academy[3]—pale in comparison, if indeed they are true at all, to the perceptual gains achieved by a careful examination of one's ideas in relation to others. This is the purpose of research writing.

Most attacks on research writing in the freshman composition class, however, do not originate from opposition to this sense of "practical," but from confusion about the practice associated with teaching writing. In an essay which is typical of such attacks, Stephen North complains that the "conventional" five- to eight-week unit on research writing placed at the end of a composition course causes students insurmountable difficulties: that they cannot write well in a form they have not studied, that students get too few opportunities to make mistakes, that research writing will not remedy students' existing problems with writing, and, most important, that young writers have a "difficult time making research material their own."[4] North's points are well taken. But are these shortcomings or veritable calamities inherent in research writing and student ineptitude, *or* in the practice of teaching composition that North characterizes? Admittedly, if instructors simply add a "block" on research papers to the end of just *any* composition class—a class constituted of practices which fail to allow students the opportunity to make mistakes, to think critically about their ideas, and so on—then the research paper will present a challenge that few students will be prepared to meet. And, in my view, this is the kind of class North describes in his essay: one marked by the disjunction between theory and practice to which I alluded earlier. He fails to recognize that assigning research writing should be the result of a teacher's judicious deployment of a practice which leads to the student's acquisition of the rhetorical and perceptual skills necessary for such discourse. And, yes, I believe that the average college freshman is capable of acquiring these skills.

What kind of practice *does* aid students in the acquisition of these skills? It might be easier to describe first what practices *do not* lead to successful research papers. One founded upon what might be termed writing as therapy or liberation of the self—this notion leads to students' keeping journals, experimenting with prewriting techniques, and composing personal meditations[5]—will seldom, if ever, prepare students for research writing. Of course, these techniques were never intended to lead to such an end. Indeed, proponents of this kind of practice are in effect rebelling against a product-oriented composition course which the research paper has too often been used to symbolize. Similarly, a system based on the emulation of classical topoi (which has given rise to a huge number of readers organized by the so-called rhetorical modes), while potentially providing students with experience in organizing their perceptions of objective phenomena, inevitably fails to help students "make ideas their own." It fails, for the most part, because of its implicit suggestion that realities can be neatly collapsed into discernible patterns: comparison, classification, process, and the like. This system too often misleads students into believing that a writer's central chore consists of matching a subject to a single "mode." I think most of us would agree that just the opposite is the case: that good writers make thoughtful decisions about the suitability of imposing an ordering principle upon a given body of information and that very few pieces of mature discourse can accurately be regarded as examples of "pure" comparison, definition, or anything else.[6] In addition, the rhetorical-modes approach generally imputes no logical or causal connection between the modes, as if one mode bears little or no relationship to another. In short, when the use of rhetorical modes constitutes the writing practice of a composition course, students seldom recognize that they see in an object of study only as much as their rhetorical model allows them to see.[7]

A composition course which leads to the students' critical examination of their own ideas, and hence to research writing, should be based then on several definable principles. First, and most obvious, we must admit that the writing of expressive essays only will not prepare students adequately for a research project. Students who have only compared the inferiority of a dormitory cafeteria's gruel to the delights of home cooking or described the psychological benefits they have derived from life in a fraternity or sorority will not be prepared to undertake a research project. Second, the course should be centered on a well-defined topic or otherwise narrowed to include readings related to each other. Thus, long before a research paper is assigned, students have been given an opportunity to develop ideas about the general subject area they will explore in more depth. (As critics of the research paper quite reasonably point out, it is virtually impossible for students to "make ideas their own" if they have no ideas about a topic before they begin a research project.) Third, if instructors do decide to use the rhetorical modes in a composition course, these modes should be applied to one or two topics. That is, rather than assigning students to write six to eight essays on six to eight topics and insisting on their employing a different mode for each essay (a practice shared for some inexplicable reason or reasons by many teachers of composition), we might ask students to write these essays on one or two topics. In effect, we must insist that our charges reconsider positions, question themselves about the origins and implications of their ideas, and weigh their former opinions in light of new evidence. Of course, these same essays can also form the basis for units on sentence combining, mechanical skills, or whatever other problematical areas seem to merit consideration. (I am not aware of any compelling hypothesis which suggests it is more effective to analyze writing problems in essays about the cuisine of dormitory cafeterias than to analyze the same problems emerging in projects dealing with more challenging, information-based topics.) In short, the practice of a composition course which includes research writing *must* make it possible for students to succeed with their research projects, and it is within this possibility that the practical benefit of research writing coincides with practice: in the writers' struggle to compare their ideas to alternate ideas and hence make ideas their own.

The issue of research writing in the freshman composition course involves more practicalities than just these two, and I might conclude by mentioning a few of these. One overwhelming "practicality" of the departments in which many of us labor involves enrollment and, ultimately, survival. Opponents of research writing in the composition course often propose a "writing in the disciplines" program as a desirable alternative. This program, they contend, would "free" the composition teacher from the burden of the research paper; the specialist in a technical field could teach majors the forms commonly used in writing within the field, and teachers of composition would go on about their business. However, this notion is replete with faulty and dangerous assumptions. First, research writing *is* the business of the composition teacher. More than anyone, the composition teacher is trained to help students with *all* the aspects of research writing: rhetorical stance, style, argumentation, diction, and mechanics. Second, while our colleagues in other departments find it all too easy to identify the writing problems of their students, it does not necessarily follow that they are equally skilled at helping these students solve them (or that they are especially eager to spend the time necessary to do so). Third, and most important, total enrollments in the English courses at many universities are bolstered greatly by those in three classes about which there exists significant doubt of the expertise of English faculty to teach them: film, business and technical writing, and, yes, even composition. Keith N. Hull and Ruth Mitchell have explained quite clearly why technical and professional writing belongs in English departments,[8] and, to cite one instance, the English Department at the University of Illinois persuaded the College of Engineering not to secede from the composition Union—at least for the moment—as it has periodically threatened to do. The point of all of this involves more than self-survival, more than the animal instinct of a teacher caught in an academic world which seems to be evolving in a way that threatens his existence. "Writing in the disciplines," at least insofar as it includes research writing, implies that an enormous chasm separates so-called practical writing and the writing our students do in the composition class. If our colleagues *really* begin to believe this—and if we allow them to—one wonders how long they will be able to endorse the freshman composition course. We *must* be practical.

This is an edited version of a paper presented at the December 1981 meeting of the MLA.

NOTES

1. Laurence Behrens, "Meditations, Reminiscences, Polemics: Composition Readers and the Service Course," *College English* 41 (1980), 566.
2. Charles Yarnoff, "Contemporary Theories of Invention in the Rhetorical Tradition," *College English* 41 (1980), 555.
3. Baker's comments appear at the beginning of his section on research papers in *The Complete Stylist and Handbook*, 297; a large number of widely used composition texts—Jim W. Corder's *Handbook of Current English*, 6th ed., and Frederick Crews's *The Random House Handbook*, 3rd ed., to name but two—emphasize the value of learning to use the library and to document sources.
4. Stephen North, "Teaching Research Writing: Five Criteria," *Freshman English News* 9 (Fall 1980), 17–18.
5. See Yarnoff, 553–556, for further discussion of these practices.
6. For further discussion of the limitations of rhetorical topoi, see Yarnoff, 556ff.; see also C. H. Knoblauch, "Modern Composition Theory and the Rhetorical Tradition," *Freshman English News* 9 (Fall 1980), 3–17.
7. The concept of modeling capacity—the manner in which a system of analysis models the object of study—is discussed frequently in Soviet semiotics. A number of essays in *Soviet Semiotics*, ed. Daniel P. Lucid (Baltimore: Johns Hopkins University Press, 1977), provide information on this topic. A more readable discussion of this topic is included in Fredric Jameson's *The Prison-House of Language* (Princeton: Princeton University Press, 1972), 15ff.
8. See Keith N. Hull, "Notes from the Besieged; or, Why English Teachers Should Teach Technical Writing," *College English* 41 (1980), 876–883. See also Ruth Mitchell, "Shared Responsibility: Teaching Technical Writing in the University," *College English* 43 (1981), 543–555.

Bibliography: More on the Research Paper Debate

Bramer, George R. "Freedom and Control in the Research Paper," *College Composition and Communication* 20 (Dec. 1969), 352–359. Discusses the general pros and cons of research paper instruction on the way to a description of an approach which is meant to achieve a balance between control and freedom.

Ford, James E., and Dennis R. Perry. "Research Paper Instruction in Undergraduate Writing Programs: A National Survey," *College English* 44 (Dec. 1982), 72–78. Ascertains how, how much, and by whom research paper instruction is given; gauges developments during the preceding five years and projects future trends; and determines the role of library-use instruction in the overall process. Concludes that research paper instruction constitutes a major responsibility and, therefore, the profession should do more to help teachers fulfill it.

French, Robert W. "Journals and Term Papers," *Exercise Exchange* 17 (Spring 1973), 7–8; reply by Betty Bandel, ibid., 18 (Fall 1973), 27–28. French believes that the research paper is a stultifying, authority-centered experience for high school and lower-level college students. Students should be asked to keep journals instead. Bandel counters that the research paper need not be stultifying if imaginatively taught, that "to go to Authority" needn't mean "to accept Authority," and research skills "cannot be switched on, like an electric light, at the beginning of the junior year in college."

McClusky, Howard Yale. "An Experimental Comparison of the New Type Test and the Term Paper," *Journal of Applied Psychology* 17 (Oct. 1933), 621–627. Early and unique experiment found students who write research papers on material to be covered in a final examination gain no real advantage over students who prepare directly for the test with regard to factual material learned, but they gain great advantage regarding processes of organization and creative expression, and having to synthesize and relate ideas in a common context.

Stevenson, John W. "The Illusion of Research," *English Journal* 61 (Oct. 1972), 1029–1032. Decries the English "research" paper because it "serves no real value as an 'English' assignment; and it promotes dishonest writing."

Willis, Veronica Tischer. "An Investigation of the Use of the Documented Research Paper in College Courses," Diss., United States International University, 1970 (for a fuller abstract, see *DAI* 139 [1970], 2137A). Reports and analyzes the results of a survey of research paper instruction in all fields at colleges and universities in California to assess "the service value of the documented research paper and identif[y] the level or levels where it is most used." Recommends dropping or deemphasizing the research paper on the undergraduate level because few such papers are assigned.

The Research Paper in Rhetorical Context

PUTTING THE RESEARCH PAPER INTO RHETORICAL CONTEXT

Thomas E. Gaston, Bret H. Smith, and Robert P. Kennedy

You are a college freshman. Your teacher has just announced that you will do a "research paper" this semester. Little you see in such an assignment that is yours. And if the teacher knew what was going on in your head, if she had any idea of the fuzziness of the knowledge, the extent of the distortions, and the number of misimpressions that you carried away last year from Miss Whoosit's "introduction" to the research paper, she would dissolve in despair.[1] Even so, it is not those misimpressions that are the teacher's most important obstacle.

Her greatest and most crucial challenge is getting students to see the *point* of it all. What, after all, can a typical high school senior or college freshman possibly know about research? Research—any kind of research—is as foreign to an average student as theology is to a typical farmer. But the farmer, according to an old joke, has an advantage the student does not. "Of course, I believe in baptism," he is supposed to have explained. "I've seen it done." The problem is that students have not seen research done.

For this reason, teaching the research paper presents the composition teacher with a problem in audience analysis that is not less tricky just because it regularly goes unrecognized. It is no small irony that those of us who confront this problem daily in our freshman rhetoric classes have proven ourselves such inept practitioners of the art we espouse. As rhetoricians, we certainly know how important it is for the writer to consider carefully the purpose, audience, and genre of each communication. Most of us iterate and reiterate to students the importance of being clear about *what* we need to say to *whom* in what kind of *document* for what *purpose*. Yet in our own communication to

them, about the research paper, we too often work from egocentric
assumptions that border on academic jingoism. And we make it
virtually impossible for many of them to see the research paper the
way we see it: as a specialized form of communication for use in a
specific rhetorical context to accomplish important work in the
world.

The innocence with which we occasionally set nursing students
and future economists to tracing the gold symbolism in *Silas Marner,*
although a genuine example, is too extreme to indicate the scope of
the problem. In one sense, however, the example is perfect. A
widespread tendency among us is to teach research methodology via
literary problems, solved by some approximation to standard critical
methods, written up according to discourse conventions that we take
for granted, and documented—of course—as per the *MLA Handbook.*
The larger point and the irony is that we, who preach to students the
importance of persuading readers to accept new ideas by aligning
them with established beliefs and values, are in this important part of
our work, so inflexibly hypnotized by our own interests.

Let no dedicated philologist mistake this formulation of our
common problem as a renewed attack from the literature-does-not-
belong-in-the-composition-classroom camp. That issue is both old and
irrelevant. Our point is different. We are emphasizing the *a*-rhetorical
(one might almost say *anti*-rhetorical) context in which instruction in
the research paper customarily takes place. And our concern over this
point extends far beyond any conflict between aesthetes and philistines.
Even the innovators among us, who would have us arrest students'
attention by assigning them to research their future vocations, or the
state of the world on the days of their births, or the spectacular crimes of
yesteryear, often contribute to our restiveness.[2]

Unless one has the sense that somebody wants or needs to know
about the crime or the vocation or the birth date he has "researched,"
the ensuing paper necessarily lacks rhetorical validity. That is why it
is easier, in our experience, to inspire interest in the research process
than to elicit good written reports. The source of the data that the
student works with is, we think, not of great importance. The
write-up can hardly be better than the student's understanding of his
genre and the possible audiences for it.

What is crucial if students are to find their rhetorical bearings is
that they see from the outset a valid educational point to their work.
This means, in practice, that all students—future scientists, real

estate agents, and engineers no less than future journalists, historians, and teachers—need some assurance that the research skills they are expected to learn in "English" will be important to them later in college and, especially, in "real life" beyond school.

It is easy enough, we realize, to get freshmen to mouth platitudes ("English is bound to help you in later life"), but it is unrealistic to expect much more unless we plan our instruction to elicit more. Even those eighteen-year-olds with firmly decided academic majors and vocational plans know too little of the details of their future work to see for themselves how the English teacher's strategies will apply to their majors, their interests, and the careers.

Sensing that this was more than a trivial problem, one of us some years ago began to introduce into his unit on the research paper a brief orientation designed to place library research and its attendant academic conventions within a larger context of intellectual and economic activity. Gradually, over a decade or so, he evolved the practice of using this orientation as his *introduction* to the research paper assignment. And he noticed in his classes a concurrent improvement in the quality of students' research and writing that seemed at first out of proportion to such a modest adjustment in the content of instruction. Since then, a number of colleagues and students to whom he recommended this approach have tried it and reported uniformly favorable results.

So we are convinced of its efficacy, and we now think we can account for its advantages in terms of two extremely basic rhetorical principles. This perspective on the research paper gives the student, first of all, a surer sense of genre. It gives him an idea of how library research operates, as it were, in its native habitat, of what kinds of information research reports communicate to what kinds of audiences for what kinds of purposes. Thus it gives him the sense of rhetorical direction that is prerequisite to all effective discourse. With these bearings, students can acquire research paper skills in the same way they acquire other communication skills, by combining common sense, imitation, reasoning, and intuition in whatever ad hoc fashion is necessary to find ways of making their evidence and their conclusions clear to their readers. In short, this beginning warrants the intellectual and communicative *validity* of the instruction to be presented on the research paper.

The second advantage of placing the research paper in this context is that doing so invites students to conceive of research in terms of their personal interests. From the outset, they are encouraged to see the research report as a tool which they can and probably will use, in one variety or another, to reach their own goals. If we allow them to see it, however mistakenly, as just another requirement, a hurdle that the English department plops between them and their degrees, we should hardly be surprised if they negotiate it unwillingly, awkwardly, and ineptly. But if we are willing to take a broader, more accurate, and for most of us a more tolerant view of research, then it becomes much easier to connect the research paper, as we know it, with the world of practical reality as our students conceive it. In proportion as we are able to transcend the constraints of departmental parochialism, we can put library research into a larger picture and thus can relate it responsibly, properly, and unmistakably to the academic and vocational goals of future scientists, engineers, and technicians. Only when this is done will the rhetoric used in our instruction square with the rhetoric supposedly being taught by our instruction.

How, then, does a teacher put the research paper into its proper intellectual and rhetorical context? We have no specific methodology to tout; we are not even convinced that the method matters much, provided that the appropriate points are made in a coherent and convincing manner. So we list below, with brief and admittedly oversimplified discussions, the major teaching points to be covered before plunging students into a detailed discussion of the rationale for, and conventions of, documentation. The points are listed more or less in the order of presentation.

1. *All human knowledge is tentative.* As a culture, we cannot simply rely on the wisdom of our forebears, because the wisdom of yesteryear comes to us tangled indistinguishably with yesterday's errors and dogmas. Intellectual and economic progress requires that old beliefs be challenged, for nobody can know in advance which of our present certainties will ultimately prove to be misplaced. Certainly no one today would attempt to cure depression by removing "bad blood' from the patient. Yet for more than a thousand years physicians practiced bloodletting as confidently as today's doctors apply antiseptic. Indeed, the case of antiseptic has about it a certain irony, for less than twenty years ago researchers discovered that the antiseptic lotion then routinely given to hospital patients was toxic when absorbed through cuts and abrasions on the skin. One day the use of that lotion constituted our most enlightened medical practice. One

year later, its use would have been considered near-quackery. Research is an ongoing quest for knowledge which by its nature must often undermine "information" from the past in order to establish new truths.

2. *What most people accept as "truths," at any point in history, will be found upon examination to derive from one of four sources.*[3] First, some beliefs are just accepted by convention, i.e., "everybody knows it." In the U.S. today, everybody "knows" that it is "normal" to stand about three feet away when talking with a casual acquaintance. Citizens of many Latin American countries "know," however, that so much distance is a sure signal of aloofness. Their conventions are different; yet both beliefs are correct because they accurately reflect the conventions of the respective culture.[4] Second, some beliefs are based on authoritative pronouncements by a source which is seldom or never questioned—a Bible, a Koran, a *Mein Kampf,* a *Communist Manifesto,* or even a constitution. Third, some "truths" are accepted simply because they seem intuitively "right." These include many religious perceptions, perhaps most personal values, and almost all aesthetic insights. Surprisingly, however, they also include mathematical relationships and scientific hypotheses which, often enough, are conceived of *before* the experiments and proofs that will later be called upon to demonstrate them.[5] Finally, some beliefs are based on the accumulation and rational interpretation of observable evidence. This, of course, is the domain of systematic research.

3. *Rational inquiry is the acknowledged and preferred source of knowledge in our culture.* An American salesperson trying to persuade a buyer to use a new product knows that she must present research demonstrating that the new product is cheaper or better. Governmental procurement officers and purchasers for businesses expect such data, and so do informed consumers. As a result, huge amounts of money are spent by corporations, universities, and government laboratories to develop the needed data.

When existing laws are questioned or new ones proposed, Senate and House committees subpoena expert witnesses to give testimony under oath on the relevant issues. The process is one of research, and the reports that are issued, though much longer, are not different in kind from the research papers you will learn to write in this course.[6] An even more familiar example of research in action is the jury trial. Here, the opposing attorneys and the judge cooperate in assembling and presenting to the jury all the relevant facts—the physical evidence, the testimony of witnesses, the opinions of experts, the wording of the law, and the significance of past court decisions—in short, everything that the jury can properly consider to arrive at a rational decision. A moment's reflection will convince almost any objective thinker that virtually every segment of our technological society depends heavily on, and values, research. Even those members of the populace who have only the vaguest understanding of rational inquiry hold research in esteem and respect its findings. They must. Why else would TV hucksters who peddle toothpaste and laxatives to the masses so often brandish research reports from book-lined studies or appear in white coats surrounded by an aura of scientism?

4. *Research is the method by which rational inquiry is used to generate new knowledge.* The point of this whole discussion is to indicate in some detail what research is. First, however, it is important to be clear about what research is not. One thing it most definitely is not is a process leading to "pure" knowledge. A common mistake is to assume that the *only* way to arrive at valid truths is via "objective" scholarly research. Most experts, however, are quick to point out that the source from which a proposition derives is not a reliable indicator of its truth value. A belief is not necessarily wrong just because it is highly conventional or is promulgated with authority or seems intuitively obvious. In fact, all the other avenues to truth figure prominently in well-conducted research. Even empirical science has its "received opinion," which compares to the common person's conventional beliefs; its Authorities, whom lesser scientists hesitate to contradict; and its geniuses, whose intuitive flashes illuminate intellectual territory that must be systematically explored by whole generations of more pedestrian researchers. The advantage of research is not that it increases the *possibility* of a true conclusion, but rather that it decreases the *probability* of a false one. By proceeding rationally and objectively, by bringing together what is already known, and by basing new claims on explicit reasoning, research produces the most probable conclusions to be drawn, in a form that can be *communicated* to any qualified person. It is this communicability that is the biggest advantage of research. Our beliefs, our faiths, and our intuitions, however valid, may be forever personal and inexpressible, but the reasoning we do from evidence can be shared and used as the basis for cooperative decisions.[7]

5. *Research uses no special forms of thought; it only systematizes and extends the common sense of everyday life.* At bottom, all research consists

of four simple operations: making relevant observations, making intelligent guesses about the relations among observed facts, testing the guesses thus made, and revising those guesses as necessary in the light of test results. These four operations are not in the least mysterious or esoteric. They are almost as natural as breathing. Suppose that on a cold January morning, you jump into your car praying that you can get it started before you freeze to the icy vinyl seat. You turn the key. A moan resonates from under the hood. You try again (i.e., you replicate the experiment). Still nothing. So you make a guess based on your observations. Hypothesis: "The battery terminals are loose or corroded." But you lift the hood, trace the ground wire to the battery, and find the connections in good shape. Scratch Hypothesis One. Hypothesis Two: "The battery is out of water." But you check the cells and find them full. Hypothesis Two rejected on the basis of experimental findings. From here on, your research proceeds in earnest. Forming new hypotheses and checking them out one by one, you proceed until you find a loose starter wire. You tighten that, try the ignition again, and beam as the engine coughs to life and settles into a purr. If you are philosophically inclined, it may occur to you as you are driving along that you still don't know for certain that the loose starter wire was the cause of your car trouble. Some other factor could have been operating—a short that comes and goes, or something of that sort. But if you are like most people, you will assume that the starter wire was the culprit unless you have further trouble. In effect, then, you do what a scientist does. You interpret your findings in light of the probabilities and trust conclusions based on your experimentation until contradictory evidence turns up. It will become clear in the next few days that *all* the specialized techniques of research, humanistic as well as scientific research, are simply methods for increasing the range and accuracy of observations and for tracing more precisely the relationships among them. They are just better ways of finding the loose starter cable and surer ways of deciding whether it caused the engine failure.

6. *There are, essentially, three kinds of research, all of which are used to some extent in every branch of scholarship, science, and technology.* You will see, as we proceed, that certain kinds of investigation are particularly suited to certain disciplines. But all researchers work with data of three kinds: data from the past, data from the present, and (surprisingly enough) data from the future.

6a. *Reports of research using data from the past include histories, biographies, case studies, and certain kinds of survey research.* Historians and literary scholars spend innumerable hours in archives, reading through old newspapers, journals, and diaries, piecing together the events of bygone days. Often it is necessary to confirm dates and establish chronology by checking public records or by reading through private collections of letters and journals. Clues carefully teased from sources like these enable intellectual detectives to assemble the biographies and histories that compose much of our cultural heritage.

An adaptation of this historical method is used in marketing, business management, clinical psychology, and medicine. A comprehensive history of a single subject of investigation is called a *case study.* Case studies are characteristically used during the earliest stages of investigation, before the development of firm hypotheses and enough received opinion to guide more definitive work. Case study researchers try to assemble all the data that seem likely to be relevant to a subject. The physicians takes a detailed medical history, and the psychologist takes copious notes on a patient's early childhood experiences, neither knowing in advance just which questions are likely to lead to the proper diagnosis.

A somewhat different method of collecting data from the past is used frequently in the social sciences. Special questionnaires or structured interviews are used in *survey* research, which is often designed to gather from informants data on such subjects as child-rearing practices, job histories, etc. In such studies the researcher reaches back through time, as it were, and brings together selected information from hundreds or perhaps thousands of persons who are total strangers to her and to one another.

6b. *Some research concentrates on understanding the significance of data from the present.* Examples include field studies, taxonomies, polls, surveys, and military status reports, all dealing with events that are currently taking place.

Field studies, for instance, are an important tool of anthropologists, who often attempt to understand the social structure of a tribe, subculture, or community by living among its members and making detailed notes of their interactions. Ethnologists also use field study data to modify, interpret, or contextualize the data on animal behavior that they've collected through laboratory experiments and through observations of animals in captivity.

Taxonomies are a special type of present-oriented research which concentrates on the classification of data. Only when observations are properly grouped can they lead us to the generalizations that spark new discoveries. If you are a psychoanalyst, it makes a great deal of difference whether you classify homosexuality as a neurosis, a psychosis, or an alternate course of normal development. Taxonomic research is particularly important to botanists and zoologists, for whom it is important to classify properly every form of life.

Perhaps a more familiar type of present-oriented research is found in certain surveys and polls designed to gather facts about the most recent events. The Nielsen ratings of TV shows, for instance, are based on viewers' most current preferences. And the question usually posed by pollsters from Gallup, Roper, et al. is, "If the election were held *today,* for whom would you vote?"

6c. *Some research concentrates on understanding the significance of data to be collected in the future.* This is the distinguishing characteristic of experimental research. Whether carried out in the laboratory or in the field, experiments are carefully planned and controlled observations. The observations must be decided on in advance, and the researcher must know which findings will confirm her hypothesis and which will disprove it. Laboratory experiments allow the researcher to control variables much more exactly so that, if suspected causes are operating, she is sure to find them. Field experiments, on the other hand, are conducted in more realistic settings. The variables cannot be so carefully controlled, but findings from a field experiment are more likely to have practical significance. That is why tire manufacturers road test their products and why agricultural experiment stations try out new hybrids in side-by-side fields. It is not uncommon for a superiority that has been demonstrated in the laboratory to be almost imperceptible in the field where unpredictable factors can work against it.

7. *The research strategies to be taught in the next few weeks constitute a particularly useful approach to past-oriented research.* You will learn how to take a topic, consider it, and find in it a researchable question. You will learn how to sleuth around in a library until you have located the information that bears on your question. What is more, you will learn to do this with the greatest efficiency and the least effort, by "pyramiding" your bibliographical work so that each source leads you to the next in a sequence that homes in on the data you need for a precise answer to your question. You will learn useful strategies for

organizing, interpreting, and reporting the data you assemble. And if you do not already know how footnotes and bibliographies function in research reports, you will learn. But most important of all, you will learn why footnotes and bibliographies are important. When you have thought about their function as intellectual insurance against error, fraud, and incompetence, you will see why scholars take them so seriously. Responsible documentation is an ethical obligation in virtually every field of inquiry, for without it the intellectual cooperation basic to all research is undermined. So you want to learn to use documentation correctly. It is an academic necessity based on simple decency and common sense.

8. *Library investigation is a variety of past-oriented research which is essential to the methodology of almost every academic discipline, every science, and every technology.* When a real estate appraiser gets down to work on a feasibility study, when a chemist gets a hunch that she may know where to look for a new molecular structure, and when a CPA is asked a new question about the IRS code, they all head for the library. One expert on research design declares emphatically that "a good library is as invaluable to a researcher in scientific problems as it is to the philosopher, historian, and scholar in the humanities."[8] Later, in describing the pattern of a scientific report, he makes clear that a "review of the literature" is almost always an essential first step. Only by considering what has already been done can the scholar be sure that she is even *engaged* in research! Research, we said in Point No. 4, is the generation of *new* knowledge. Unless the researcher begins by familiarizing herself with what others have already investigated, she may simply repeat their work.[9] This may not render her work useless, but it certainly diminishes its value. What is worse, if she is naively replicating work that was not well planned in the first instance, she may repeat errors that would have been easily recognized by a thoughtful reading of reports on the earlier research. It is a waste of time to do again what has already been done unless it will be done better, more definitively, or more elegantly. Even to judge whether that is the case, the researcher must be familiar with past work. That appraiser does not want to waste his time working out in Des Moines techniques which have already been perfected in Schenectady. The chemist will get little satisfaction from being the *second* discoverer of her molecule, and the CPA's professional reputation depends on his coming back from the firm's library with answers that his client can depend on. For all these purposes and for a hundred others that you

will encounter in years ahead, if you are alert enough to recognize them, library techniques constitute an extremely important research tool. Almost every educated person is a regular consumer of research. And most educated people find themselves, occasionally at least, in situations requiring that they prepare written reports of research. When that happens to you, the proposal or staff study you write is likely to be of special importance in your career. So you can expect to use the conventions for documenting, organizing, and interpreting data that you learn in this course—or close approximations to them—no matter what field you enter.

After these points have been made, we begin by assigning a very short "documented theme" and follow up with practical exercises designed to help students understand the logic as well as the techniques of footnoting.[10] Only then do we begin with the usual research paper assignment, at which point we proceed in somewhat different directions. One advantage of our preparatory instruction is that it can be used to introduce almost any kind of research assignment. Most of the assignments we read about seem workable enough, when evaluated on their own terms. However, those terms are not always the determinants of an assignment's success in the classroom. For the research paper, we consider some sense of rhetorical context to be an important prerequisite. That seems to be why an initial understanding of the points outlined above is so helpful to both the instructor and the student. This understanding makes it much less likely that freshmen will see the research paper as academic busywork and more likely that they will see it as a step toward intellectual maturity.

NOTES

1. In assigning gender to the hypothetical persons mentioned in this article, all teachers at any level are assumed to be female. This decision derives not from occupational stereotyping but rather from a decision to accord the status role to the female. Conversely, all students—who come through in this article as naive and highly dependent, to say the least—are assumed to be male. Gender will be randomly assigned to other hypothetical persons. Readers inclined to quarrel with this decision are petitioned for largess. Though our cogitations over the stylistic nuances of sexism are admittedly confused, our consciousnesses are raised. *Pax vobiscum.*

2. For detailed information on research assignments of this type, see W. Keith Kraus, *Murder, Mischief, and Mayhem: A Process for Creative Research Papers* (Urbana: NCTE, 1978); Arnold Leslie Lazarus, "Termpaper or Term Project?" *National Education Association Journal* 40 (Feb. 1951), 138; and William F. Woods, "Freshman Histories: A Basic Research Assignment." *FERN* 3 (Summer/Fall 1977), 1–3 (revised from ERIC ED 155689).

3. These classifications are adapted from Fred N. Kerlinger, *Foundations of Behavioral Research: Educational and Psychological Inquiry* (New York: Holt, Rinehart and Winston, 1965), 6–8.

4. Edwart T. Hall, *The Silent Language* (Garden City, N.Y.: Doubleday, 1959). Hall considers the "silent language" of cultures crucial to successful cross-cultural communication. He argues that American diplomats should be trained by anthropologists familiar with the cultures in which their consulates are located. The nature and scope of Hall's examples are so impressive that one can plausibly argue that issues of war and peace sometimes hinge on whether sociological and anthropological research is well conducted and whether its findings are clearly communicated.

5. Arthur Koestler, *The Act of Creation* (New York: Dell, 1964), 147, 163, et passim. On the same subject, see also James Austin, *Chase, Chance, and Creativity* (New York: Columbia University Press, 1978).

6. An assignment that we have planned but not yet tried involves having students examine a number of reports from government commissions and private agencies in order to get a sense of how research is conducted and communicated. We are particularly interested in the reports of consumer advocate groups and of such governmental investigative bodies as the Warren Commission, the Kerner Commission, the Walker Commission, and the Commission on Obscenity and Pornography.

7. The importance of communicability in research is stated compellingly by S. I. Hayakawa in "Communication and the Human Community,"

ETC: A Review of General Semantics 16, no. 1 (Autumn 1958), 5–16, and also in the book that Hayakawa reviews at length in that article, biologist J. Z. Young's *Doubt and Certainty in Science* (New York: Oxford University Press, 1951).

8. J. William Asher, *Educational Research and Evaluation Methods* (Boston: Little, Brown, 1976), 216–241. The quotation is from page 219.

9. Sometimes this scholarly wheel spinning reaches comic proportions. Thus Richard D. Altick writes on page 147 of *The Art of Literary Research* (New York: W. W. Norton, 1975):

> A gaffe that was more comic than anything else occurred when Alan Clutton-Brock noted in the Times Literary Supplement (January 19, 1951) that in *Murder in the Cathedral*, T. S. Eliot borrowed fragments of Conan Doyle's story, "The Musgrave Ritual." In the next issue, J. Isaacs commented that this was nothing new: Grover Smith, of Yale, had pointed out that borrowing in Notes and Queries for October 2, 1948. A month later (TLS, February 23), Smith declined credit for the "discovery," because Elizabeth Jackson had made it still earlier, in the Saturday Review of Literature for January 25, 1941. Here was a clear case of two scholars independently publishing a fact that each honestly thought he had been the first to come upon, whereas actually a third person had beaten both of them to it. Although this TLS correspondence was promptly listed in the standard annual bibliography of research in Victorian literature, four years later (MLN, 70 1955, 269–71) still another scholar, observing that "apparently attention has never been called to the fact that ten lines of *Murder in the Cathedral* are taken with very little alteration from the Sherlock Holmes adventure '*The Musgrave Ritual*,'" proceeded to dish up the parallel once again. We can expect it to be rediscovered any day now.

10. These exercises, originally developed and written up by Thomas Gaston and others in a paper entitled "Bringing the Research Paper Down to Earth," are now in widespread use at Purdue. The authors of the present paper are now creating similar exercises so that the teaching points enumerated above can be covered via a variety of different activities focusing on inherently interesting textual materials. Interested persons may write to Tom Gaston, Department of English, Purdue University, West Lafayette, Ind. 47907.

"THE RHETORICAL SITUATION" AND THE RESEARCH PAPER: AN INTEGRATIVE APPROACH

Marcia Noe

For several years I have used Lloyd Bitzer's notion of the rhetorical situation as the focal point and organizing principle of my freshman rhetoric course.[1] The rhetorical model that Bitzer outlines in "The Rhetorical Situation" has been useful as a theoretical framework for the principles of argument and persuasion that are introduced as well as a vehicle for teaching the research component of the course. Using Bitzer's model, the teacher can better integrate the rhetorical aspects of the course with the research skills that are taught and demonstrate to the students that rhetoric is not merely another textbook term to memorize but a complex of factors that interact in our lives and are capable of effecting change.

I work within a system that "tracks" freshmen rhetoric students according to their English ACT scores. Teaching the advanced class provides an opportunity to teach rhetoric, in the Aristotelian sense of discovering the available means of persuasion in a given case, to students who have already mastered basic composition skills and who are capable of responding to the stimulation and challenge of rhetorical theory. Although a comprehensive course in rhetoric, as defined by Aristotle and developed by Perelman, Burke, Kinneavy, and others, might be too ambitious an undertaking for any freshman student, Bitzer's model of the rhetorical situation provides a workable teaching tool in dramatizing to students how rhetor, audience, and discourse interact in various life situations.

In "The Rhetorical Situation" Lloyd Bitzer shows how situation is the controlling element in generating discourse and how the standard aspects of rhetorical method (rhetor, discourse, audience) are primarily governed by situation. Bitzer asserts that rhetorical discourse should not be viewed as an isolated example of eloquence but, within the total context of its origin, as a way of solving a problem or meeting a need. This need or problem, which Bitzer terms the exigence, is what actually brings about the discourse. Other constituents of the rhetorical situation are the audience, those persons who, through hearing and responding to the discourse, are capable of resolving the exigence; and the constraints, factors that are inherent in the situation or that the rhetor uses to motivate the audience.

A rhetorical situation may be simple, bringing forth only one piece of discourse, or complex, involving several types of discourse developed to meet more than one need. Bitzer uses the example of President Kennedy's assassination to illustrate the latter type of rhetorical situation. Shortly after the assassination occurred, the type of discourse that prevailed was primarily informative, in order to quell the confusion about what had happened; later, eulogies were given to comfort the American people, and analyses of the event were offered to satisfy the public's need to know why their president was killed. Thus, different kinds of discourse arose at different times to meet different needs.

Rhetorical situations may be as public as the Kennedy assassination or as intimate as an argument with oneself about a life decision; regardless of their nature, they abound in our lives and provide excellent opportunities for students to learn how rhetoric works. During the first week of the semester, students read and discuss "The Rhetorical Situation," brainstorming to compile a list of actual rhetorical situations that meet Bitzer's criteria. Each student then chooses one rhetorical situation to investigate and analyze for the semester research project.

The first step is to identify the constituents of the rhetorical situations the students have chosen; they can easily identify the rhetor, audience, and exigence but have difficulty with the concept of constraints. At this point, Aristotle's taxonomy of inartistic and artistic proofs is brought in as an analogue to Bitzer's theory of constraints: inartistic proofs correspond to constraints inherent in the situation, such as facts, traditions, beliefs, attitudes, and motives; artistic proofs are those constraints the rhetor develops, such as evidence of his personal character (ethos), his modes of reasoning (logos), and his style of discourse or use of emotional appeals (pathos). This taxonomy then becomes fundamental to the course as students learn about deductive and inductive arguments; rules of evidence;

and arguments involving generalization, definition, cause and analogy, fallacies, and propaganda devices. Students practice rhetorical analysis by using Bitzer's model to examine such fictional rhetorical situations as Franklin's "The Speech of Polly Baker," "To His Coy Mistress," and Mr. Casaubon's proposal in *Middlemarch*. Students demonstrate their understanding of rhetorical theory and their ability to use Bitzer's model in analyzing a rhetorical situation in their final course project, the research paper.

Using the Bitzer model, the teacher can avoid several perennial problems encountered in teaching the research project. Requiring the students to choose a specific rhetorical situation to investigate rather than a topic to write about helps them avoid the trap of choosing a topic that is too broad, becoming overwhelmed by an abundance of sources, and writing a vague, unfocused paper. The student who chooses to examine how newspaper coverage of chemical leakage in Love Canal, New York, prompted business and government to assist that community is more likely to develop and support a thesis successfully than the student who chooses to write about "pollution."

Another concern is avoiding repetition of what students have already learned in high school. By the time they are college freshmen, most students have already written at least one research paper, but the Bitzer model gives students a fresh perspective on research by introducing them to a new kind of project, the rhetorical analysis. Previous research papers they have written have involved compiling and organizing the comments of several writers on a topic; this research assignment gives them the opportunity to create a piece of original research and analysis, using the concepts of rhetoric and argument studied during the semester as analytical tools.

Because they must analyze the actual rhetoric used in a given situation, students are compelled to work with primary sources, another new experience. They learn how to locate the transcript of a trial or the text of a speech, how to order and use microfilmed newspaper accounts of an event, how to contact their congressional representative to obtain government documents, how to order a book through interlibrary loan, how to locate the address of a special interest group in the *Encyclopedia of Associations*. They are introduced to bibliographical tools and sources of information they have never used before: the student who is writing a paper on "the energy crisis" may never venture beyond the card catalog or the *Readers' Guide*, while the student who is analyzing the rhetorical strategies President Carter used during the summer of 1979 to persuade Americans to support his energy program will learn to use such sources as *Facts on File*, the *New York Times Index*, the *Public Affairs Information Service*, and the *Gallup Opinion Index*. They also learn new research skills: the student who is writing a paper on "nuclear energy" will probably use the same research procedures learned in high school, while the student who is examining the ways a local citizens' group for safe energy is attempting to organize their community against nuclear power will learn how to gather and document information from personal and telephone interviews, letters, television and radio talk shows, public meetings, lectures, and promotional literature.

The Bitzer model is also useful in integrating the development of research skills with the rhetorical component of the course; too often, the research paper is taught in isolation from work in composition or rhetoric, as an appendage rather than as an integral part of the course. Students must learn how to work with rhetorical concepts such as proofs, audience, and exigence in order to write their research paper; they must also learn to locate sources, take notes, and document information in order to put the rhetorical concepts they have learned into practice; thus, both aspects of the course become interdependent and equally important as students develop research skills along with their ability to analyze rhetorical discourse.

This approach also demonstrates quite effectively to students that rhetoric is a mode of altering reality at work every day in everyone's life, a more complex and sometimes paradoxical process than the communication triangle suggests. The student who examines how lifers at Rahway State Prison in New Jersey use rhetoric to turn juvenile offenders away from crime finds that language can change behavior, even when used by poorly educated, unsophisticated rhetors, while the student who investigates Clarence Darrow's defense of John Scopes finds that even the most skillfully devised rhetorical strategies sometimes fail when other constraints are more powerful. The student who analyzes Gerald Ford's speech justifying the Nixon pardon learns that sometimes the ostensible exigence in a rhetorical situation (the need to unify the country) has been contrived to mask the actual exigence (Ford's need to put Watergate behind him before he could be elected president). Likewise, the student analyzing the effect of feminist rhetoric used to rally women to the cause of Inez Garcia, on trial for killing one of her assailants after being raped, finds that the rhetors were more concerned with focusing public attention on rape than on Inez's innocence.

Bitzer's theory of the rhetorical situation is useful in showing how rhetorical theory is a description of how rhetoric works in real life rather than a rhetorician's ivory-tower conception of how language works. Aristotle's belief that ethical proof is the most effective rhetorical constraint can be verified by students who look at the way Charles Manson, the Reverend Sun Myung Moon, or the Reverend Jim Jones of the People's Temple persuaded large numbers of people to act against their own best interests. Kenneth Burke's notion of identification, the process by which rhetor makes common cause with audience, can be seen at work in Richard Nixon's successful prosecution of Alger Hiss through identifying with and playing upon Americans' fear of communism. Students can also see how failure to identify with one's audience can undermine an otherwise well-planned rhetorical strategy in the experience of an international mining conglomerate's attempting to persuade the residents of a mountain community through expensive advertisements and promotional brochures that it is as concerned as they are with preserving the quality of their environment.

Many students, through their work on this project, discover that a rhetorical situation can become more complex than Bitzer's model suggests. A student who chose to examine the 1968 Democratic National Convention found a spiraling effect was produced, with one rhetorical situation generating another until the public's attention was focused on quite a different exigence than was originally intended. She noted that the traditional rhetorical arena provided by the convention, ordinarily dominated by delegates competing to nominate successfully a presidential candidate, was co-opted by antiwar demonstrators intent upon dramatizing another exigence: the need to end American involvement in Vietnam. Still another rhetorical situation surfaced when reporters who came to the convention with preconceived ideas about the demonstrators began to portray them in a more positive way after becoming angered by the police brutality they witnessed and sometimes experienced. Thus, the original exigence, the need to nominate a candidate, was overshadowed by the demonstrators' need to mobilize public opinion against the war, which gave way to the media representatives' need to show the public that police brutality was occurring. The student concluded that this spiraling effect of rhetorical situation creating rhetorical situation was, in part, responsible for the decision to end America's involvement in the war. "In Chicago, by reaching the reporters to carry their message, the demonstrators accomplished their purpose. Only after many such happenings around the country before and after Chicago did the people become aroused enough to begin to put pressure for change on their congressmen and individuals of authority. This pressure, although not the primary reason, was a factor in terminating the open conflict in Vietnam. Therefore, Chicago and other demonstrations like Chicago, proved to be a truly rhetorical situation."[2]

In many ways, Bitzer's theory of the rhetorical situation is useful to the teacher of rhetoric; students, too, have recognized the benefits of a course based on this approach. "I feel writing a research paper based on Bitzer's ideas was a good assignment," wrote one student in her evaluation of the course. "It required thought, time, and, of course, a paper of that type always requires work and a knowledge of writing principles." Another student voiced the initial misgivings shared by many of her peers: "At the beginning, the rhetorical situation seemed perplexing. I was unsure of what was required. However, after going over the various rhetorical devices, I began to see how things were to go together." One student's evaluation reflected his new awareness of an unpleasant fact of rhetorical reality: "This research paper on a rhetorical situation helped me see the effects language can have. It seems that it's not what the facts are, as much as how they are expressed and interpreted." Another response raised the question of the student who learns the lesson all too well.

> People, when trying to argue a point of view, use any type of reasoning which will work to their advantage. They will be vague for the moment so as to buy time to prepare a more definite view later. They will use statistics which may not be complete or totally factual. They might even use their position of authority to influence their audience. Rhetors use these and other factors to gain their audience's approval. Now, as I was examining the editorials of the *New York Times* concerning women's suffrage, I saw where they would use these methods. This will make me able to analyze any other claim or opinions which I come in contact with in the future. It will be easier to decide upon the validity of their claims. Of course, I will be able to use these same methods, as politicians do, when it is to my advantage, too.

NOTES

1. Lloyd Bitzer, "The Rhetorical Situation," *Philosophy and Rhetoric* 1 (1968), 131–144.
2. Martha Keenan, "The Rhetorical Situation in Chicago: August, 1968," research paper, English 101A, Nov. 1976, 6.

A PROCESS-ORIENTED RESEARCH ASSIGNMENT: I-SEARCH BEFORE RESEARCH

Bernadette M. Glaze

Introduction: How Can Teachers Use I-Searching?

I teach American Civilization at Lake Braddock Secondary School in Burke, Virginia. American Civilization is an eleventh-grade interdisciplinary, team-taught course which combines the teaching of American literature and American history. My classes are heterogeneous, with students from middle to upper-middle socioeconomic backgrounds. In 1978, Fairfax County Public Schools adopted a teacher's guide for teaching writing and research in social studies, *Writing and Research in the Social Studies*. One of the objectives on the eleventh-grade level is: "The student will write a multi-paragraph, documented research paper on a topic designated by the teacher. Use a minimum of five sources, at least one of which must be primary" (1: 85).

Since the implementation of the writing program, I have searched for ways of teaching the research paper that would help students produce lively, interesting, honest writing. I read books and articles on teaching research papers. I found advice on developing a controlling purpose and preliminary outline. I read sample calendars and exercises on fact vs. opinion, distinguishing between primary and secondary sources, note-taking, and avoiding plagiarism. I talked with fellow teachers also searching for a better way. My colleagues and I shared hours of dialogue on how to improve student research papers. We also shared frustrations about:

- students' inability to formulate an original hypothesis
- students' inability to develop a controlling purpose or thesis statement
- plagiarism

75

- cardboard writing
- an increasing number of students refusing to turn a paper in

Each year we finely tuned our teaching of the research process, but we still complained about the end result: dull student papers which were simply summaries or reports with "thesis sentences" stuck on for effect. There had to be a better way.

At a Northern Virginia Writing Project meeting last September, Marian Mohr and Don Gallehr announced the publication of a new book by Ken Macrorie, *Searching Writing*. Don wanted someone to review the book for the NVWP newsletter—"preferably someone in social studies, since this is a new approach to teaching research."

We each got a chance to glance through the book during the meeting, and when my turn came, I opened to the preface.

> I Search. That's the truth of any inquiry. Research doesn't say it, rather implies complete detachment, absolute objectivity. Time to clear the miasma and admit that the best searchers act both subjectively and objectively and write so that professionals and the public can understand their searches and profit by them. Time to get down to basics, which are not footnotes, but curiosity, need, rigor in judging one's findings and opinions of experts and helping others test the validity of the search.
>
> For many decades high schools and colleges have fostered the "research paper," which had become an exercise in badly done bibliography, often an introduction to the art of plagiarism, and a triumph of meaninglessness—for both writer and reader. As a teacher I've helped to bring about such inane productions myself. Now I look forward to reading I-Search papers because they tell stories of quests that counted for the questers and they're written in a way that catches and holds readers, as examples in this book make evident. (Preface)

What Macrorie had written really hit home. He was describing the frustrations and was offering a solution: an I-Search paper of teaching research. What was an I-Search paper? I found a brief description in chapter 2:

> In the last four years other teachers around the country and I have been challenging students to do what we call I-Searches not Researches, in which the job is to search again what

> someone has already searched—but original searches in which
> persons scratch an itch they feel . . . a search to fulfill a need, not
> one that the teacher had imagined for them, but one they feel
> themselves. (2: 14)

The examples of I-Searches spread throughout the book were
written in first-person narrative style on topics of personal interest
and were based on questions such as: Would I have a hard time
owning and training a wolf? Could I become a firefighter? Could I be
a disc jockey? Should I be an architect? Macrorie talks about
possibilities for I-Searching. "To start students in history, social
science, or science, for example, with *Searching Writing* would enable
them to become writers instead of jargoneers, and to retain and
increase their natural human curiosity and initiative in searching"
(Preface). This was a fresh response to my yearly search for a better
way to teach the eleventh-grade research requirement. I offered to
review the book for the newsletter.

One of my favorite chapters was "Objectivity and Subjectivity." It
told the story of the objectivity, or complete detachment, which has
come to be associated with the traditional research process. Macrorie
claims that this supposed detachment is what is wrong with how we
present searching. A search should take place, not out of complete
objectivity, but because "somebody needs to find out something. . . .
Somebody's got a question and wants to answer it" (2: 162).

My colleagues and I had the best intentions but we seemed to be
working against ourselves. Often I railed against college professors—
we were making the kids write these papers because of them. I agreed
with Macrorie's analysis:

> As a teacher I've been that hypocritical without realizing it. I
> thought I was helping students learn to use the library and
> master the form of research reporting. I had been told that
> people have to know them [these skills] in order to go through
> college, graduate school, and make a go of a profession. Now I
> realize that other teachers and I have given so many instructions
> to students about the form and length of papers that we've
> destroyed their natural curiosity. They don't want to grab
> books off the shelf and taste them. (2: 55)

I enjoyed the style of the I-Search papers. They tell stories of
experience written in narrative rather than expository form. I had
often looked for good professional expository writing to use in the

classroom. The only place I could find models of expository writing
was in composition texts. Not even our history text was written the
way we ask kids to write. I did find one history text written the way
we tell kids to write, and it was as dull and boring as the student
writing. I-Search papers are different.

> When you write a first-rate I-Search paper, you'll not only be
> developing a useful lifetime habit and carrying out an intellec-
> tual task, but you'll also be getting experience in writing the
> sort of account often published in magazines and books these
> days. More and more editors are ignoring the old essay and
> article forms. Readers are buying magazines and books which
> tell the story of experience rather than present reports that
> consist mainly of abstracted or generalized points and statistics
> accompanied by an anecdote or two. (2: 77)

I-Searching seemed to offer a fresh approach to both finding
information and writing about that information, an approach that
would encourage interesting, lively, honest writing.

While I was reading *Searching Writing,* my partner and I were
preparing our students for a trip to Williamsburg as part of our study
of colonial America. The trip was intended to inform as well as to
provide inspiration for students in developing colonial history
projects. To accommodate those who could not go on the trip, our
librarian put together a reserve book cart on colonial history. The day
before the trip, I called together the stay-at-school group for
instructions. I told them they should use the books on the cart to help
them choose a topic for the project. They should hand in note cards
and bibliography cards to the substitute. One young man spoke up,
"But, Mrs. Glaze, what if we don't have a topic by the end of class?"

"Well, just turn in the notes you've taken so far."

Not satisfied, he got right to the point. "But what if you spend
your whole time looking through the books for ideas and don't have
any note cards or bibliography cards?"

He was not looking for a way around the assignment. He was
being very honest and logical. What to do? I replied, "Oh—good
point, Kurt. Let's see . . . I know—write me the story of your looking,
browsing through the books. Yes, that's it. Write me the story of
what happens. A 'browse paper.' "

The idea seemed to take. Kurt grinned, "O.K. That sounds easy
enough."

I didn't know what to expect from the browse papers, but they certainly seemed appropriate. They answered a need and the students seemed responsive. The idea of writing the story of your "browse" through the cart was based on the idea of I-Search—tell the story of your search. The next day, I told the students who went on the trip to write the story of their topics so far. Both the topic stories and the browse stories reflected a natural, genuine voice. Students either gained a clearer idea of what they needed to do next, or in some cases, "discovered" their topics through writing the browse papers.

The basic idea of I-Searching soothed my frustrations with the traditional research paper. But what about the county objectives? And what about the students' twelfth-grade government teachers next year? I would have had to deal with these doubts, but it was October and second semester seemed far away. The day-to-day demands of teaching put thoughts of I-Search versus research on hold.

At a midwinter department meeting, our chairman reminded us of the county research paper requirement. We discussed library use, deadlines, length, use of class time, and methods of evaluation. None of this sounded very much like I-Search. I still had time, though. The papers weren't due until the middle of May.

My office-mates assigned the research paper soon after the department meeting, and for weeks I heard discussions about bibliography cards, hypothesis, and preliminary outlines. I felt uncomfortable during these discussions. I didn't want to do it that way this year, but I was worried about what would happen if I didn't. I rechecked the county guide to see if I-Search could meet the objectives of the required paper. I read the familiar list:

- develop an original hypothesis from the given topic
- use the library to locate primary and secondary sources
- take notes on properly labeled note cards
- refine hypothesis into a clear purpose or thesis statement
- arrange supportive details in a topic outline which indicates a structured method of development
- develop and state controlling purpose in an introductory paragraph
- present researched data in three or more supporting paragraphs
- use statistics, opinions, or reasons (2: 85)

I-Searching would certainly accomplish all of these goals, but I still had doubts about the first-person narrative style. And what about those twelfth-grade teachers?

I was struggling with a Fairfax County–Macrorie compromise when I had a conversation with Anne Wotring, a colleague at Lake Braddock. Anne knew I had read *Searching Writing* and asked when I was going to start the I-Search paper with my students.

"Well, Anne, I'm thinking of a compromise of some sort. Maybe have the kids do an I-Search journal but keep the traditional format. Your kids did I-Search papers, didn't they? How did they do?"

"They were wonderful papers. We all enjoyed them. But why aren't you going to do I-Searching?"

"Frankly, I'm concerned about what will happen next year. I'm worried that the I-Search is out of context in the schoolwide program."

"Bernie, don't worry about the twelfth-grade teachers. The kids will learn more doing I-Search and will be able to adapt easily."

I thought long and hard about that conversation. Can an I-Search paper be a valuable thing for a social studies student to do? The only way to find out was to teach I-Searching and learn with my students. They would be the source for my search. I decided to keep a journal of class activities and of student reactions to help answer my questions.

Throughout the year, my students learn to write history by writing in journals so I used the same approach with the I-Search papers. The day before I introduced I-Searching, students brought fresh journals to class and did a ten-minute free writing on the "Research Paper."

I asked for volunteers to read their free writings aloud. There was some hesitation. I think they were afraid of offending me. A brave soul broke the ice with this:

> When someone says the words "Research Paper," the first thing that comes to my mind is "Yuck." They seem to me to be boring, boring papers that take two full weeks to complete in which you get nothing out of it but frustration. I don't think we should have to do time in high school or college. ·

Someone added quickly, "Pick a minor subject and explain it majorly!" We all laughed. There was some applause and shouts of "O.K., Creston!" and "You said it!" Other volunteers read reactions that were just as negative.

The research paper? The first thing you hear from me is a groan. It's a lot of hard working, reading, rewriting, and a plain pain in the neck!! I hate them.

Work, work, work . . . going to far-off libraries and rummaging through back issues of *Boys' Life* for one sentence on your topic. A research paper also means our eleventh-graders will have to plagiarize their brains out copying their thesis sentences from last week's *Head Lines* and forgetting to give the author credit. This is a research paper.

When I think of the research paper, I think of a lot of hard work, bibliography cards, footnotes, note cards and rough drafts. In doing a research paper, you need to spend a lot of time in the library and find the books you need.

Something that I don't want to do because all I've ever heard about them is complaints. People that have already done them just laugh when they know I have one to do still.

I told them I agreed with them, and we were not going to do things that way this year. There were many sighs of relief and an immediate lightening of the atmosphere.

After school, I asked Bea Kirby, our librarian, to talk to my classes about using libraries in the context of an I-Search paper. Bea had read *Searching Writing* and said she would be delighted to prepare such a presentation. I arranged for her to come in the day I introduced I-Searching to my classes. I also arranged to go back and interview Anne Wotring. Anne is a first-rate teacher and writer. I was eager to talk further about the I-Search papers her students had done. She started the interview with three pieces of advice:

> 1. Have the students write the introduction (the what-I-knew and what-I-wanted-to-find-out parts) before their searches. Give them class time to do this.
> 2. Read plenty of samples of I-Search papers in class. Macrorie includes many in *Searching Writing.*
> 3. Emphasize style—tell it as a story.

I asked about time. "Is ten days long enough for the search?"
"Yes. That's plenty of time for a paper this length."
I asked Anne how long her papers were.

"Believe me, Bernie, you'll have no trouble with length. Once they get started . . . We all naturally know how to research if we are curious enough. That's what the I-Search is all about. That's also why the best topics are those which are of immediate concern."

I asked Anne if she required note cards and bibliography cards. Anne said she didn't since many of the I-Searches were primarily interviews. Anne also emphasized that since most of the searching was done outside of class, we should use class time to write.

Anne then talked about collecting the first drafts. They fit into one of three categories.

1. those which needed editing
2. those which told the sketch of the search but forgot to put in what the students learned
3. those which needed more searching

Anne was enthusiastic about the results of the I-Searching in her classes. This enthusiasm and her experience with I-Searching made her an invaluable source for my search.

I needed to review *Searching Writing* to prepare the introduction of I-Search to my classes. I wanted the introduction to go well because I knew this could determine the students' attitudes toward the whole project. My quick review reminded me of some essential Macrorie:

- Let the topic choose you by asking what you need to know these days.
- An I-Search paper should be valuable to the writer and her readers, not be done just to fulfill the instructions of a teacher.
- Research—you search again what someone has already searched.

I decided to photocopy an excerpt from *Searching Writing* for the kids to read: "Sketch of I-Searching" (2: 62–64), a list of eight important elements of I-Searching. I felt ready.

I introduced the I-Search assignment by putting two terms on the board:

I-SEARCH

RE-SEARCH

I asked the kids what they thought the differences would be.

They picked up on it quickly. "I-Search is more personal." "It's something I do." "Re-search is someone else's search."

They all looked interested. I told them of my decision to change the emphasis of the research paper. This year they were going to do I-Searches on something they needed to find out. It should be something they really needed to know—now. I expected snickers and a rolling-of-the-eyes reaction to "Let the topic choose you," but the room was silent.

I distributed the "Sketch of I-Searching" (2: 62–64) I had photocopied and asked them to read. Once again the room was silent. Each student seemed engrossed in the reading. When they were finished, we talked about the importance of choosing the right topic—that is, searching something you honestly needed to know. I used a topic from Anne Wotring's class as an example: How can I get a basketball scholarship? Andy Baines dropped her chin to her chest and raised her hand like a shot.

"Mrs. Glaze, pardon me, but how can the answer to that question be a three- to five-page paper?"

In response, I put the four steps or divisions of an I-Search paper on the board:

1. what I knew
2. what I wanted to find out: Why I'm writing this paper
3. the story of the search
4. what I learned

The reaction was positive: sighs of relief, interested eyes, good feelings all around. One student asked if it was permissible to use "I" when writing the paper. When I said yes, there were more audible sighs of relief.

Next I referred the students to step no. 2 in "Sketch of I-Searching:

> Find experts or authorities. Ask them where to locate the most useful books, magazines, newspapers, films, tapes, or other experts on your topic. (2: 62)

I then introduced our first expert, Bea Kirby. Bea had developed a "Search Strategy Check Sheet" after reading *Searching Writing*. She focused her presentation on how I-Searchers could use the resources of the library. She pointed out the *Washington Information Directory*, which has the names and phone numbers of many experts on various topics and includes an excellent subject index. She discussed reference works and the best way to use the *Readers' Guide to Periodical Literature.* Bea referred constantly to I-Searching and told the students how lucky they were to be doing such an assignment. I offered information about resources when I could, and I think our mutual interest and enthusiasm was good modeling. We finished our introduction with an assignment: By Friday, let a topic choose you. This had been a good beginning. My students and I felt comfortable and upbeat about I-Searching.

I knew students needed to read models of I-Search papers. I ran off three examples from *Searching Writing,* and for the next two class periods students read and wrote journal reactions to the papers.

Students liked the I-Search papers. After conference time each day, we shared journal reactions.

> These papers are written in a mild tone like there's no pressure on the authors. The author seems like he is eager to learn all about what he is researching and he is trying to answer a question he has on the topic. The papers are fun to read because they seem like the person is talking to you about his problem and how he answers it. I think once I get my topic on what to write about, this is going to be a very enjoyable paper to write.

> When you said we were writing an I-Search paper, I thought, "Oh, wow, another research paper, just change the re to I and you get an I-Search paper." Well, I was wrong, but now I think I know what an I-Search paper is. It's a short story filled with facts, what fun! Now instead of just collecting facts and putting them into a well-constructed mechanical paper, I have to be creative! Me creative, well, I'll give this thing a shot and come up with some kind of I-re? search paper.

> Today I read some entries of I-Search journals. I noticed that the key objective for a person is you get out and talk to people to get to the right sources. Both papers of the D.J. and the camera were very interesting. The architect paper was probably better written then the other two. It sounded more organized.

> An I-Search paper is an excellent idea. I like it a lot better and I think it won't be as *BORING* as writing a research paper. It will be very interesting. It seems much easier and more comfortable to write. I am very glad we're doing I-Search—it's a lot better!

A couple of students in each class noticed that the papers read like stories. We talked about good nonfiction having the same characteristics as good fiction. I asked students to point out where the learning was and what skills were involved in I-Searching. I wrote the responses on the board: interviewing, making judgments about what you read and hear, reporting, writing, finding the answer to your question.

The topic conferences proved invaluable. I asked, "What do you need to know right now? and "Why do you need to know this?" and "What do you want to find out about it?" and helped students find topics and formulate questions. Because of the time of year, many topics were college or career related:

> Should I become an aeronautical engineer?
> Are military academies for me?
> What's the best used car for me?
> Can I get a soccer scholarship to college?

One student wanted to do a search on gun control because of all the controversy surrounding the issue. When I asked what she wanted to know about gun control, she couldn't answer. I suggested some background reading and told her to try to have a question in a couple of days. She came back to my desk minutes later with her question already formulated: "How do I feel about gun control?" We were both pleased. In fact, I thought that question, "How do I feel about ———?" would be a good way to begin investigating many such issues.

Two students wanted to do more traditional topics: the space shuttle and World War II weaponry. These students needed more time to read background information and to narrow their topics before they could formulate questions.

Choosing a topic was a soul-searching experience for students who said they had no special interests or questions about anything. I'm sure they watch too much TV. My response to this was always, "You are a walking-around, live human being and as such are a unique individual. In the name of Henry David Thoreau, of course you have interests!" For these students especially, walking-around-thinking-about-it time was important. I assigned the paper on a Monday and by Friday most students had let a topic choose them.

Friday was Source Day. The air was full of space shuttle excitement and spring break anticipation. The topics were due and we were going to share topics, help one another develop questions, and trade suggestions on sources and how to get started. I arranged a circle of twenty-five chairs in one corner of the room. On each chair I had placed a ditto, which looked like this:

Source Day

Name_____
My Question:
Group Suggestions:

Name	Topic	Question

There was enough space so that we could write in the information for each student in the class. Each student was to state his or her topic and question, and the rest of us were going to offer suggestions on how to get started. A soft spring breeze reminded me of the gorgeous day and time of the year. Was I-Searching powerful enough to keep the group going with an open-ended discussion like the one I had planned?

When class began, I directed students to the circle of chairs, explained Source Day, and told them how to fill in the ditto. The sharing sessions proved productive and honest. There was risk taking I hadn't predicted. The topics were personal, thus revealing. We found out new things about one another: hobbies, career directions, college preferences. The sharing was spontaneous, with kids who had never spoken to one another exchanging names, addresses, telephone numbers. A typical exchange went like this:

Mrs. Glaze. O.K., Jim, your turn—what's your question?
Eric. Wait, Mrs. Glaze, what's his last name?
Mrs. G. Damico. D, 'A—.
Jim. No, Mrs. Glaze, it's "Damico."
Mrs. G. Sorry, Jim Damico. D, A, M, I, C, O. O.K., what's your question?
Jim. Well. I've decided to do it on "Should I be a veterinarian?"
Mrs. G. Do you know anyone you could interview?

Kent. My sister's a veterinarian. She lives in Baltimore.

Mrs. G. Do you think she'd mind? Could Jim give her a call or write?

Mark. How old's your sister? Maybe Jim should take her out to dinner!

Kent. She's twenty-four. No. She wouldn't mind.

Mrs. G. Jim, why don't you talk to Kent after class. Also there's someone else doing a similar question. Do you know . . . ?

We had many such exchanges. Not only did the kids help one another get started, but they also helped one another refine questions. Some had topics but no questions yet. Caroline Cangolosi wanted to do something on San Diego because she was moving there in July. The kids talked about this for a couple of minutes and someone said, "Hey! How about, 'What is life like for a teenager in San Diego?' "

Someone else offered, "And guess who is sitting in this very room who lived his whole life in San Diego? O.K. Pat, that's right, isn't it?"

Pat nodded. Caroline had her first source.

The best part was the way the kids talked with one another. They were mature, responsive. They were discussing ideas and concerns that were theirs. They were the experts, not the teacher. I felt as good about Source Day as I have felt about any day in twelve years of teaching.

Two class days after Source Day, I assigned the introduction. I reminded students of the purpose of the introduction: tell the story of how you got into the search, what you knew or didn't know, and what you wanted to find out. Greg Jones asked if we were going to write the papers the same way the samples were—like stories. I said yes and then decided another reading from *Searching Writing* would be helpful before they began to write. I distributed an excerpt from chapter 9, "Tell It as Story." As the title indicates, this chapter talks about how to write the I-Search. The students read and wrote journal reactions. Just as with other I-Search reading times, I could hear the proverbial pin drop. I asked what they found most interesting.

- The reader could tell when the writer wasn't interested. (Macrorie included an I-Search paper that was superficial.)
- The introduction to one of them was dull because the person wasn't in it.
- They sounded like talking.
- They sounded natural.
- The introduction should be interesting and exciting and catch the reader's attention.

- It's from your memory—more personal—it actually happened.
- The introduction captures the readers' attention—the guy wrote like he was interested in the paper—not just *like* he is but he *is*.
- It seems like the more you're into your topics, the easier it is to write.

The students picked out the characteristics of good I-Searching. They were ready to write their introductions. I gave them class time to write. They read their introductions in reading/writing groups using these questions as a guide:

1. Is the introduction written as story?
2. Is there any part of the introduction your group would like to know more about?
3. Does the introduction include an incident(s), people, places?
4. Does the introduction tell the story of how you got into your topic?
5. What do you want to know about the topic?

By one week after Source Day, the kids had written first drafts. I gave them the weekend to revise based on group suggestions, and collected the rough drafts of the introductions the following Monday. After reading through a dozen or so rough drafts, I decided to assign a v-, v, or v+ indicating the degree to which the paper needed revising. I made few comments on the drafts. Asking questions was more appropriate—Can you tell me more about this? or, Why (when) did this happen? Who was this?—clarifying questions meant to help the searcher tell the real story of his or her topic.

By this time, the kids were into their searches. Some things that helped with this stage were:

Flexibility. Many students wrote letters and needed time for the replies. Students arranged interviews with counselors, teachers, veterinarians, soccer coaches, sports announcers, farmers, and college deans. I had to be sensitive to the appointment schedules they were given and adjust due dates accordingly.

Interviewing. We devoted a couple of class sessions to determining the characteristics of good interviewing. We discussed questioning techniques; how to record and compose the interview; and the best preparation for an interview.

Periodic Source Checks. I conferred with students on the progress of their searches. Since the searching was done out of school, I needed to build in some accountability. This enabled me to see who wasn't searching at all and to prod, suggest—whatever I thought would motivate. Few students were doing nothing.

Periodic Free Writing. These helped clarify where the searcher was and what he or she had to do next. For some students, these free writings were the first drafts of their I-Search papers. We wrote on the story of my topic, my search so far, and composing the introduction.

Documentation Day. I used Macrorie's suggestions on documentation because they seemed simple yet thorough (2: 64–65). I spent fifty to seventy-five minutes discussing documentation. The length of time depended on the number of questions. Students were relieved to find out that we weren't going to use footnotes. "For short papers, footnotes . . . aren't appropriate as documentation. What makes more sense is 'Back-notes' that appear at the end of the paper" (2: 64). I told them to list the sources they used in writing the paper in alphabetical order, putting interviews last, and to number each source. I gave them examples of bibliographic entries for books, magazines, encyclopedias, and interviews. Then I said, "O.K., now let's say you have listed five sources. What would this mean, then?" And I wrote "(2: 15)" on the board. They easily figured out that this would mean page 15 from the second source listed in the bibliography. I told them to place the source number and the page number in parentheses at the end of the passage when needed or simply include the source number if they were referring to an interview.

Four weeks after I assigned the I-Search papers, the first drafts of the search were due. This four weeks included the week of spring break. The searchers read the drafts in their reading/writing groups and used these questions as guides:

1. What sections would you like to know more about?
2. Is the search told like a story? Is the narrative written in clear chronological order? Does the author use direct quotes and dialogue?
3. What are the sources of the search?
4. Has the author checked more than one side of the issue? That is, did the author compare the words of differing experts?
5. What are the group's suggestions for the search? Experts, magazines, books?

Students wrote journal entries on "What I need to do next" as an assimilation of the reading/writing group session. I gave them the weekend to revise, and collected the first drafts on Monday.

I read approximately one hundred first drafts in a week. The papers were easy reading because of the narrative style. There were fewer grammar errors than usual. I thought this had to do with the more natural style of writing. Most papers ran well over the five handwritten or three typed pages we had originally planned. Because they were stories of searches, just how much thinking, analyzing, reading, judging, and interviewing were done was apparent after a quick reading. I had told the students that the conclusion—what I learned—did not have to be part of this draft. Some were still awaiting replies to letters, others interview appointments. I was reading the stories of their searches so far, even though there were a good number of searches complete at this time. There were car searches, family-history searches, and one diet search. There was one very painful why-did-my-father-leave-us search. One of the best searches was the "How do I feel about gun control search?" The student read articles on both sides of the issue and interviewed several policemen who had different opinions on the issue. Her paper shows analysis, critical judgment, and real, honest, live thinking. One student searched his way into a summer job at a veterinary clinic, another into a job on a dairy farm.

The student who wanted to search World War II weaponry had asked, "What was the impact of WW II on weapons technology?"

I told him he had an encyclopedia-length paper on his hands and should narrow the question. The paper he wrote was the story of his search for a way to narrow the question. He learned that he had started too broad and ended up formulating a much more appropriate question. He had searched his way into a good question for a more traditional research paper.

My interview with Anne Wotring really helped at this point. I, too, found that some papers needed editing, others more searching. Some students told the story of the search but forgot to put in what they had learned. I wrote comments and questions like these:

> Have you checked the *Readers' Guide*?
> Do you have an interview lined up?
> What did you find out here?
> Could you put this in a dialogue?

Is there another expert you could talk with?
How did you find out about this expert, book, magazine?
What do you need to do next?
Are you satisfied that your search is complete?
Where are you in the search?
Have you asked the librarian for help? Or the counselor?
Would you like a conference?

I returned the rough drafts in a week and gave students another week to revise and write the conclusion.

I was going to forgo a reading-writing group session for the final drafts because we were getting close to final exams, and I wasn't sure how seriously they would handle the class time. I took an informal poll and was told emphatically that yes, they wanted reading-writing group time. I was amazed at how they reacted to one another's papers. They clamored for more class time. This was one of the most successful reading-writing group experiences in my class. They showed genuine interest in listening to one another. We ended up reading the papers for three days. These were important papers; they were proud of them and wanted to be heard. Their enthusiasm was worth all of our work. And so were the end results. The I-Search papers were interesting, lively, and detailed. They were honest. Not counting one dropout and one runaway, only 2 students of 130 did not do papers. The I-Search papers were hands-down the best papers of the year.

Just before I returned the I-Search papers, I assigned a journal writing on "What would you tell a rising eleventh-grader about I-Search?" Students wrote:

It sounds like a lot to do an I-Search paper. Just forget about how long the final form will be, in fact don't even think about it. First think of a subject—not just any subject but something that really interests you. Pick your subject with care, one that you don't know everything about. Then start the fun! See how creative you can get trying to figure new and different ways of searching out your topic. After you find something out, write it so you don't forget details, it's awful hard to sit down and write your whole search after you're done. Write a few sentences here and there—before you know it, you'll be done. Remember to keep a record of your sources.

If I was talking to a lowly, seamy underclassman, I would tell them that the I-Search papers were a good experience and a whole lot "funner" than writing research papers. Even though interviews are necessary, the usual busy work associated with research papers is completely avoided. The interviews are much easier than hours of boring information.

You really have nothing to worry about. This will probably be one of the easiest papers you'll ever write. All you have to do is pick a topic that you're *really* interested in and want to find more about. Then just go on your way finding out things about it. Try and find out every possible thing that will affect you. But be sure that while you are finding this out to write down everything you do. This paper is essentially a story of how and what you're finding out about your topic.

Well, first of all, I'd say it's a heck of a lot easier than a re-search paper. But be sure to pick a good question, it'd be better if you had something to do with a question you *really* want to answer. You know, a personal question. The papers themselves are so much easier and a lot more fun than the re-search. But don't put it off to the last minute. If you keep everything together and do the introduction, search, and conclusion when they're due, you've really got everything done. All you have left to do is rewrite it or to type it.

What I Learned

I learned that students not only enjoy but also learn from I-Searching. Here are some comments from a journal we did on "What I learned from I-Searching."

Doing my I-Search paper, I learned something very disappointing. I thought that people who had been working in their fields for a long time would know what they were doing. The people that spent out thousands of dollars making the (Alaskan) pipeline didn't know what they were doing. Today the pipeline is really of no use to us. We (U.S.) don't get much oil from it. Japan gets 75% of it. Before the pipeline was built, the engineers should have thought about the fact that there were not proper facilities to transport the oil over the U.S. Instead of thinking of this before, they spent millions of dollars, they thought of it after. Now, our money is spent and we have a flop up in Alaska. Besides that, it is embarrassing that other countries know of our stupidity.

All in all, I have learned something I never thought before. The arts (theatre, etc.) is where I belong. When talking with "L" I realized how much I enjoy theatre. He got me remembering mostly all the fun I had, where my closest friends were and so on. I also learned that teaching is not the best of jobs. Wouldn't it have been great if I could become a professional? I think about that all the time. I also learned that in order to go anywhere with theatre, I need lots of training.

I really learned that I don't have to get all flustered when someone asks me what college I'm going to and what field I'm majoring in. I'm really sorry I didn't put this in my I-Search itself. I know I cut the ending short. But I can't correct it, so I'll do my best here. I found that I will be good for a music program in my college and I won't go to a college without a fairly decent music program. I learned that I shouldn't jump the gun and make the decision now that could determine my future, but wait and let it develop itself rather than forcing it. I learned patience in myself. To be patient with my inside turmoil and not let others goad me into a quick decision.

I learned as much about my family as I could gather from my parents. I picked up a little history from what my parents told me—but basically I was pretty familiar with that history before hand. This paper was a new experience in writing. It wasn't hard at all. Once I started writing, everything flowed right out. It sounded natural because I just wrote what I thought without having to translate into a higher vocabulary bracket. No one likes to do research papers of any kind, but if you have to do it, the I-Search is the best alternative yet.

These free writings underscore the value of I-Searching. I learned that when students are given an opportunity to search something important in their lives, they will do a good job. They will also find out what good searching involves:

Formulating a question to be answered through searching
Finding and interviewing experts (people or books)
Judging the opinions of experts (people or books)

Testing the statements of experts against those of other experts
Using primary and secondary sources
Developing good interview techniques
Documenting what they find
Taking careful notes
Answering their questions based on what they've found in the
search

After my students handed in the final drafts, we discussed the
differences between what we did this year and what they would be
asked to do next year. "Let's see if we can adapt your I-Searches to
what your senior teachers might ask next year. Think about what you
wrote in your 'What I Learned' section. Now write a thesis sentence
that would be appropriate in an expository, multi-paragraph, research paper." After a few seconds of blank stares, they began to
write.

In order for one to teach theatre, one must have patience, a
caring attitude, and the time to give for the concern of
students.

The Alaskan pipeline is a failure.

Dairy farming is a diversified field of study requiring training
in business, science, and medicine.

Biomedical engineering involves dedication, hard work, and
desire.

This country needs uniform gun control laws.

Not everyone could come up with an instant thesis sentence, but I
didn't expect them to. However, with more time I think most could
have.

I wanted my supervisor, Frank Taylor, Social Studies Curriculum
Specialist for Fairfax County, to read these papers. I called Frank and
told him about *Searching Writing* and emphasized how impressed I
was with the papers. Frank said he was interested in the concept and
would like to see the results. A few days after school was out, I took
two dozen I-Search papers to Frank's office. We sat down in a quiet
conference room. Frank had a copy of *Searching Writing* and the

Fairfax County Social Studies Program of Studies. I asked him how he liked the book.

"The book is great, just great. But, Bernie, I have a couple of questions for you. First, do you think we can use it in social studies?"

"Absolutely. I'm glad you enjoyed the book, Frank, but before I answer any questions, I want you to read the papers I brought."

I spread six I-Search papers out on the table, and Frank read. He smiled a lot. He even chuckled once or twice.

"Frank, when was the last time you laughed like that when you were reading student papers?"

"Well, the last time I laughed like that wasn't while I was reading student papers, but that's another story."

"O.K., Frank what do you think?"

"Terrific. The papers are terrific. They're easy to read. Well written. You can tell they've learned a lot about writing. Are they all this long?"

"Frank, length was never an issue. And I read over 120 papers in a week."

"That's a selling point right there. I bet plagiarism wasn't a problem, either."

"No, there is really no way to plagiarize these. I was never concerned about it anyway. The kids enjoyed doing them too much for that to be an issue."

"Bernie, how would you like to do an in-service in September?"

"On the I-Search? I'd be delighted."

After we discussed the details of the in-service, Frank said, "O.K., now there's just a couple of things. I think this I-Search is just great, and I don't want in any way to jeopardize the integrity of the papers. But my job is to implement the Program of Studies objectives, and the county research paper is supposed to be on a Program of Studies objective." Frank opened to eleventh-grade American Studies, and we scanned the long list of objectives. Frank said he felt the objectives were broad enough that we could adapt the idea.

"Now, how are we going to write this up for the in-service program? What's the title?"

"How about, 'I-Search Before Re-Search'?"

" 'I-Search Before Re-Search'—I like that. Now what are we going to say about it?"

" 'I-Search: an exciting new approach to the introduction of research skills.' "

I-Searching works because it taps the natural curiosity of students. By personalizing the search process first, students learn the value of using primary sources, finding experts, and judging information. They learn the process of selecting topics that truly interest them, formulating questions, and searching for the answers. Writing in first-person narrative enables them to think about what they are doing and avoids mechanical note-taking.

A couple of days before I sat down to write this conclusion, I received a copy of James Moffet's latest book, *Active Voice: A Writing Program Across the Curriculum.* The program sequences three groups of writing assignments from the concrete to the abstract. The third group of assignments interested me immediately: narrative into essay.

> This group of assignments goes from concrete narratives to more distilled ones and thence to the ultimate distillation of narrative-generalization. So the shift is from the past tense to the present tense of generalization—*what happened* to *what happens.* (3: 72)

I-Searching bridges the gap from the concrete to the abstract and prepares students for the more abstract research tasks they will be assigned later. I will assign two I-Searches next year: one just like the one we did this year and another which will make more use of the library and will be on a topic related to American history.

I am sitting in the marbled and columned Main Reading Room of the Library of Congress as I finish this up, thinking about what I learned from this experience. I learned a lot more about my students. The sharing that went on created a comfortable, open atmosphere in my classroom. I liked that feeling. But back to the point. There are signs in the Main Reading Room which indicate the purpose of each alcove and section of the stacks. There are "Science and Technology—Special Searchers: Special Search Section, Alcove 7; and Search Facilities Office." This wonderful institution was designed for searchers. I-Searching is an excellent way to introduce students to the pleasures and satisfaction of searching. I like the sign in the alcove in front of me: "Special Searchers." Teachers who use *Searching Writing* will be encouraging all the special searchers in their classrooms.

SOURCES

Fairfax County Public Schools, Department of Instructional Services, Division of Curriculum Services. *Writing and Research in the Social Studies.* Fairfax, VA: County School Board of Fairfax County, 1978.

Macrorie, Ken. *Searching Writing.* Rochelle Park, N.J.: Hayden Book Co., 1980.

Moffet, James. *Active Voice.* Montclair, N.J.: Boynton/Cook Publishers, 1981.

Taylor, Frank. Personal interview. June 23, 1981.

Wotring, Anne. Telephone interview. Apr. 7, 1981.

THE RESEARCH PAPER AND POSTMODERNIST PEDAGOGY

James C. McDonald

The freshman research paper, I believe, is the most institutionalized single writing assignment in the academy, with the possible exception of the dissertation, and the research paper in general (of which the dissertation may be a subspecies) is the most institutionalized genre of student writing, at least in the humanities. The freshman research paper is usually the longest, most time-consuming (taking up over one-third of the average composition course, according to a 1982 survey by James E. Ford and Dennis R. Perry [828]), most intimidating, most frustrating, and sometimes, incredibly, the most satisfying paper that a freshman writes in composition, and finishing it (thank God!) marks the climax of the course. Almost all freshman writing programs (78.11 percent) require it (Ford and Perry 827), and frequently the research paper is the only assignment specifically required in each section of freshman composition. The research paper chapter is usually the textbook's longest and may receive the closest scrutiny by textbook selection committees. Teachers spend far more time in class, in conference, and going over bibliography cards, notes, outlines, and drafts with the research paper than with any other assignment, and the English department, the library, and other parts of the university often have an unusually heavy investment in this one assignment. Almost every library (87 percent) offers at least a tour to students learning to write the research paper, and at most schools (66 percent for freshman courses, 69 percent for advanced) librarians lecture writing classes on research methods and materials, and more than half of the schools provide special training for instructors and/or librarians in teaching and supporting the student writing a research paper (Ford and Perry 829).

98

My own experiences teaching at five different schools reveal a variety of involvement of library staff, writing centers, teaching assistants training programs, even regional accrediting associations in the teaching of the research paper. At Winthrop College each librarian prepared to conduct two classes with students in a composition course on research methods and starting a research paper, commenting on students' responses to a library exercise designed by the library and giving each student individual attention in the library as the student began to comb through abstracts, indexes, and the card catalog, and the librarian was specially available to these students for help until the paper was finished. After much consideration, the library at Northern Illinois University began to permit second-semester freshmen writing research papers for their composition and literature course to use the library rather than casebooks and developed a class and handouts on how to research works of literature in various British and American periods. At the University of Southwestern Louisiana, new teaching assistants taking the practicum course are assigned to observe a composition course taught by a professor or instructor *and* to teach the research paper in that course. The University of Texas at Austin, in grand Texas fashion, has an entire library geared to helping freshmen with the research paper. The librarians are trained to watch for freshmen who look like they need help, and the Undergraduate Library has developed brightly colored pamphlets and exercise sheets to help students with each stage of the paper. The Undergraduate Library has multiple copies of books on popular research paper topics, monitors the topics students like to write on to guide new acquisitions, and regulates the topics available for students to write on in each class to avoid overburdening the library. Writing Center tutors often go to classes to give workshops on compiling a bibliography or developing an outline from note cards.

Certainly the peculiar and intense institutional regulation of and involvement in this one freshman assignment needs study, but, in fact, there has been little theoretical discussion of the research paper of any kind, as a quick look at the Longman bibliographies, Gary Tate's *Teaching Composition,* and a 1980 ERIC bibliography on the research paper by Ford, Sharla Rees, and David L. Ward show. Ford and Perry note that *College English* and *College Composition and Communication* have averaged under one article on the research paper every two years, and that the CCCC and NCTE conventions usually fail to devote a single session to the research paper and almost never offer more than one (826). Most articles discuss methods to help students avoid plagiarism and to make writing the research paper more interesting and successful. Articles debating the validity of the research paper as a genre and its value as an assignment, such as Richard Larson's 1982 "The 'Research Paper' in the Writing Course: A Non-Form of Writing," are fairly common, going back almost to the time when the assignment originated, about seventy years ago. Discussing the arguments for and against the research paper by respondents to their survey, Ford and Perry conclude that this debate reflects "that the research paper is at the center of the controversy over whether English faculty should fulfill a 'service' role to other departments" (830). But articles concerning the validity or wisdom of assigning research papers tend to ignore the institutional entrenchment of this assignment. There has been some theoretical work on the genre, mainly by cognitive theorists, including a fine article by Margaret Kantz recently in *College English.* Almost no historical work has been done, and postmodernist theories and pedagogies, such as critical pedagogy and deconstruction associated with such figures as Paulo Freire and Jacques Derrida, generally have not been applied to the genre.

The current-traditional concept of the research paper developed and hardened soon after its beginning in the 1920s. The now-familiar steps for composing a research paper—choose a subject and narrow it, compile a bibliography, take notes, write an outline, and finally compose the theme—appeared in 1930 in the first article on the subject in *English Journal,* James M. Chalfant's "The Investigative Theme: A Project for Freshman Composition." Chalfant's few words about the final step, writing the theme, were concerned about mechanical problems of incorporating and documenting quotations and paraphrases to avoid plagiarism. In essence, the current-traditional research paper has been an exercise in researching and reporting what others have written to produce a paper that conforms to the course's conventions governing documentation—the concerns of most discussions of the assignment in textbooks and articles. James Berlin, in a brief discussion of the research paper in *Rhetoric and Reality,* writes that "the research paper represented the insistence in current-traditional rhetoric on finding meaning outside the composing act, with writing itself serving as a simple transcription process" (70). Students and teachers have commonly viewed the research paper as an expository essay that stitches together words, facts, and ideas, provided by authorities. Although instructors and textbooks often have taught the research paper as a persuasive essay or an assignment in problem solving, as Robert A. Schwegler and Linda K. Shamoon report, "students generally view the research paper as informative in aim, not argumentative, much less analytical, as factual rather than interpretive; designed to show off knowledge of library skills and documentation procedures . . . as an exercise in information gathering, not an act of discovery" (819). Students have often been told and often strongly believe that a research paper should not include their opinions. (I remember my high school history teacher telling this to my class, explaining that there was nothing new he could learn from high school boys, unless we were writing about sex, and he didn't let us write about that.) With the research paper, then, the writer is merely a reporter of information, and invention is mainly a problem of becoming familiar with the resources in the library, taking accurate and complete notes from these sources, and organizing this material effectively. Current-traditional textbooks like McCrimmon's *Writing with a Purpose* and Brooks and Warren's *Modern Rhetoric* sometimes briefly discuss the student's responsibility to understand, evaluate, and synthesize the material he or she has collected, but once that statement is out of the way, the textbooks concentrate on the real business of composing a research paper— finding sources, taking notes, and avoiding plagiarism—and ignore problems of interpreting and evaluating the texts that the student finds on a subject and composing one's own text out of the texts of others.

From a current-traditional perspective, in fact, interpreting these texts should not be a problem, for language is merely a conduit for transferring thoughts from speaker to hearer. Writing is a simple matter of translating thoughts into words and reading a matter of translating the words back into thoughts. If the writer has written clearly, transmission to a reader should be automatic. In the first edition of the *Harbrace College Handbook* John Hodges gave students this advice for reading and using the texts that they discovered in their research.

> Seldom will a whole book, or even a whole article, be of use as subject matter for any given research paper. To find what the student needs for his particular paper he must turn to many

> books and articles, rejecting most of them altogether and using
> from others a section here and there. He cannot take time to
> read each book carefully. He must use the table of contents and
> the index, and he must learn to scan the pages rapidly until he
> finds the passages he needs. (370)

Hodges' advice to students not to read carefully, but just to scan pages quickly in search of useful passages assumes that reading is merely a matter of recognizing words and the ideas they represent and that knowledge is a commodity that one possesses. The assumption that knowledge is a commodity of course, explains the current-traditional obsession with plagiarism and acknowledging proper ownership of ideas. Knowledge can be stolen. Books and articles here are merely containers of bits of knowledge and data which can be labeled and located by indexes. (Berlin points out that composition instructors began teaching the research paper shortly after many important bibliographical indexes began to be published and to appear in libraries [70].) Hodges' advice suggested that students use indexes much as shoppers use signs and directions in a giant mall to guide their searches to the right stores and aisles for items they "need." Hodges did insist that students "evaluate" their sources, but mainly along the lines of checking to make sure they do not buy bad merchandise: "One important consideration always is the reliability of the source. Does the author seem to know his subject? Do others speak of him as an authority? Is he prejudiced? Is the work recent enough to give the information needed?" (370). Some knowledge, like milk, has an expiration date. Once a text was certified, the information should be good. Knowledge here is information, facts, easily perceived through a see-through package of language. Chalfant suggested that the research paper was a valuable assignment because "the real distinction between the educated or trained man may often be not so much a matter of actual possession of facts as a knowledge of where and how to find what one wants to know at the time he needs to know it" (42). The writer here is like Sergeant Joe Friday on an investigation—"Just the facts, ma'am."

Paulo Freire has called such a view of knowledge and education "the banking concept of education," which turns students "into 'containers,' into 'receptacles' to be 'filled' by the teacher" (58). Banking education is "an act of depositing, in which the students are the depositories and the teacher [and in the research paper, library sources] [are] the depositor." Students are not involved in communication but instead "patiently receive, memorize, and repeat" "communiqués." The "scope of action allowed to the students extends only as far as receiving, filing, and storing the deposits," writes Freire. "They do, it is true, have the opportunity to become collectors or cataloguers of the things they store." But, for Freire, "knowledge emerges only through invention and re-invention, through the restless, impatient, continuing hopeful inquiry men pursue in the world, with the world, and with each other" (58).

Compare Freire's description of students as "receiving, filing, and storing the deposits" of knowledge to the treatment of compiling a bibliography, gathering note cards, and composing an outline and rough draft, not only by Chalfant and Hodges, but by most current textbook chapters on the research paper. Freire's words are echoed in Schwegler and Shamoon's summary of students' descriptions of writing a research paper:

> You usually don't get around to it for a while, but when you do you start out with a little bit of an idea; then you get a lot of books and put the information on note cards; you keep the note cards and bibliography sorted out; then you put together the pieces of information that are related, start on a rough outline, and finally write the paper. (818)

Banking education, Henry A. Giroux writes, is more interested in students " 'reproducing' history rather than learning how to make it" (120) and does not recognize "that knowledge is a social construction so that students can learn to play an active part in its production both in and out of the classroom" (121). "Implicit in the banking concept," writes Freire,

> is the assumption of a dichotomy between man and the world: man is merely *in* the world, not *with* the world or with others; man is spectator, not re-creator. In this view, man is not a conscious being (*corpo consciente*); he is rather the possessor of a consciousness; a empty "mind" passively open to the reception of deposits of reality from the world outside. (62)

The student's role is essentially to "adapt" "passively" to the world, and "the educator's role is to regulate the way the world 'enters into' the students, . . . to organize a process . . . to 'fill' the students by making deposits of information which he considers to constitute true knowledge" (62–63).

When the research paper is no longer conceived as strictly expository or informative discourse and students are expected to write evaluative or persuasive research papers, the concepts of knowledge as commodity and banking education create problems for teachers and writers. By assigning persuasive and evaluative papers, teachers now expect students not to be passive, but to take an active role in evaluating, shaping, and creating knowledge. But the teacher and textbook generally teach the same process of researching and writing found in the first edition of *Harbrace*. Though teachers normally do not determine what knowledge students receive, the elaborate step-by-step process of finding sources, taking notes, composing an outline, and drafting and revising the paper with close attention to rules governing documentation, paraphrasing, and inserting quotations under the watchful eye of the teacher closely regulate how students receive and transmit knowledge. Kantz and Schwegler and Shamoon both describe students and teachers frustrated because students who go through this process normally summarize and synthesize, in other words, merely reproduce the knowledge of their sources, when the teacher expected "original" evaluations and arguments. Though these writers recognize the complicity of teachers and textbooks in creating this problem, they tend to locate the problem in the student rather than in the nature of the research paper or the dominant concept of knowledge in education. This tendency has led many teachers to the conclusion that students simply "can't think," at least not "critically." But, as David Bartholomae writes, most of the written work that students must do "places them outside the working discourse of the academic community, where they are expected to admire and report on what we do, rather than inside that discourse, where they can . . . participate in a common enterprise" (278).

"Students need to read source texts as arguments and to think about the rhetorical contexts in which they were written," Kantz states, "rather than to read them merely as a set of facts to be learned" (78). But drawing from Linda Flower, Kantz goes on to argue that teachers and students should conceive writing a research paper as a problem-solving activity. The concept of intertextuality in postmodernist theories offers a richer view of the research paper, focusing on just what current-traditional instruction has ignored. Research paper

instruction informed by postmodernist rhetorical and literary theories would treat reading sources as a creative and critical act and
would closely connect and identify reading with writing. Writing a
research paper could involve more than merely gleaning information
from sources; it could be a study of the discursive practices of texts on
a particular subject in which writers consciously situate their own
text in the discourse of others. I find the language of deconstruction
particularly appropriate for discussing the research paper. "No
matter how much a text struggles to keep itself pure and different
from other texts," Jasper Neel writes in *Plato, Derrida, and Writing*,
"it originates as a weaving of prior texts. It must graft itself onto
something else in order to become itself" (128). In "Derrida,
Deconstruction, and Our Scene of Teaching," Sharon Crowley writes
that when students go to the library to read about the subject for a
paper, "they try to enter into the chain of signification which
surrounds, and amounts to, discourse about their subjects" (176). All
writing requires weaving and grafting of prior texts. Writers and
teachers can pretend that texts are autonomous and words original
with a personal essay or an expository essay based on personal
knowledge and observation. They cannot pretend this with the
research paper (at least not so easily, although the image of the writer
as an objective reporter of information standing outside the discourse
of others, not situated within it, certainly has disguised the intertex-
tual nature even of the research paper for many writers and teachers).
In a current-traditional course, the research paper is more complex to
write than other types of writing—research is an added element to
the writing process, and the writer must grapple with the problem of
preserving her own voice and style as she incorporates the voices and
styles of many writers into her text. From a postmodernist perspective, creating a voice while appropriating the discourse of others is a
constant problem in the creation of any text. Neel writes that every
discourse has two voices, "the 'I' of the discourse" and "the semiotic
system into which the text must fit so as to be recognizable *as* a text
. . . by providing rules for how texts operate, defining such roles as
writer and reader, and setting boundaries within which the concept
'text' becomes thinkable" (121):

> These two discourses struggle continuously. The "I" attempts
> to make a unique statement, to reveal whatever "knowledge"
> the text has been shaped to carry. The system, on the other

hand, constantly reveals how this particular discourse is woven into the web of similar discourses. By providing any given discourse with the context of all the other discourses that precede and surround it, the system reveals what this discourse borrows, what it lacks, and how it speaks only by using words and patterns that come already loaded with uncontrollable connections. (121)

The research paper could permit teachers and students to focus on the problems of learning a system and establishing a voice. Most students writing a research paper soon know how difficult it is to make a "unique statement" or "original argument," and many do unconsciously acquire many of the rules and conventions of the discourses that they study in their research. Many obviously do not. This paper is one of my first attempts to make any extensive use of the language of deconstruction or critical pedagogy. Like many freshmen, I find the language still feels alien and uncomfortable, and like many freshmen, I have wondered if I have gotten in over my head, whether I am making any sense or saying anything worthwhile. But I have also incorporated some strategies for self-protection, making plenty of use of quotations and using the rhetorical ploy of confessing my uncertainties humbly to gain the sympathy of possible critics. But this strategy is more than just a ploy for sympathy, for it has allowed me to find a way of connecting comfortable and familiar language to the still alien and uncomfortable language that I am learning. (I am also very aware that, unlike most freshmen, I have chosen to try to appropriate a language such as deconstruction only after reading and hearing dozens of arguments about the political and moral implications of this discourse.)

A postmodernist pedagogy also would demand that the class examine the language of the texts that they use to interpret the texts and to question their authority. A pedagogy influenced by deconstruction or critical pedagogy would encourage students to ask what is missing from the texts they read, to reject the idea of an objective or disinterested report, and to explore the ideologies of texts. The importance we usually give to the *Readers' Guide to Periodical Literature* in composing a research paper presents an opportunity to teach students critical readings of news reports and popular and influential magazines. Current-traditional pedagogy instead has encouraged a dangerous uncritical acceptance of the authority of these magazines and the news media as a whole. Freire, in contrast, holds that analyzing newspaper editorials is "indispensable" "so that people will react to newspapers or news broadcasts not as passive objects of the 'communiqués' directed at them, but rather as consciousnesses seeking to be free" (116). Neel writes that good writing teachers, like it or not, are usually practicing deconstructionists, pointing out to students what is missing from their texts. I don't see how we can do that with students' texts and not with the texts we have them read and use without encouraging a false and debilitating sense of distance and difference between the texts of students and the texts of authors.

Both critical pedagogy and deconstruction would demand that the writing course and the research paper, as Crowley puts it, "engage students with issues that concern them directly, socially, and politically, and would direct the resulting discourses into the communities where such things matter" (38). Like Kantz, Freire advocates a "problem-posing" education (66–67), but with a difference. Students, he argues, should be "increasingly posed with problems relating to themselves in the world and with the world [and] feel increasingly challenged and obliged to respond to that challenge" (68–69) as "critical co-investigators in dialogue with the teacher" (68).

Examining the current-traditional rhetorical and epistemological assumptions behind the origin of the research paper and trying to discuss the research paper from other rhetorical perspectives have problematicized this assignment for me, and at this point I can offer only a sketchy set of goals and practices. Given the extent of its institutionalization, the research paper is not an assignment that we can simply abandon, yet the assumptions behind this genre and the ways it is normally taught are now untenable. I believe that we can work out pedagogies informed by postmodernism that can transform, if not explode, the genre of the research paper to help students become better readers, researchers, and writers.

BIBLIOGRAPHY

Atkins, G. Douglas, and Michael Johnson, eds. *Writing and Reading Differently: Deconstruction and the Teaching of Composition and Literature.* Lawrence: University of Kansas Press, 1985.

Bartholomae, David. "Inventing the University." In *Perspectives on Literacy,* ed. Eugene R. Kintgen, Barry M. Kroll, and Mike Rose. Carbondale and Edwardsville: Southern Illinois University Press, 1988. 273–285.

Berlin, James A. *Rhetoric and Reality: Writing Instruction in American Colleges, 1900–1985.* Carbondale and Edwardsville: Southern Illinois University Press, 1987.

Burton, Mary E. "The Evolution of an English Problem," *English Journal* (coll. ed.) 27 (1938), 60–65.

Chalfant, James M. "The Investigative Theme: A Project for Freshman Composition," *English Journal* (college ed.) 19 (1930), 41–46.

Crowley, Sharon. "Jacques Derrida on Teaching and Rhetoric," *ATAC Newsletter* 2, no. 1 (Spring 1990), 1–3.

———. "Derrida, Deconstruction, and Our Scene of Teaching," *Pre/Text* 8, nos. 3–4 (1987), 169–183.

———. *A Teacher's Introduction to Deconstruction.* Urbana, Ill.: NCTE, 1989.

———. "writing and Writing." In Atkins and Johnson. 93–100.

Derrida, Jacques. *Dissemination.* Trans. Barbara Johnson. Chicago: University of Chicago Press, 1981.

———. *Margins of Philosophy.* Trans. Alan Bass. Chicago: University of Chicago Press, 1982.

———. *Of Grammatology.* Trans. Gayatri Chakravorty Spivak. Baltimore: Johns Hopkins University Press, 1976.

Donahue, Patricia, and Ellen Quandahl, eds. *Reclaiming Pedagogy: The Rhetoric of the Classroom.* Carbondale and Edwardsville: Southern Illinois University Press, 1989.

Ford, James E., and Dennis R. Perry. "Research Paper Instruction in the Undergraduate Writing Program," *College English* 44 (1982), 825–831.

Ford, James E., Sharla Rees, and David L. Ward. *Teaching the Research Paper: Comprehensive Bibliography of Periodical Sources,* 1980 (ERIC ED 197363). Reprinted in *Bulletin of Bibliography* 39 (June 1982), 84–98.

Freire, Paulo. *Education for Critical Consciousness.* New York: Continuum, 1973.

———. *Pedagogy of the Oppressed.* Trans. Myra Bergman Ramos. New York: Continuum, 1970.

———. *The Politics of Education.* South Hadley, Mass.: Bergin and Garvey, 1985.

———, and Donaldo Macedo. *Literacy: Reading the Word and the World.* Critical Studies in Education Series. South Hadley, Mass.: Bergin and Garvey, 1987.

Giroux, Henry A. *Schooling and the Struggle for Public Life: Critical Pedagogy in the Modern Age.* Minneapolis: University of Minnesota Press, 1988.

Haas, Christina, and Linda Flower. "Rhetorical Reading Strategies and the Construction of Meaning," *CCC* 39 (1988), 167–184.

Hewitt, Rosalie. "Composing Research," *Journal of English Teaching Techniques* 12, no. 2 (Winter 1984), 23–30.

Hodges, John C. *Harbrace College Handbook.* New York: Harcourt, Brace, 1946.

Kantz, Margaret. "Helping Students Use Textual Sources Persuasively," *College English* 52, no. 1 (Jan. 1990), 74–91.

Kennedy, Mary Louise. "The Composing Process of College Students Writing from Sources," *Written Communication* 2, no. 4 (1985), 434–456.

Knoper, Randall. "Deconstruction, Process, Writing." In Donahue and Quandahl. 128–143.

Larson, Richard L. "The 'Research Paper' in the Writing Course: A Non-Form of Writing," *College English* 44 no. 8 (Dec. 1982), 811–816.

Mathewson, Angell. "Long Compositions Based on Research," *English Journal* (coll. ed.) 30 (1941), 457–462.

Miller, J. Hillis. "Composition and Decomposition: Deconstruction and the Teaching of Writing." In *Composition and Literature: Bridging the Gap,* ed. Winifred Bryan Horner. Chicago: University of Chicago Press, 1983. 38–56.

Neel, Jasper. *Plato, Derrida, and Writing.* Carbondale and Edwardsville; Southern Illinois University Press, 1988.

Olson, Gary A. "Jacques Derrida on Rhetoric and Composition: A Conversation," *Journal of Advanced Composition* 10, no. 1 (1990), 1–21.

Ong, Walter J., S. J. "Ramist Method and the Commercial Mind." In *Rhetoric, Romance and Technology: Studies in the Interaction of Expression and Culture.* Ithaca: Cornell University Press, 1971. 165–189.

Schwegler, Robert A., and Linda K. Shamoon. "The Aims and Process of the Research Paper," *College English* 44 (1982), 817–824.

Sherbourne, Florence. "Vitalizing Freshman 'Research' Themes," *English Journal* (coll. ed.) 27 (1938), 755–760.

Shor, Ira, ed. *Freire for the Classroom: A Sourcebook for Liberatory Teaching.* Afterword by Paulo Freire. Portsmouth, N.H.: Boynton/Cook, 1987.

Starbuck, A. "Experience Enriched by Reading," *English Journal* (coll. ed.) 27 (1938), 114–121.

Ulmer, Gregory L. *Applied Grammatology: Post(e)-Pedagogy from Jacques Derrida to Joseph Beuys.* Baltimore: Johns Hopkins University Press, 1985.

Winograd, Peter. "Strategic Difficulties in Summarizing Texts," *Reading Research Quarterly* 19 (1984), 404–425.

Winterowd, W. Ross. "Black Holes, Indeterminacy, and Paulo Freire." In *Composition/Rhetoric: A Synthesis.* Carbondale and Edwardsville: Southern Illinois University Press, 1986. 307–313.

BIBLIOGRAPHY: MORE ON THE RESEARCH PAPER IN RHETORICAL CONTEXT

Dickerson, Mary Jane. "The Implications of Collaborative Writing: A Dialogue" (ERIC ED 305644). By negotiating the processes of joint authorship students reconsider their own identities and the nature of composing as a social act.

Nelson, Jennie, and John R. Hayes. "How the Writing Context Shapes College Students' Strategies for Writing from Sources" (ERIC ED 297374). An ethnographic study of the strategies, goals, and processes of two groups of students. The teacher's role is very influential.

Overview: The Research Paper in the Nineties

THE VALUE OF THE RESEARCH PAPER IN THE NINETIES . . . AND BEYOND

Greg Larkin

Unlike many of my colleagues in English departments, I love to teach the research paper. In fact, I enjoy research paper teaching more than teaching literature, composition, or linguistics. When under consideration for my present position, my most serious error, which almost cost me the job, was my unwise claim that I could teach the research paper to freshmen, and as if that weren't questionable enough, my downright naive assertion that my freshmen could also learn how to write effective research papers.

Many published sources were quoted to me in an attempt to get me to see the error of my ways. For instance, I was shown a ferocious anti–research paper article condemning inadequate libraries, and student inability to distinguish between useful and useless information, to organize, and to document.[1] Or, as another published essay put it: "for all its lofty purposes its results are enervating and self-defeating."[2]

Why are research papers so widely hated by students and teachers alike, and can these reasons, if brought out in the open, be examined and refuted? And beyond these pragmatic considerations, are there any larger issues, beyond the mere possibility that we can teach research papers, to suggest that we should teach research papers? I have researched these questions quite carefully, and for over ten years taught the research paper at the university and consulted in technical writing at many businesses outside the university. I still believe a defense can be made.

The practical and philosophical objections to research papers that I have encountered included the following:

1. The students can't read well enough to extract relevant materials from outside sources.

2. The library doesn't have adequate holdings or staffing to support the topics students want to write about.

3. The students can't integrate borrowed materials with their own writing, so they just plagiarize.

4. Research papers can be bought and sold openly, so the teacher can never tell who actually wrote the paper the student turned in.

5. There is no agreement at all about what constitutes proper format on a research paper, i.e., footnote and bibliography forms, outline form, pagination, etc., etc., so it is both impossible and unwise to teach these matters.

6. Research papers are inherently schoolroom exercises that have no relationship to the kinds of writing actually required in the real world; hence employers have to unteach what English teachers so laboriously try to instill.

I believe the same basic answer applies to all these objections: the research paper may make us aware of the various problems listed above, but that does not imply that the research paper itself causes those problems. In fact, I will show that each of these problems, to the extent that it is a real problem in the first place, is not so much the product of the research as it is inherent in our educational systems and methods as a whole. Indeed, we may bury our heads in the sand, eliminate the research paper, and hope or believe that therefore these educational problems will go away, or we can face the fact that eliminating symptoms does not cure diseases. The research paper does demand certain fairly sophisticated skills, but by the same token it allows us a perfect opportunity to teach those skills, which while sophisticated and hard to learn, are also very basic in the sense that the skills required in research and research writing are basic to success in almost any endeavor, especially any educational endeavor. It should be our business as educational professionals to solve problems, not to run away from them.

The research paper can present specific problems, but it can also be the context in which students learn skills that solve not only research paper problems, but many others. The research paper is an ideal assignment through which to teach critical reading, integration of borrowed materials into student writing, and focusing and narrowing, to name only a few skills. Rampaging research students, hungry for relevant materials, can be a most effective (and in my experience, most appreciated) means of inspiring a library staff to update its collection and keep it current. The one-to-one conference method of teaching, which the research paper at least in part demands, only forces the teacher to adopt an individualized approach, which is increasingly being recognized as a superior method of instruction anyway. Finally, from my experience with dozens of major businesses and government agencies in the past few years, research and research writing are viable skills and valuable commodities in the real world.

But let us examine the specific objections more systematically:

1. *Students can't read.* Indeed, by and large they can't. No one who has administered a *CLOZE* test on a tenth-grade reading passage to college seniors, as I have, and found only 31 percent of them passing it, can deny that in general our students can't read. Shall we then stop asking students to read? After all, they can just use computers, can't they?

Or, should we ask ourselves why our students can't read, and then, armed with that understanding, help them to learn to read. If we do this, I think we'll find that the research paper assignment is tailor-made to help students learn to read.

As Constance Weaver has shown beautifully, one reason students can't read is that virtually all the traditionally used methods to teach reading in school take a word-by-word or even a sound-by-sound approach. As a result, students and teachers define "reading" as "getting the sounds right," while meaning is largely ignored. The student, being taught only to "sound things out," has little motivation for understanding the reading at all. Hence over a period of years we develop students who can read a passage flawlessly out loud, but have no idea what it means.[3]

But the very nature of the reading one must do for a research paper implies reading for meaning. As was pointed out at least twenty years ago, a good research paper can come only from good reading.[4] If students can't read well, they can't write well.[5] If teachers don't teach critical reading, i.e., if they don't distinguish between "research" as an intellectual investigation and "research" as a technique of sticking in documented bits of information, can they expect anything else but weakly based research papers?[6] But is the weakness of such papers inherent in research papers, or in students, or in the teacher's simplistic methods?

The research process can be used to teach reading. The research teacher can design exercises in which the student is supplied a research topic and a detailed outline and then told to find the parts of a carefully selected reading passage that bear on each part of the outline. The student can be trained to select different parts of a passage and place each with the part of the research outline that treats the same idea. In so doing, the student is getting valuable instruction in reading for meaning, as he or she works on the research paper. By the very nature of the assignment, the research paper can be the best reading teacher many students have ever had, if teachers choose to make it so.

And this effective reading instruction can lead to learning both facts and insights as well or better than more traditional, "objective" ways of teaching.[7] Some creative teachers have even designed entire research paper courses specifically intended to use research to support, teach, and demand critical thinking, and critical interpretation of sources.[8]

Thus, it seems quite important to me that we not join the ranks of teachers who insist that research is really the business of the social studies teacher and that the English teacher should only be "responsible for the correction and grading of the finished product."[9] Surely the English teacher has more to offer than mere copyediting. Surely we can, and should, teach critical reading and critical thinking, and surely the research paper is a context in which we can do so.

2. *The library is no damn good.* I guess if we aren't supposed to teach any content, but only final form, then we have no business in the library either. But if research papers include both a content and a form about which English teachers may have something valuable to offer, then we can take the same basic approach to the library "problem" that I just took above to the reading "problem," i.e., the library relates importantly to both the form and the content of the research paper, and the effective teacher will use the library from both points of view. As MacGregor and McInnis put it, "This approach to the teaching and learning of library research methods through a synthesis of methodological and epistemological principles centers on the idea that any body of knowledge has both a substantive and a bibliographic structure, which stand in a logical, predictable relation to one another."[10]

Many librarians, as well as English teachers, have written syllabi for courses combining library instruction with content-area instruction.[11] The "library connection" is just one answer to the charge discussed above that the English teacher, not knowing any content area, hence shouldn't be involved with research. Joining research and content-area instruction is advantageous to both the librarian and the

English teacher: "Effective and efficient use of the library does not merely call for orientation, but rather demands education. Placing such education within the context of what is happening in the classroom is by far the most sensible way to proceed."[12] Cooperation between library and classroom has been urged in many places.[13]

Of course, one practical objection to this cooperation is that many libraries aren't very good. But the research paper gives the library not only an excuse to, but a method of, improving its holdings. The trick here is to steer research students into their own majors or content areas for their research topics. Not only are they more familiar and comfortable with their own majors, they also can be turned loose on their major professors, who in turn can hit the library staff when they determine that indeed Johnny or Janey can't possibly complete a simple research paper on the subject in which he or she is supposedly majoring at the university.

In my own experience, I have been instrumental in designing and implementing a course taught jointly by the library staff and the English department. I have found that librarians like to teach as well as to order books and that they are very efficient at both. However, they don't know exactly what to teach or which books to order (except those in library science), so they tend to depend on faculty members, who presumably are keeping up with their own areas of specialization, to let them know what to teach and what to order. In my experience, the librarians know what resources are in the library and they will teach effectively whichever of the available resources I tell them my students need. Furthermore, the library resources are in general just as complete as the faculty chooses to make them. If there should be a reluctant or inefficient library staff somewhere, I believe that some inroads into that problem could be made by sending large groups of angry, frustrated research paper students in to request materials which should be available or usable, but aren't. From a librarian's point of view, required research papers force students to use library materials, and use is one of the ultimate justifications for adding any item to the library's holdings.

3. *Integrating borrowed materials and the problem of plagiarism.* Once again, my basic approach to plagiarism is that while it is true that the research paper attracts this problem, that very fact implies that the research paper provides a great opportunity to eliminate not only the problem but the underlying cause. As with the first two objections discussed above, the fruitful way to approach this problem is not

from the negative side—i.e., plagiarism is evil or immoral or whatever—but from the positive side—i.e., teach the students how to integrate borrowed material clearly and effectively with their own opinions. I have seen very clever negatively based checklist approaches to stopping plagiarism, which are almost inevitably based on a very mechanical, symptomatic concept of what plagiarism is and what causes it. Such lists include things like checking bulletin boards for advertisements for research papers for sale, knowing all the source books on a given topic in the library, and a host of other sneaky "tips."[14] Frankly, I think it would be quite fun to trick these pharisees, and I don't blame students for trying to trick such teachers at all. When documentation and integration of borrowed material are taught as an idiotic game, the natural response is to reject and beat the whole system.

A far superior approach to plagiarism, both philosophically and pragmatically, is to stop considering the research paper as a mere puzzling numbers game involving no originality or insight on the student's part.[15] To do this, the teacher must present the research paper as a question to be answered rather than a body of information to be rehashed.[16]

This approach to the research paper implies several things about plagiarism. First, for the "honest" students who nonetheless plagiarize, the problem is that they can't distinguish their ideas from others' ideas.[17] As Stevenson has pointed out, not knowing themselves, they can't tell what is theirs and what isn't. The students only know they don't really know anything about the subject, and so they are forced by the research paper assignment to adopt a false persona of "expert" on the subject. Hence they write dishonestly both in a philosophical sense (i.e., they pretend to know the subject) and in a practical sense (i.e., they plagiarize).[18] Stevenson's answer to this dilemma is to drop the research paper, but I don't believe that's desirable or necessary. Rather, we must train our students both in the process of becoming expert and in the recognition of limitations, both of which are quite important ideas for the student to learn and to apply.

Such methods of training in expertise and its limitations are available. Students can be given very practical exercises in which a research thesis and outline are provided, along with several relevant quotations, statistics, or paraphrases from other clearly indicated sources. In the beginning stages of training, the teacher can even provide the student with ideas that could be inserted as the author's own additions and connections between the research thesis and the borrowed materials. Then, in subsequent exercises, the teacher can remove first the provided authorial comments, and later the relevant materials from outside sources (especially if the research paper is being used as a reading teacher as described above). Such methods can and do work: "Students taught by this method are not only able to construct sophisticated diagrams . . . but also able to write research papers of a consistently high quality that exceeds any standards familiar to the authors in ten years of undergraduate teaching."[19]

In a sense, it boils down to individualizing instruction, not as many research paper teachers put it, so as to catch prospective or actual plagiarizers,[20] but rather as a positive part of an overall strategy for systematically helping the student to see not so much that good writing is not plagiarizing, but to see that good writing is maintaining authorial control over the smooth mixing of borrowed and authorial ideas. We can and should teach good writing much more effectively than not plagiarizing. And best of all, in most cases if we teach good writing effectively, we won't have to worry so much about plagiarism, because we will have dealt with its cause, not its symptoms.

I have discussed the nuts and bolts of instruction in research writing elsewhere.[21] At the end of this writing instruction the teacher can remove the provided research thesis and outline and simply say to the student, "Write a research paper," and the student can do so, because he or she has had concrete practice and instruction a step at a time with thesis, outline, borrowed material, and authorial commentary. As for plagiarism, the student will have had the instruction necessary to avoid thinking of or presenting other people's material as his or her own. In the larger context of effective writing, the students will have had the instruction necessary to help him or her generate prose which effectively integrates various types of materials, from various sources. And that is a skill well worth our teaching and our students' learning.

4. *Who wrote the paper?* While it is true that ready-made research papers can be easily obtained from both public and private sources, it seems clear to me that if a research paper course is being taught on an individualized basis in the context of a process rather than a product, the teacher will know long before the paper is handed in whether the student is working on his or her own paper. If the teacher sees the

initial proposal, the working outline, the note cards, the first draft, etc., then there is a record all along the way of the student's progress. Many articles talk about individual conferences, but few do so in the context of helping the student to see the research paper as a series of steps in one process, in which each step prepares for the next in conceptual as well as mechanical ways.[22]

The point is that if the teacher is teaching the course from the point of view of individualized instruction in a process, the issue of who wrote the paper is largely defused. If the teacher thinks it necessary, the entire record from proposal to note cards can be hauled in with the final paper, although I have never found such a load of extra stuff to carry necessary. In fact, in over ten years of teaching the research paper, I have yet to have any doubts about who wrote the paper, except in the case of students who either suddenly produce a paper in a few days or suddenly change their topic overnight, especially toward the end of the semester. So after a few cases like that, I simply stopped accepting such last-minute efforts.[23] But again, the point I'm making is not that we become suspicious of every student and set up a series of hurdles. Rather, the teacher has individual conferences with the student in order to help him or her see and think through the whole paper as a process, rather than as a series of checkpoints that in some mystical way result in a research paper product, after the student suffers through the full rite of passage.

Of course, the student could start the semester with a finished paper and laboriously fake the proposal, note cards, etc., but to do so successfully would require nearly as much effort as actually writing the paper and might be almost as effective a teaching device anyway, because the student would not just be handing in a finished product, but going through the generation process (albeit backward).

5. *No universally accepted format.* Although it has been argued that there is a consistent, universitywide form for written reports,[24] I doubt very much if that is actually true, and if it is true, it shouldn't be. Having worked very recently with professional engineers, geologists, accountants, computer programmers, and many others, I am quite certain that every discipline has its own typical documents and forms. Footnotes, bibliographies, margins, pagination, outlines, etc., etc., etc., are all the subjects of innumerable discrepancies from text to text, year to year, and company to company. Why should we torture ourselves and our students into mastering a certain form when it's almost certain that next year, next teacher, or next job, they will

just have to unlearn our form in order to learn another? The answer is, we shouldn't. We must teach something larger and more meaningful than any one form, and that is the principle of adherence to the form set by whoever is in authority, and the process of selecting a consistent and appropriated form on our own if no one is in authority. As Samuel said to Saul (1 Samuel 15:22), "To obey is better than sacrifice, and to hearken than the fat of rams." If we can teach our students the process of *following* a form rather than the product of following *the form,* we will prepare them very well for the style sheets and in-house guidelines that so many employers demand today.

Before going on to consider a final objection, let me add here that there are many other classroom-oriented practical problems associated with the research paper that can be approached in the same basic way as the five problems I've discussed above. Such problems as "students always pick too broad a topic," "students don't know enough about anything to do research," "the sixteen-week semester is too short," and a host of other typically small-minded problems can all be solved with a modicum of effort and ingenuity. Of course, we won't be successful with every student every time, but we will be successful with many often. So in response to practical problems such as these I say, "Don't cut off your head because you have a headache." Solve problems instead of running from them. If topics are too broad (and they usually are), devise ways to help students learn to narrow them; if students don't know anything about anything, let the research paper be a guided chance for them to learn something about how to learn something; if the semester is too short, adjust your curriculum, both in terms of how many classes in research you teach and how much of which parts of the research process you teach in each. Some problems are harder than they look. And some are easier.

I have saved the most philosophical charge against the research paper for last. I believe the various philosophical objections to the research paper can be summed up in one sweeping statement:

> Research papers are inherently schoolroom exercises that have no value or significance in any context outside of the university or high school classroom.

I believe this statement is true in a very narrowly defined sense, and untrue in a much larger and more important sense. It is true that there is no immediate use for the products of student research papers:

the endless rehashes on abortion, inflation, and the environment. No such papers are written in the "real world," in part because of the practical objections discussed above. Nonetheless a strong case can be made for the research paper on three simultaneously practical and philosophical grounds: product vs. process, freedom vs. control, and utility.

Product vs. Process

By now, no English teacher should be teaching product orientation in any English class, including the research paper class or unit. Surely, by now, we are all aware of the importance of teaching English from a process orientation.[25] A. E. Malloch is on the right track when he identifies the problem with research paper teaching as being a view based on the research paper itself as an empty form.[26] Rather than teaching product, we must teach process: "our primary purpose throughout such a project will be to teach methodology (rather than any specific set of facts)."[27] In writing a research paper, unbeautiful product that it is, the student can learn to think, to read, to evaluate, to combine, to judge, and to write, just to name a few of the more important processes. Our job, as Marilyn Samuels points out, is to teach the research paper as a series of tasks, each of which prepares the student for the next step in the overall process, which is the true aim of the instruction in the first place.[28]

Freedom vs. Control

If teaching process is our aim, then we must have a special relationship in our teaching between freedom for the student and control over the student. Too much control, while it may turn out effective products, won't train students in the process of writing effectively. Hence, I can't agree with teachers like Block and Mattis, who insist on rigid control over student research activities.[29] No doubt, especially with younger students, Block and Mattis will turn out better papers, but they won't turn out better writers.

Of course, I don't advocate simply turning students loose either. As Farrison says, in general students "are not yet sufficiently matured in judgment to investigate 'sources,' deal critically with 'the literature on the subject,' evaluate facts and theories, and draw 'conclusions.' "[30] But I can't agree with his conclusion: "So why teach them to play at these things?"[31] The teaching value of play is well established. We don't teach students to play, we teach them through play. "Sesame Street" is serious business underneath all the fun. When we allow students to "play," we are giving them control in the rules of the game, but also freedom in the chance to learn through mistakes that "don't count for keeps." This "playful" approach is advocated seriously by Bramer as "graduated freedom, or diminishing control."[32] Bramer goes on to delineate four skill levels, or "plateaus," through which he guides the students. Each plateau provides a certain framework but also increasing freedom for the student.[33] The student moves from being controlled to self-control, which is freedom.

If we are teaching process, this movement from control to freedom will most naturally and effectively take the form of a series of steps, such as identified by Marshall,[34] Schroeder,[35] or Saffioti.[36] The exact order or steps are less important than the view which must be given to the student of the research paper as a process with subskills that can be learned.

Thus the only research teaching proposals I am firmly against are those which wish to cut out some part of the process, on what always seem to me to be rather arbitrary grounds. For instance, Rivlin urges us to forget the actual writing of the paper, since once the paper is set up and researched, the writing is merely mechanical.[37] On the other hand, Brickman urges just the opposite by suggesting that some "assistant" gather all the data and let the student do only the writing.[38] Or, Wells refuses to allow his students a thesis,[39] while Taylor insists that they write strictly from a personal point of view.[40] I am not absolutely opposed to any of the above approaches, as long as they are used as steps in an overall process of teaching, rather than as ends in themselves as their authors seem to intend them. We can teach research paper writing effectively if we lead the student from external control to internal control (freedom) through a series of skills making a coherent process.

Utility

But when we have done it, when "students taught by this method are able . . . to write research papers of a consistently high quality,"[41] have we done something worthwhile, or is even our process of research paper teaching ultimately itself only a useless product? No doubt students cannot turn in their school research papers on their first day of "real work" outside the schoolroom. Of course, their undergraduate research skills must be retooled on the job, in realistic contexts that we can't usually generate in the schoolroom situation. But the student who has learned to think about the impacts of marijuana on our society can adapt that thinking ability to analyze the impacts of an offshore oil rig on the environment around it. The student who has learned to read critically a fiery sermon against abortion can use that critical reading ability to separate the facts from the opinions in an environmental impact statement submitted by an eager developer. The student who can write a schoolroom research paper on vitamin C and the common cold can research and present a cogent defense of a client in a court of law. In the cases sketched above, the skills used in each pair of topics are different in depth and complexity, but not in kind. In doing a schoolroom research paper, a student can learn, in a relatively simple context, the same skills that he or she will be able to use later on, out of school, in more realistic and serious contexts. Hence, I cannot agree with teachers like Taylor, who claim that "the research paper is of no value in the high-school English class."[42] Taylor's own reasons for his statement are the best indication of its incorrectness: "because reasonably correct and creative writing—the goal of instruction in composition—cannot be developed by teaching students to regurgitate the thoughts of others."[43] "Correct and creative" writing is not some mystical product that by definition excludes research paper writing. And research writing is not merely regurgitating the thoughts of others. Or, to cite another example, Stevenson claims that the research paper "serves no real value," because it is "pretentious."[44] The research paper can be taught pretentiously, but it need not be. It must not be if the teaching is to be effective. It seems to me that teachers who object to the research paper in terms of value are looking at it strictly in terms of judging the products which the students create. The value of research writing in high school and college is largely in terms of process, not product.

This is not to say that we ought to be unconcerned with the quality of the work the students produce, and that we ought not to encourage students to avoid schoolroom topics as much as possible. On the contrary, we ought to try our best to keep the university and high school from being any more insulated from the rest of the world than they already are. The more accurately we can duplicate in our classes the conditions outside the school, the more useful our training will be to students when they are not students any more.

On the other hand, there is some virtue in giving a student a simple, safe environment in which to develop basic skills, especially if the student is largely unprepared, as so many research paper critics insist. If we are focusing on teaching processes to students, then we need not become terribly defensive about the products they turn out. We must accept our students where they are in terms of intelligence, background, and skill, and use our teaching to move them to new heights.

For this reason, I disagree strongly with teachers like Kitzhaber, who state that research into secondary sources is not critical to English studies.[45] On the contrary, the research paper can benefit our students a great deal in every language process that is important to us as English teachers: reading, writing, listening, and speaking, plus many subskills, such as logical analysis, documenting, and a host of others. These language skills are valuable to our students—far more valuable than any particular area or material they have studied in "English," and immensely more valuable than any product they might turn out. Our students' success in any job, and even more importantly, in any role they may play in life—as parent, spouse, employer, or friend—depends in large measure on just the language skills that research paper writing can help to develop.

May I give just one example? I recently consulted with the Army Corps of Engineers, who are employing an English major (with no technical background at all) as an editor and writer of their reports. Her language abilities won her the job, and have won her the respect and cooperation of her technically oriented peers. The reports she writes every day are based on the integration of researched facts from published sources with the field observations and interpretations of engineers. Her language skills, developed in part through research paper writing in school, as well as the equally important literary and personal essay writing, are of enough value to her that they are the skills she uses in the "real world" to earn her living. She never intended to write for the Corps of Engineers when she took her degree in English, but because she learned processes, among them what I've called research paper writing, she has a satisfying job today. Not every student wants or needs to become a technical writer in order to justify or utilize the language skills developed in school, but the fact is that those students who do have those language skills are ahead of the game in businesses and in private life.

Thus, both pragmatically and philosophically, I believe strongly that we ought to require students to do research papers, not from a defensive and apologetic position, but from a position of strength and a commitment to our best sense of the true value of the education we want our students to gain.

NOTES

1. W. Arthur Boggs, "Dear Principal," *English Journal* 47 (Feb. 1958), 86–87.
2. John W. Stevenson, "The Illusion of Research," *English Journal* 61 (Oct. 1972), 1029–1032.
3. Constance Weaver. *Psycholinguistics and Reading: From Process to Practice* (Cambridge, Mass.: Winthrop, 1980).
4. Dorothy C. Hockey, "Thwarting the Ventriloquistic Freshman," *College English* 14 (Oct. 1952), 24.
5. This point was one of the major bandwagons of the 1980s. For instance, the February 1982 edition of *College Composition and Communication* is largely devoted to the reading-writing connection.
6. Fred E. H. Schroeder, "How to Teach a Research Theme in Four Not-So-Easy Lessons," *English Journal* 55 (Oct. 1966), 898.
7. Howard Yale McClusky, "An Experimental Comparison of the New Type Test and the Term Paper," *Journal of Applied Psychology* 17 (1933), 621–627.
8. See, for instance, Robert Palmer Saalbach, "Critical Thinking and the Problem of Plagiarism," *College Composition and Communication* 21 (Feb. 1970), 45–47, or Mark E. Blum and Stephen Spangehl, "Introducing the College Student to Academic Inquiry: An Individualized Course in Library Research" (ERIC ED 152315).
9. Thomas E. Taylor, "Let's Get Rid of Research Papers," *English Journal* 54 (Feb. 1965), 126.
10. John MacGregor and Raymond G. McInnis, "Integrating Classroom Instruction and Library Research," *Journal of Higher Education* 48 (Jan./Feb. 1977), 20.
11. For instance, see Lennart Pearson, "What Has the Library Done for You Lately?" *Improving College and University Teaching* 26 (Fall 1978), 219–221.
12. Bruce Morton, "Beyond Orientation: The Library as Place of Education and the Librarian as Educator," *Improving College and University Teaching* 27 (1979), 163.
13. Haskell M. Block and Sidney Mattis, "The Research Paper: A Cooperative Approach," *College English* 13 (Jan. 1952), 212–215.
14. Patricia C. Bjaaland and Arthur Lederman, "The Detection of Plagiarism," *Educational Forum* 37 (Jan. 1973), 201–206.
15. R. G. Martin, "Plagiarism and Originality: Some Remedies," *English Journal* 60 (May 1971), 621–625.
16. George Arms, "The Research Paper," *College English* 5 (Oct. 1943), 19–25.
17. Saalbach, 45.

18. Stevenson, 1032.
19. MacGregor and McInnis, 33.
20. For instance, see Edgar F. Daniels, "The Dishonest Term Paper," *College English* 21 (Apr. 1960), 403–405; A. E. Malloch, "A Dialogue on Plagiarism," *College English* 38 (Oct. 1976), 165–174; or Eileen N. Wagner, "Outfoxing Fraud: Research Papers Without Repression" (ERIC ED 143015).
21. Greg Larkin, "Fact, Transition, and Comment: A Practical Approach to Research Paper Writing," *Freshman English Resource Notes* 4 (Fall 1978), 6–7.
22. One notable exception to this is Marilyn Schauer Samuels, "A Mini-Course in the Research Paper," *College English* 38 (Oct. 1976), 189–193.
23. This policy was urged long ago; see Harry N. Rivlin, "The Writing of Term Papers," *Journal of Higher Education* 13 (June 1942), 316.
24. Nancy Arapoff-Cramer, "A Survey of University Writing Assignments," *College Composition and Communication* 22 (May 1971), 165.
25. The importance of the process orientation has been a central concern of English teachers at least since Janet Emig's seminal monograph, *The Composing Process of Twelfth Graders* (Urbana, Ill., NCTE, 1971).
26. Malloch, 169.
27. Arms, 263.
28. Samuels, 191.
29. Block and Mattis, 213.
30. W. Edward Farrison, "Those Research Papers Again," *Journal of Higher Education* 16 (Dec. 1945), 487.
31. Farrison, 487.
32. George R. Bramer, "Freedom and Control in the Research Paper," *College Composition and Communication* 20 (Dec. 1969), 355.
33. Bramer, 352–359.
34. Colleen Marshall, "A System for Teaching a College Freshman to Write a Research Paper," *College English* 40 (Sept. 1978), 87–89.
35. Schroeder, 899.
36. Carol Lee Saffioti, "Modular Approach to Teaching Research in Freshman Writing Courses" (ERIC ED 153251).
37. Rivlin, 319.
38. William W. Brickman, "Turmoil over Term Papers," *Education Digest* 38 (Nov. 1972), 57.
39. David M. Wells, "A Program for the Freshman Research Paper," *College Composition and Communication* 28 (Dec. 1977), 383.
40. Taylor, 127.
41. MacGregor and McInnis, 33.

42. Taylor, 126.
43. Taylor, 126.
44. Stevenson, 1030.
45. Albert Kitzhaber, *Themes, Theory, and Therapy* (New York: McGraw-Hill, 1963), 147.

. . . TO PRACTICE

Libraries and Librarians

133

A GENERAL RESEARCH MODEL FOR RESEARCH PAPER INSTRUCTION

James E. Ford

A topic as solemn as research paper instruction demands something like a biblical introduction:

26. And [on the sixth day] Teacher said Let us make one project in our image, after our likeness: and let the project have dominion over the other projects and over every subject of the college student.

27. So Teacher created the research paper in her own image, in the image of Teacher created she it; boring and difficult created she it.

28. And Teacher blessed it, and Teacher said unto the research paper, Be fruitful, and multiply, and replenish the supply of dropouts, and subdue the remainder of the college students: and have dominion over the other projects, and over every single grade that the student receives.

29. And Teacher said, Behold, I have given you every lesson on English grammar, which will help you in preparing your paper, and every lesson on English usage which will help you to get a passing grade on your paper; to you it hath all been given.

30. And to every beast of the earth, and to every fowl of the air, and to everything that creepeth into the classroom, wherein there is life, I have given every rule and principle for good English; and it was so.

31. And Teacher saw everything that she had made, and behold it was very good. And the Bib cards and the final draft were the sixth day.

Chapter 2

1. Thus the verbs and the nouns were finished, and everything had its purpose.

2. And on the seventh day Teacher ended her work, which she had made; and she rested on the seventh day from all her work which she had made.

3. And Teacher blessed the seventh day and sanctified it: and all the students who had worked also, rested from their work.

135

4. And on the seventh day Teacher sat down on a nearby stone to begin the drudgery of correcting the freshman research papers: and the freshman students saw that it was so, and they smiled. It was very good. (Pauline Erickson Mortenson, *College English* 32 [1970], 58–59)

This section from the First Book of Gramesis, written by a student when she was a junior, reflects a condition engraved as painfully on my own memory as on the faces of students I have met in past semesters. One aspect of this condition is the distressful confusion of writing research papers on topics one does not really understand. The other is the high discomfort of struggling through the library. The two are of course closely, even causally, related.

Let me tell you with an analogy what I think is the source of the second problem. It relates to the way students are usually taught—if they are taught at all—to "use" the library. It is as though student drivers were told by their instructors: "Here is the clutch and this is how it works. Here is the carburetor and here's how it works. Here is the transmission and this is how it works," etc. Then the instructor says, "Now, drive!" I suggest that something very like this is what is usually done in orienting students to the library, either by teachers or by librarians or in research paper guides. The instructor says: "Here is the card catalog (the key to the library!)"; "here is the *Readers' Guide,*" etc. "Now, research!"

The result is described by Patricia Knapp: "motivation of independent inquiry through assignments. which [call] upon students to formulate their own questions and seek their own answers in the library, with minimal guidance, often produce[s] not learning but confusion, frustration, and hostility." No wonder a student looks upon having to grade research papers as suitable revenge for assigning them. And, as we all know, in most cases the student is right.

I can make particular Knapp's generalized description with an experience from last spring. In a pilot project for freshman English I began that term, I taught and required the completion of a research paper in a three-week period, but using only four class periods for instruction. Here are some responses to Question no. 4 from a questionnaire filled out by each student after the unit was completed. The question was, "What was your initial attitude about the assignment?" And here are a few typical responses:

> I thought it would be really hard and beyond my capabilities. I did not want to do it.

> Scared at first, and confused, lost.

> Scared and incompetent.

> Surprised, upset.

Question no. 5 asked, "What is your attitude about the assignment now that it is completed?" I'll repeat each student's "before" answer and then the corresponding "after" response.

> I thought it would be really hard and beyond my capabilities. I did not want to do it. / It was easier and more beneficial than I had previously anticipated. It really wasn't bad.

> Scared at first, and confused, lost. / Total relief.

> Scared and incompetent. / I feel more adequate and comfortable in the library.

> Surprised, upset. / I am glad I had the opportunity to learn about doing research. I am pleased.

Why the change? I believe it was because the students were not "called upon to formulate their own questions and seek their own answers in the library, with minimal guidance." They were taught adequate principles embedded in a relatively simple research strategy model (Figure 1). I don't mean to suggest that what follows is the only way, or even the best possible way, to guide student research; but it is a workable way.

The principles which structure the model are:

1. The library is organized from the general to the specific, in whole and over and over in its parts.

2. These parts (departments, sections) are made up of the same classes, or categories, of works.

These two principles make it possible to learn the use of the library. The research-related conclusion to draw from them is: Do your research from the general to the specific. Beginning at the general is the only way students can ensure themselves, and their instructors, that they know what they're writing about. Another conclusion has to do with attitudes: anyone who really understands the way the library is organized will feel that the library *wants* to give the researcher the information he or she seeks, not hide each needle of information randomly in a chaotic haystack.

As they begin, students don't know much about their topic—what's more, they don't know what to think *about* their topics *with*. That's okay; that's why they are doing research. But they must first acquire the tools with which to think about their topics in order to narrow them to real subjects and then form theses. What they need to know first are the kinds of things at the top of the first segment of the mode: historical context, relationships within the topic and between it and other topics, terms and their definitions, issues, and authorities.

And where do they find this information? In the kinds or classes or categories of works listed in the content compartment of Section I. It is important for them to know—and act upon the knowledge—that they should work from more to less general within each section and not just between them. That is, there are more general (universal) content sources and less general (subject) content sources. Figure 2 gives examples of each kind of work listed here and elsewhere on the model. (Notice that the most general—universal—sources are in the left column. Subject-specific works are in the right column, examples from many different fields given first and then, below them, examples all of which are drawn from English studies—literature, language, or pedagogy.) A student who, for example, wants to write on some aspect of adoption should move quickly from the *Encyclopaedia Britannica* to the *Encyclopedia of the Social Sciences,* where such usable real subjects as interracial adoption and private vs. public agency adoption are raised.

And how are these general content sources to be found? By consulting the kinds of works listed in the source department of Section I of the model. They also come in universal and subject-specific formats. Again, Figure 2 gives examples of each. Take, for instance, Sheehy's *Guide to Reference Books* (which librarians refer to simply as "Sheehy"). "Sheehy" collects and organizes according to subjects for efficient retrieval virtually every class of reference work in the library. If the goal is to make the student more self-sufficient in research, this work, usually kept at the reference desk, is invaluable. Or, take the much underused *Bibliographic Index,* which twice a year assembles bibliographies on nearly every subject from books and from articles in over 1,900 periodicals. Both works will direct the many students who evidently are interested in the topic of abortion to the *Abortion Index,* a yearly volume of thousands of substantial scholarly articles on the topic—thus freeing the student from *Cosmopolitan* and *Redbook.* Or, finally, *Ulrich's International Periodical Directory* is a most useful listing by subject of 60,000 periodicals. One special feature of this work is that it tells in its annotation of each periodical where that work is indexed.

Now (boyfriends, girlfriends, and rock concerts willing), the students have acquired the thought machinery—the context—which will make it possible for them to knowledgeably work toward specific material which will support their theses. In fact, having begun with only a general topic, they have used the background study to narrow the topic and then form a thesis about it. I require proof that this procedure has been followed in the form of a one- to two-page background study, including a bibliography listing a specific title corresponding to every appropriate category of work in Section I, before students can begin working on the research paper itself. The student desiring to treat the topic "Should Parents Read Fairy Tales to Their Children?" who does not list Bruno Bettelheim as an authority, or the one who, writing on abortion, is ignorant of the *Abortion Bibliography* can be rescued at this point, while there is still time.

The bridge from the general to the specific sources (Section II) is constructed of the subject-organized tools—all indexes of one sort or another—located in the source department of Section II. Once again, there are universal and subject-specific subcategories here as well. Students treating all but the most popular topics will want to move quickly through the *Readers' Guide,* if they do not skip over it completely, to get to more specific indexes. Some articles on women's issues in literature will be indexed in *MLA Bibliography,* but *Women's Studies Abstracts* give a narrow focus in this area. Nor should those powerful tools, the citation indexes, be ignored. The *Science Citation Index,* which has long been a standard tool among scientists, has been joined by *Social Science CI* and, quite recently, the *Arts and Humanities CI.* Each work as the standard subject index, though the entires are generated from keywords in article titles and are thus more accessible than is usual; but they are unique in allowing the researcher to find all references cited *by* a particular author in a particular work and all references *in which* an author is cited. There is presumably a close subject relationship among such chains of citations. And all students should become familiar with *Essay and General Literature Index,* the only work solely dedicated to indexing parts of books (collections of essays and even chapters).

Students can use the indexes to harvest titles of books and articles and move immediately (through the card catalog and the library's list of serials) to these ultimate courses. Or, after collecting titles, they can stop off at Section III to preselect the ones actually to be read. Reviews and abstracts, found through the appropriate indexes, give what can be called qualitative evaluations. Citation indexes furnish—in a very rough way, to be sure—a quantitative measure of the impact a piece of writing has had on the writer's peers.

But does what I have described here really work as smoothly as I have made it seem? Only for those of us with tenure-track appointments at Utopia U. I assure you, however, that it has worked, more or less well, for most of my students; at least it has worked better than any other system I know of. Here are some real-world observations about the system.

The biggest problem is still and always getting students to engage the cogs of their minds with those of the research model. But the mere fact of having the model in their hands, to which the teacher and librarian can physically point, seems to increase the confidence level so that more students will at least begin to get seriously involved. Also, the model must be adapted to the capacities of the students. I use the version presented here for the most advanced undergrads and graduate students. I omit some features—abstracts, for example—for less experienced students. But even freshmen must get through all the stages. Also, the model shows the rule, not the infinite exceptions and overlaps which can only be experienced, not taught. Finally, the model won't compensate very well for the instructor's lack of familiarity with the kinds of sources listed on the model. My belief is that we should continually be striving to reduce the gap between teachers and librarians, librarians becoming more knowledgeable about the research process as it relates to actual writing assignments and teachers learning more and more reference sources and the ways they are organized in the library. The best thing to do is pick a topic yourselves and work it through the model, or any other system you can find or invent. As you have the time, choose others, and still others, until the best reference guide the student can have is—you.

Figure 1.

RESEARCH STRATEGY MODEL
Work from general to specific—step by step

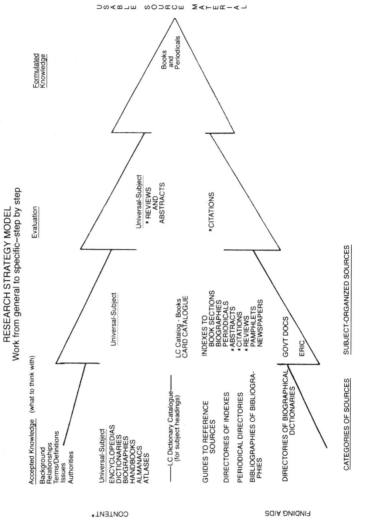

Figure 2.

SECTION I		SECTION II		SECTION III	
Universal	*Subject*	*Universal*	*Subject*	*Universal*	*Subject*
E. Britannica	E. of the Social Scis.			Current Book Rev. Digest	Mental Health Book Rev. Index
	E. of Poetry & Poetics				Combined Retro. Index to Books in Scholarly Journals (hums. & s.s.)
OED	Dict. of Economics			Dissertation Abstracts	Abstracts of Popular Culture
	Dict. of Am. Slang				Lang. & Lang. Behavior Abstracts
Internat. Who's Who	Who's Who in Am. Art				
	Contemporary Auths.				
	Occupational Outlook Hdbk.				
	Handbook to Lit.				
World Almanac	Women's Rights Almanac				
Times Atlas	Oxford Economic Atlas				
	Mapbook of Eng. Lit.				

Sheehy, Guide to Ref. Books	Info. on Music Ref. Guide to Eng. Studies	Essay & General Lit. Index		Science Citation Index
Ulrich's Internat. Periodical Dir.	Chicorel Index: Indexing & Abstracting Services (hums. & s.s.)	Biographical Dict. Master Index	Journalist Biog. MI Writers for Young Adults MI	Social Science Citation Index
		Readers' Guide	Applied Sci. & Tech. Index / Ed. Index (for articles on composition)	Arts and Hums. Citation Index
Ulrich's Standard Periodical Dir. (US & Canada)	Ed/Psyc Journals: Scholars' Guide MLA Periodical Dir.	Abstracts		
World Bibliog. of Bibliogs. Bibliographic Index	Bibliog. of Bibliogs. on Iranian Studies / Bibliog. of Biblios. on Children's Lit. (Abortion Bibliog.)	Review Indexes / Citation Indexes		
		Vertical File		
Slocum, Biographical Dictionaries		Facts on File / Newsbank	N.Y. Times Index	

THE RESEARCH WRITING PROCESS: AN UNDERGRADUATE ASSESSMENT TOOL GROUNDED IN TEACHING STAFF/LIBRARY COOPERATION

Carol Lee Saffioti

Over the past decade at regional and national conferences, reactions to the competence-based writing program at our campus of the University of Wisconsin system have varied widely, especially concerning the issue of the research requirement. After considering the program and format described here, readers may reflect the same spectrum of views, and as I indicate in the conclusion, the debate continues even on our own campus. Some may ask, "Why haven't we tried something like this?" Others may ask, "Why would anyone try something like this?" As a full-time faculty member in English for over seventeen years who has also served as department chair, I hope I can address the issue related to both stances, since I have been actively engaged in curriculum development in this area since 1975 (Saffioti 131; Berge and Saffioti). Also, I would like to suggest that despite concerns reflected by some of the literature relating to plagiarism, artificial constructs, and extra work for department faculty, nevertheless writing skills related to research remain a primary, if sometimes unstated, concern of university education (Crawford 79; Phelps 76; Steffans 239). Teaching a separate composition course housed in the English department and devoted to basic college research I have been able to contribute to the knowledge and skills of my students; I have enjoyed sharing with students my own experiences writing and doing research; and I have expanded my own knowledge of the complex system of sources and resources, computerized and otherwise, which we call a library. Thus, though others make a case for housing such instruction in other courses, including

144

freshman seminar or freshman orientation (Cuseo), I find that by having the opportunity to teach the course as a faculty member I have seen, in addition to the benefits to students, the benefits and rewards related to my own teaching as I have been able to apply them to my own research, writing, and teaching in other courses.

A typical load for the instructor teaching our research paper course is three one-credit sections of the course, with the enrollment total approximating the enrollment of one three-credit course, in addition to whatever other course the instructor has been assigned that semester. The course consists of library use instruction, which is evaluated through the completion of a workbook developed specifically for use in our campus library, and introduced both in the classroom and in the library through the teaching and support of the library staff, with a guided approach to research writing which allows instructors (who come from the full-time faculty as well as the part-time teaching staff) leeway within university-established guidelines to structure the course and its assignments to suit their teaching styles and interests. It is a course which carries credit toward graduation, but is not required of all students, though most students choose to take it, as the most popular of several options students have to demonstrate their ability to carry out a college-level research writing project.

A small percentage of students (less than 5 percent) are able to demonstrate their proficiency in these areas of college-level library use and research writing by submitting evidence of their high school work which satisfies our college-level requirements. Papers submitted from high school undergo scrutiny by a panel of faculty and library staff who review the work and interview the student, evaluating research and writing skills, as well as making every effort to assure that the paper is the student's own work. Also, students may do a paper in conjunction with a general degree-level course they are taking, and submit it for consideration under the same guidelines, provided that the instructor of the course agrees to monitor the process and that the student fulfills all requirements for the project as stipulated in the university requirements. In order to have this option, students must have received a B− or better in their college-level composition course at Parkside, or its equivalent if they are transfer students. The percentage of students who take this option varies somewhat from year to year, with the writing coordinator estimating an average of twenty or thirty papers completed this way per semester across the entire university, though not all are approved the first time round. Students are free to revise and resubmit papers under this option with no penalty. By far, the largest percentage of students take the course tailored specifically for the purpose, though some students do not successfully complete the course the first time.

The workbook developed by the library staff for the purpose of teaching library skills took its present form over a five-year period and is based on a model developed by Miriam Dudley in the late 1970s, for which both she originally, and our campus as one of the first to implement its design, gained national recognition. ("Self-Paced Library" 330)

Since then, we have had the opportunity to evaluate the success of the course, our approach, and the tools we have developed to help students meet their goals as we have continually updated the information and the implementation of the dual assessment we use: the first addresses mastery of individual skills, and the second is process oriented, as students integrate those skills into a single research-related writing project, or a series of shorter ones within the syllabus of the course. Because the guidelines emphasize the rhetorical mode of writing (that is, students must be able to argue persuasively on an issue or subject selected in consultation with both teaching faculty and library staff, with convincing, timely, appropriate evidence), the students may find themselves involved in doing several related smaller projects leading to one final paper, or may engage in such activities as debates, classroom simulations, or questionnaires or poll taking and interviewing, in order to apply research skills in ways which they are later asked to summarize in written form—all without sacrificing the principles or the purpose of the universitywide assessment process.

Student evaluations are of course mixed, but the faculty and staff who teach the course most frequently, and are most successful at it, indicate that although attitudes toward the course and the process are often very strongly negative to begin, the students themselves comment at the end of the course concerning their increased confidence in using a university library, and in their ability to handle more complex issues and materials in longer writing assignments by the time they finish.

The key phrase here is, of course, "by the time they finish," for indeed, some students drop the course and retake it later but before the credit deadline. Faculty who see firsthand, and understand the rather painful process of development most students undergo, are often met with challenge by administrators impatient to see quicker results and more efficient ways of assessment. Those of us who teach the course have been able to withstand the scrutiny of administrators' eyes so far when they attend to such things as enrollment figures and grades, but we sometimes feel that our purposes are at odds with those of administrators.

The debate goes on, even within the English department over the years, as to the efficacy of a course which essentially serves the needs of other departments at the level or point at which students are readying to enter a major (students must demonstrate their competence in library use and research writing by the time they have accumulated forty-five credits). We also struggle to make the course relevant to students who often perceive it as a bureaucratic hoop to jump through, especially when they are impatient to begin their majors. We do not, in fact, restrict students to completing the course before declaring the major, but it is a fact that students who apply the assignment to at least the general subject area or areas most related to their prospective major, or to their interests, write better papers, and we tell them that.

Nevertheless, when English department faculty have been ready to give up the task and responsibility not only for the teaching but also for the assessment process which is inherently a part of it, the university through the faculty governance process has indicated in several major rounds of discussion of the purposes of general education that faculty across the campus have some faith in the process and the manner in which we carry it out, stressing the importance of assessment long before graduation. They see these basics in terms of reasoning and writing skills which will prepare students for higher-level tasks performed later, and more appropriately assessed by course work and faculty within their chosen major.

We have found several factors contributing to the success of such a course within the framework of a universitywide requirement to demonstrate competency: 1) support of the general faculty, not only in the school of liberal arts, but also across the campus in the schools of education, business, and science and engineering; 2) close cooperative efforts between teaching faculty and library staff; 3) a process of identification of the persons who are most successful teaching the course as the "core" of instructors who do teach it on a regular basis; 4) the commitment of full-time instructors to the course, who are in fact the ones who tend to do the best teaching in the course; and 5) a university-supported program which provides students options appropriate to their level of skills.

Throughout the years we have discovered the importance of the administration and key faculty members in leadership positions who are committed to consensus building. This core of people needs to be involved in encouraging faculty and librarians to work together to plan course materials and curriculum goals, and to participate in collaborative efforts to expand their own skills. In addition, college or university administrators should encourage endeavors by groups of faculty and staff to garner support for curriculum development through grants small or large. Also, they should be willing to provide career incentives and rewards for faculty and librarians to strengthen their teaching skills in this critical area. Finally, incentives as well as rewards for students who complete the process are important and should be widely publicized, including exemption for superior students after a separate evaluation or screening process which involves more than admissions staff or counselors.

The evaluation of a program's success should be ongoing; for instance, while we have been actively pursuing the rewarding of better students for many years, and the preparing of all students, we still have serious thinking to do about the motivation of students who enter with deficient skills from their previous educational experiences, and usually with some negative experiences related to libraries.

In comparison with other programs nationally, our campus does not use the "clinic" approach, nor the "mini-course" structured within a more general writing course, nor a noncredit, or voluntary, approach of many other campuses. The English department has accepted the responsibility for administering a course integrating areas of study which go naturally together: that is, learning to use a library and learning to write up the results of one's findings. Our approach is also somewhat different from that at the University of Alabama, where the format of self-instruction for integrated library instruction does not include writing skills in the same program (Keever and Raymond 185), or from that of the University of South Carolina, which incorporates library instruction into the freshmen seminar program (Cuseo).

Specifically, the entire faculty has defined goals which state that students must demonstrate mastery of skills in the area of research-related writing as well as library use. Within the writing area, assessment continues on two levels, since students are involved with rhetorical skills and shorter research assignments in their preceding college-level writing courses (one or two semesters of course work, depending on the student's skills level at admission).

Exposed to the individualized instruction involved in the workbook process and its development as I have worked with library staff, I have gained much of value to my teaching. The self-paced workbook approach appeals to students, yet they find they also want classroom time with instructors to discuss more general issues related to the actual subject matter they are researching, and to the struggles they have in making the transition from finding information and getting it onto the computer and ultimately into hard copy. I found I was not alone (Phipps 41) in virtually abandoning the material provided in the large, cumbersome rhetoric handbooks of the typical English 101 course. My own curriculum development and text writing began with a university and later a systemwide grant to develop materials for my own teaching of the course, and I found the collaboration with a colleague from the library to be rewarding in ways which had an impact on my upper-level teaching as well as my general education teaching (Berge and Saffioti).

Against the background of this description of our approach to one type of assessment at the level of general education requirements, let me now address some issues related to adopting and adapting it. First, the question arises of the need for the course itself. Several arguments could be made in support of it, but perhaps the most convincing is that to offer a course in research writing as part of general education course work is to indicate to students that research writing and library use are essential to college success. Often in some nook or cranny of the campus is the short course, the workshop, or the module on library skills, frequently offered at orientation time when students are both distracted by and bored with the general format and method of presentation. The objectives for an integrated writing program can stress the continuing process of developing skills which apply from lower- to higher-level course work, as students develop more sophisticated arguments with more complex tools, both technologically and teleologically. For those departments with a two-semester first-year writing program (that is, excluding remedial or noncredit work), this plan of instruction is adaptable to the syllabus of the second semester, and often is adapted. However, many campuses do not have two three-credit courses; the approach described here is adaptable either as a fourth credit attached to a specified set of general education courses (that is, the one-credit English course can be taken in conjunction with a designated set of courses), or it can be freestanding in the curriculum. In either case, the aspect to stress is the need for some planning, discussion of campuswide expectations, goals, and standards, as well as the time necessary to gain universitywide support for such goals and standards as they apply to all students at a level in their college work where the experience can prove of further use to them, and not merely as an "instrument of assessment" for administrators and state legislators.

Another issue to resolve involves the granting of credit for the course. Making the course part of the general education process or requirement gives authority and visibility to the goals and standards set by faculty and staff, who in advisory settings, as well as in the classroom, need to reinforce the value of a one-credit course, emphasizing that it amounts to much more work outside the classroom than in. Indeed, it is not an unusual amount of time to spend on a one-credit course (if that is the decision made), when a student finds herself putting in fifty hours of work outside the "one shot a week" that they may associate with the course when they register for it. One can argue the merits of offering more than one credit for the course, though the faculty on our campus continue to view it more as the "fourth credit" which enhances their other three-credit course work. However, offering the course as a noncredit addendum to the curriculum, no matter where it is housed, lessens the significance of the course as students view faculty interpretation of its value. As a departmentally housed option or requirement the course encourages students to associate their work with work done in other courses, especially other writing courses; they know that their work will be evaluated by teaching faculty who are serious about the course and involved in their overall development as students maturing and growing in skills and interests.

When considering the course structure, it is also important to address questions of plagiarism. Integrating bibliographic instruction and writing instruction helps teachers monitor student work in both. The literature reflects three elements which serve to control plagiarism: monitoring of work, relationship of work to other assignments and goals, and control of topics (Idol 202, et al.). The step-by-step process which integrates mastery of the library with using and writing about what students find offers more suitable opportunity to assess student work along the way, rather than arbitrarily at some end point. Because our program is set up so that librarians work with faculty, we are better able to evaluate jointly a topic in relationship to the students' ability to conduct the actual research and write about it. Since students are coached through the process, their rough drafts are evaluated, and they consult with library staff through visits to the classroom or through conference times for students and staff to get together, there are simply fewer chances that students can, or will, plagiarize. Being able to present to the students at the semester beginning a universitywide policy concerning the assessment of research-writing skills also gives a context for any university policies regarding plagiarism.

The next issue to address is that of cooperation between teaching faculty and library staff. The literature on the development of instructional material related to library use is legion and frequently not read by faculty (Fox). Nevertheless, familiarity with materials available from a source such as the Library Orientation Exchange (LOEX) is extremely useful in the planning and development of curriculum. LOEX also holds a conference each year open to faculty as well as librarians (Ames; LOEX).

The focus of such a course toward the goals of good research skills and good writing behooves us to avail ourselves of all the help we can get to continue to improve the teaching of the course. Thus, faculty development time and rewards are important to the design and implementation of a successful program. More specifically, the following points are useful to consider in the planning, implementation, and evaluation stages of developing an assessment model based on integrating library skills and research writing:

Administrative Support

Long before a new or revised course has been implemented, faculty and staff should be consulted and involved in the process of setting goals for any assessment of research-related skills. This issue affects all levels of university or college experience, and the beneficiaries of the efforts of library staff and English department faculty are primarily, but not solely, the students, for faculty in other departments benefit from well-prepared students. Grant money, seed money, or released time may be necessary to foster curriculum development in this area. The role of the administrator is critical in the support process, but should be just that—supportive, not directive—encouraging the development of consensus as the result of shared governance and many opportunities for discussion across curricular and departmental divisions.

Information Gathering

The faculty involved in teaching research-related methods and skills at the upper-division level should work with those who teach at the level of general education requirements, comparing methods of assessment as well as criteria and expectations for student success. Ideally, those who do teach research methods at the upper-division level (that is, within specific majors) should be involved in the actual teaching of more basic skills at the level of general education requirements as well. Meetings with library folks should be incorporated at every step of the way so that teaching faculty and librarians do not view themselves at odds with one another in terms of goals and methods of instruction. Time for joint meetings and rewards for such information sharing are critical.

Goal Setting

Departmental and library administrators should facilitate the outlining of standards related to assessment of library skills integrated with writing skills. These standards will add support both to the work of the librarian and to the work of the writing instructor in their efforts to help students succeed. In addition, the setting of standards for an acceptable research project in terms of thesis, scope, content, structure, and format will help ensure that students do indeed learn to do solid research, especially if instructors for the course are replaced, as is sometimes the case in the writing curriculum. It is not useful to discuss and then set these standards as a department, only to find significant variance elsewhere on the campus as to what these standards ought to be. The process will take considerably more effort as a core group works toward consensus, but the longevity of our program (since the mid-1970s) attests to the value of the long, and often heated, discussion and negotiation process. We have monitored the process of assessment, we have periodically reviewed our standards, but we have not significantly changed them, and certainly have not abandoned them; faculty have confidence in the process as well as the results, and seem to take some pride in the fact that the standards were developed locally on our own campus, for our own students.

Improvement of Teaching

Grant writing, workshops, and curriculum development meetings seem to occur in an intense manner over a relatively short period (one or two years) during the planning stages of such assessment programs. If I have learned anything by taking on responsibilities of department chair as well as teaching, I have learned that a certain kind of inertia sets in once a program is in place. Though now a full-time faculty member again, I am still convinced that we need to devote time, energy, and resources to the continued assessment of the success of the course and the curriculum, as well as students' success in any such program. The longer a program lasts the more difficult it may become to create excitement about new ways of teaching course work that appears to be successful, or at least stable, already. A renewal of such commitment on the part of administrators to course and faculty development, as both the program and the faculty approach the middle years and beyond, is critical for the liveliness and relevance of a program, and the intellectual growth of the faculty and staff who teach.

Would such a course work if we did not have the highly structured set of other competency-based assessments which we do, in general writing skills, math, and even reading? Undoubtedly, fewer students would embark upon learning more about the library and the research-writing process if it were absolutely voluntary, but an impressive number consistently report that they understand the importance of closing gaps and moving ahead, well prepared for their majors. Thus, involving undergraduates in the discussion, planning, and implementation of general education goals and assessment is important—something we, and probably faculty on many other campuses, do not in fact do sufficiently, or sufficiently well. Perhaps others can learn from our lack and can involve students more and earlier than most would consider doing—which is ironic, because the audience for such instruction is of course the students themselves.

Here are several other questions to help determine needs: Do you want to require students to demonstrate competency in research-related writing as well as library use? Do you want to incorporate extensive instruction in what librarians call bibliographic instruction into a writing course, or keep the two separate? Why, or why not? How many credits should such course work carry? Should it carry graduation credit? Why? And finally, if you prefer not to have a research-writing course, should you assess library use as well as research writing in first-year composition course work as your program is now structured, or elsewhere? How will you do that?

With or without a competence-based writing program, or a formal assessment program, the need for formal, guided instruction in library use and applications to writing is real for many if not most students in their first two years of college. Because the preparation of students entering college varies widely, any assessment process should take into account alternative methods of assessing students' skills depending on their previous experience. It is important to set, and use, standards which apply equally to all students, but which allow them to demonstrate competency, and to provide evidence for assessment purposes which is integrated into their current course work as college students, and commensurate with their abilities, without making them perform extraneous tasks. Assessment of college-level skills should be the goal: the purpose of creating an early, or exemption-based, option for first-year students should be to verify that they already have attained the skill level commensurate with a first- or second-year college student's experience (that is, the level of competency of students completing, or almost completing, general education requirements), not that they have attained some minimal level of mastery at the high school level. Thus, though fewer students will be exempted from any university requirement or course work, those who are will be on a par with those students who go through a longer process of development.

English departments already faced with heavy demands for service-oriented teaching in composition may not be able to justify new courses. Those which have been able to in the past are facing financial and other constraints that mean that administrators are taking a much harder look at the justification for such staffing. However, the above questions can lead to useful discussion and revision of curriculum, even if the number of courses remains the same. Let me close with an offer to provide help to those developing teaching materials, even for use within an individual syllabus. I continue to enjoy my teaching of this course, and I have felt a part of the process as I have contributed in a small way to the development of improved teaching and assessment methods at our own campus.

REFERENCES

Ames, Gregory P. "A Pilot Workshop on Term Paper Writing: A Proposal and Final Report" (ERIC ED 176310), Apr. 1979.

Berge, Patricia, and Carol Lee Saffioti. *Basic College Research.* New York: Neal Schuman Publishers, 1987.

Crawford, Janet. "Redefining the Research Paper and the Teacher's Role," *English Journal* 81, no. 2 (Feb. 1992), 79–82.

Cuseo, Joseph. "The Freshman Orientation Seminar: A Research-Based Rationale for Its Value, Delivery, and Content—The Freshman Year Experience." Monograph Series No. 4. Columbia: South Carolina University, Center for the Study of the Freshman Year Experience, 1991.

Dudley, Miriam. "The Self-Paced Library Skills Program at UCLA College Library." In *Educating the Library User,* ed. John Lubans, Jr. New York: R. R. Bowker, 1974. 330–335.

Fox, Peter K., ed. *Library User: Are New Approaches Needed?* London: British Library and Research Development Department, 1980.

Idol, John L. "Conversation and the Lively Art of Research," *CCC* 28, no. 2 (May 1977), 202–203. See also Colleen Marshall, "A System for Teaching Freshmen to Write a Research Paper," *College English* 40, no. 1 (Sept. 1978), 87–89; Robert Anderson, "Inside the Term Paper Factories," *Change* 8, no. 4 (May 1976), 19–22; and Sandy Landsman, "The Term Paper Companies Revisited," *College Journal* 41, no. 6 (Oct.–Nov. 1974), 110–115.

Keever, Ellen, and James Raymond. "Integrated Library Instruction on the University Campus: Experiment at the University of Alabama," *Journal of Academic Librarianship* 2, no. 4 (Sept. 1976), 185.

LOEX (Library Orientation Exchange), located at Eastern Michigan University, Ypsilanti, Michigan 48197. Catalogs of publications and proceedings of conferences are available upon request, as is information concerning annual conferences and calls for papers.

Phelps, Terry O. "Research or Three-Search?" *English Journal* 81, no. 2 (Feb. 1992), 76–78.

Phipps, Shelley. "Why Use Workbooks? or, Why Do the Chickens Cross the Road? And Other Metaphors Mixed," *Drexel Library Quarterly* 16, no. 1 (Jan. 1980), 41–53. See also Mary Biggs and Mark Weber, "A Proposal for Course-Related Library Instruction," *School Library Journal* 25, no. 9 (May 1979), and Joyce Merriam, "Helping Students Make the Transition from High School to an Academic Library" (ERIC ED 176783), 1979.

Saffioti, Carol Lee. "Basic College Research: A University Teacher's View." In *Teaching Library Use Competence: Bridging the Gap from High School to College,* ed. Carolyn Kirkendall. Ann Arbor: Pierian Press, 1982.

Steffans, Henry. "Helping Students Improve Their Own Writing: The Self Conference Sheet," *History Teaching* 24, no. 2 (Feb. 1991), 239–241.

BEYOND ORIENTATION: THE LIBRARY AS PLACE OF EDUCATION AND THE LIBRARIAN AS EDUCATOR

Bruce Morton

The narrowness of a recent article in *Improving College and University Teaching*[1] makes it apparent that there is disagreement and misunderstanding of the role of the library in undergraduate education. There exists a need to inform, indeed, raise, the collective conscience of teachers of higher education in this regard. Library orientation suggests a minimal introduction to the physical attributes and gross services of the library. Orientation is not, as Frederick suggests in *IC&UT*, a means by which students may gain a meaningful working familiarity and understanding of the research skills and tools necessary to perform adequately in a particular course of study. I believe that library orientation, on the contrary, is most appropriately undertaken extraneous of all course work, preferably during freshman orientation week. It should be expected to accomplish nothing more than to show freshmen where the library is located, what it looks like inside, that it contains resources which will be necessary to their education, and that there are persons employed there to help them in the use of those resources.

Education in the Library

Integration is the key concept. Merely to wish to teach a student how to use the library is an abstract expectation. The expectation must be related to a specific need to use the library. The student then will have a contextual frame from which a sense of educational purpose may develop. Various disciplines and cross-disciplines form a matrix with a variety of bibliographic tools to make learning to use

157

the library effectively and efficiently a formidable aspiration for the undergraduate student.

Institutions build library collections to complement and supplement what takes place elsewhere on campus, particularly the teaching and learning of the classroom. If this is so, then it makes little sense to engage in instruction regarding the use of the library in a manner which is non sequitur to classroom activity. Teaching is that activity which justly generates the most concern for the quality of the undergraduate library and its use. It is important that students understand that the library represents and embodies the cumulative knowledge and information systems of the various constantly evolving disciplines. All such information systems are interrelated, and it is through these systems of communication that students must wend their way in order to become informed—in order to learn. Too often the maze of disciplinary literature is circumvented by faculty with the best of intentions—reading lists are made available on the library reserve shelf—the contemporary counterpart of the Harvard Classics' five-foot shelf.

Method

How then to teach the effective and efficient use of the library to the undergraduate student within the context of an educational philosophy and specific educational objectives? There are several methods which are presently being employed, either exclusively or in combination with one another, at institutions across the nation. Among those most prevalent are:

- *Course-integrated library instruction:* Based primarily on the prototype developed at Earlham College, this program calls for the collaboration of professor and librarian in developing a series of workbook exercises which simultaneously engage the student in progressively more sophisticated use of the library while proceeding through the course syllabus. Completion of workbook assignments is a requirement for successful completion of the course. Workbooks are designed specifically for a particular discipline and for particular levels of that discipline.
- *Class-oriented library instruction:* The format for a one-class-period presentation on materials and methods relevant to

assignments in a course can vary greatly according to the preference and style of the professor. Instruction may be presented in the library or in the classroom, consist of audiovisual complement, a tour and hands-on experience (dependent upon class size), or hybrids or mutants of any of these formats. Handouts in the form of lengthy bibliographies or short research guides may also be provided. It is essential that the presentation by the librarian be designed to address the needs of the specific discipline, course, and level of study.

- *Research methods and materials presentation:* This type of instruction may be offered in the classroom or another forum. It is directed at upper-level students based on a declared major or other common interest. Instruction is geared to the nature of the research methods and literature in a particular discipline and is not related to any specific course syllabus. Time(s) and place of meeting are determined by the academic department and the library.

- *Course on library resources:* Some institutions have added full-credit courses on the use of the library, irrespective of discipline, to their curricular offerings. The course is taught either by librarians only (more likely at colleges where librarians are considered to be faculty) or team taught by librarians and faculty lecturers.

- *Librarian as seminar participant:* The involvement of the librarian as seminar participant stems from a desire to establish a trialogue. Students, professor, and librarian all contribute to the *discussion* of research materials, methods, and problems.

Prior to the librarian's appearance in the seminar, the library prepares a "Study and Research Guide" of no more than one sheet, both sides. The guide is designed as a starting point for student research on topics which are relevant to the seminar. The "Study and Research Guide" is comprised of sections addressing broad reference collection categories, e.g., encyclopedias and guides, bibliographies, statistical sources, biographical sources, indexes and abstracts, as well as a part devoted to suggested subject headings in the card catalog. This document is given to the students when they are given their research assignment, one or two weeks before the scheduled appearance of the librarian in the seminar. Students, therefore, have ample time and direction for preliminary research on their paper topics.

At the scheduled time, the librarian becomes a member of the seminar, not to give a presentation, but rather to be a participant. It is made clear that the day's discussion will be devoted to student research papers. Students are encouraged to avail themselves of this opportunity in whatever manner they choose. The result has been rewarding discussions directed variously by student, librarian, and professor in response to student-generated perceptions of problems encountered or anticipated. The skillful librarian is able to cover the same major resource materials and strategies in a nonstructured ad hoc response to student discussion as if he or she were to have given a formal presentation. Students often respond to one another based on their own research experience, and the professor and librarian are able to interject comment or suggestion based on their own knowledge or experience with particular titles, subject, or research methodology.

The immediate and residual effectiveness of the seminar format is remarkable. Students provide the context for everything which is said and therefore are inclined to see an immediate relevance to their own individual library needs. They have not been presented with a lecture containing what the librarian or professor believes they need to know about the library.

Responsiveness is a critical consideration. The library and the professor are not responding to preconceived notions of student needs, but rather are responding to the research needs which the students themselves have had an opportunity to experience and articulate. The results are students who are more excited about digging for information, and who are better able to assimilate and interpret that information in their papers.

Communication and Cooperation

With the realization that the library is, indeed, an integral part of the educational endeavor of a college or university, and an integral part of a student's educational experience, there should be a desire to ensure the encouragement and development of the use of this valuable learning resource. In order to do this, faculty must communicate their educational objectives to the library in order to open a dialogue about the specific needs of a class, and to determine what the best mode of library instruction is for the teaching style of the professor, for the discipline being studied, for the class size, and for the material to be covered. Once these factors are considered, decisions can be made and implemented. Cooperation between librarian and professor is crucial to successful library instruction. The librarian cannot, and should not, function independently in providing library instruction. Good instruction is that instruction which most effectively meets a professor's and students' perception of their own library needs.

Effective and efficient use of the library does not merely call for orientation, but rather demands education. Placing such education within the context of what is happening in the classroom is by far the most sensible way to proceed, for learning to use the library is another aspect of the undergraduate academic experience.

NOTE

1. Ronald D. Frederick, "Library Orientation," *Improving College and University Teaching* 26 (Summer 1978), 200.

THE CREATIVE RESEARCHER

Douglas H. Shepard

One of the more intriguing aspects of an involvement with research tools is what might be called the "tangential" insights that may be gained by examining them in a way, or for a purpose, for which they were not originally intended. In the field of literature, for example, there was a brief but provocative study—buried in a 1957 issue of *Fantasy and Science Fiction*—dealing with the development of science fiction as a genre deserving serious attention. What the author, C. W. Hart, Jr., did was to search the *Readers' Guide* for matter that might now be classified under the "science fiction" rubric to discover under what headings it had originally appeared. As Hart said of the *Guide,* "aside from merely being an index to periodical subject matter, it can also furnish some interesting insights into our changing customs and tastes." What he was able to discover and demonstrate was the attitude toward such material, an attitude which originally pigeonholed it under the condescending heading of PSEUDOSCIENTIFIC stories. Only gradually, as the fantastic in fiction became transmuted into the technological in our everyday lives, did the entries which revealed this shift begin to change.

Because of the relative unavailability of the original article, it may be worth pausing briefly here to outline its main points. The first reference to the subject of science fiction in the *Readers' Guide* is under the PSEUDOSCIENTIFIC stories heading in Volume 10 (1935–1937). In Volume 12 (1939–1941), the heading SCIENCE IN FICTION is used for the first time, but merely to refer the reader to Pseudoscientific stories as the main subject entry. Volume 13 (1941–1943) used the heading SCIENCE IN FICTION but still referred to Pseudoscientific stories. Volume 14 (1943–1945) had no entries for the subject in any guise. Volumes 15 and 16 (1945–1949) used SCIENCE in literature, *see also* Pseudoscientific stories. In Volume 17 (1949–1951) SCIENCE

FICTION is used as a heading but with the cross-reference to SCIENCE in literature. This may have been felt to be too bold a move because in the next volume, Hart points out, there is a reversion to type with the old SCIENCE fiction, *see* Pseudoscientific stories entry. Finally, with Volume 19 (1953–1955), SCIENCE FICTION appears as a legitimate heading without apologetic cross-reference. Indeed, although Hart does not mention it, the reversal is complete. There is still an entry for PSEUDOSCIENTIFIC stories, but it now has the cross-reference "*see* Science fiction." He does chronicle the attendant rise (sporadic at first) in the number of entries under those headings ranging from the single entry in Volume 10 to the twenty-six entries of Volume 19. Thus, as Hart has described, without ever intending to do more than provide access to some current periodical material, the compilers of the *Readers' Guide* have preserved in a kind of silhouette a significant shift in popular cultural attitudes.

Hart's article is a small but illustrative example of the point of this present study, which is to suggest that material similarly significant remains to be discovered in other, equally unexpected sources by the interested students. For example, what is the significance of the choice of the 207 authors provided with individual bibliographies in Spiller's *Literary History of the United States* (1948) and of the 16 additional bibliographies added in the 1959 *Supplement?* And why did 33 of the original 207 *not* need bibliographical supplementing? Perhaps the question should be framed as, "Why was nothing written on them in the intervening ten years although they had been thought important enough to include in the original selective list?" Is there, perhaps, in the first instance, a sign of a shifting sense of importance? Of the 33 in the latter case, are they perhaps to be discarded as, on reflection, not worthy of note and thus of study, or do they rather deserve more attention than has recently been afforded them? (Should one, for example, make a point of recommending them to the attention of young scholars searching for areas in which to explore?) To put one of the questions more directly by way of illustration, why were the following writers included but then not, apparently, written about subsequently: Zona Gale, Joseph Hergesheimer, Mary N. Murfree, O. E. Rölvaag, George Sterling, Sara Teasdale, and Elinor Wylie? Or, to reverse the focus, why did the original bibliography *not* list Booth Tarkington or Albion W. Tourgee? Examination of these and similar questions might yield interesting results.

Remaining within the field of American literature for the moment, there is the important serial bibliography entitled "Articles on American Literature Appearing in Current Periodicals" which began in *American Literature* in November 1929. It chose to see its most recently rounded-out literary period as ending in 1900, and the "contemporary" period as beginning at that point. Thus its listings were divided chronologically, ending with the recent period described as: 1900– [preceding year]. Why? Was it merely the mystical neatness of the termination of a century that seemed to suggest a more meaningful termination of a literary period from the vantage point of twenty-nine years beyond it? Then how does one explain the changed perspective which revealed itself in 1951 when the third section was altered to cover 1870–1920? In that gesture the contemporary period, "our" period, was deemed to have begun not fifty but only thirty years before (despite the fact that the prestigious MLA *Bibliography* retained the earlier limits). That sense of the order of things seems to have been altered once again, as witness the bracketing dates adopted by the relatively new *American Literary Realism,* which uses 1870–1910.

Interestingly enough, Howard Mumford Jones in his *Guide to American Literature* sees the cohesive period as beginning in 1890. However, some of the general histories he cites designate the period variously as 1900–1950, 1896–1946, 1865–1962, 1877–1913. Some of the literary histories additionally use 1870–1910, 1890–1930, 1885–1915, 1920–1960; and for novels: 1920–1951, 1890–1915, 1915–1925, 1925–1940, and 1900–1950. Is this apparently chaotic picture an accurate depiction of something not clearly noted before, that the field has become essentially chaotic? Or perhaps we are looking at the evidence of current reappraisal which will ultimately lead to new, acceptable alignments, such as in the definition of the "New Realists" of England, the writers who are dealt with in "Bibliography, News and Notes," in *English Literature in Transition,* those who bridge the gap between the Victorians and the moderns, 1880–1920.

Another potentially fruitful field is the study of changing taste in poetic diction as reflected, for example, in the increased attention paid to John Donne. Although Spenser, Shakespeare, and Milton have had separate sections of the "Literature of the Renaissance" bibliography in *Studies in Philology* annually since 1917, only since 1957 (Volume 54) has Donne been so honored. This immediately suggests increasing "popularity" for his work. If that were to be established as true, then it might be revealing to look for other indexes to change to explain the *source* of Donne's increased popularity. A quick examination of the standard *Bibliography of Dr. John Donne* by Geoffrey Keynes gives dramatic testimony to support the evidence in *Studies in Philology*. Toward the end of the bibliography Keynes has provided a list of the bibliographical and critical works about Donne for the periods 1597–1699, 1700–1899, and 1900–1957. A count of the items in each reveals that for the first 102-year period there are 124 items; for the next 199 years, only 81 items; but for the following 57 years, a staggering 632 items!

Someone should rearrange the last section, changing it from alphabetical to chronological order. Once that was done, a chart could be constructed revealing the patterns of density (and thus, presumably, of interest and appreciation) of Donne criticism, against which could be placed a similar structure for those twentieth-century poets for whom kinship with Donne and the other Metaphysical poets has been claimed. Is the increase in one matched by an increase in the other as one might predict? It would be valuable to know.

One is aware of the developing attitudes toward some American poets whose work had first to be made available, of course, before appreciation could grow: Anne Bradstreet, Edward Taylor, and Emily Dickinson. But why has the work of the colonial poet John Saffin remained virtually ignored? Anne Bradstreet's work was not really available until the edition of 1867; Emily Dickinson's in the first, procrustean editions of 1890, 1891, and 1896; and Edward Taylor's in 1939. The poetry of John Saffin (1632–1710) was made available first in 1928. However, unlike the increasing critical attention paid to the three former, there is no mention of Saffin whatsoever after 1928 until Professor Harold S. Jantz's *The First Century of New England Verse* in 1947. Subsequent to that work, nothing but silence once again for almost another twenty years until Alyce Sands's dissertation on Saffin in 1965 and the inclusion of selections from the 1928 edition in Kenneth Silverman's *Colonial American Poetry* of 1968. Why did it take forty years for an anthology to include some work by a poet about whom Jantz could say:

> [He] attained to greatness in a few of his poems. . . . Indeed, one might venture to say that when the best of his verse becomes known to literary historians, his name will have a place high in

the second rank of early New England poets, with two poems at
least which were unsurpassed in their time.

If this judgment is correct, then perhaps we have here once again an
index to popular taste in poetry. Is there, perhaps, some element of
Saffin's verse, excellent as it may be, that is unappealing to contemporary ears? In what does Saffin differ from Bradstreet and Taylor, or
even Winslow and Wigglesworth? Therein may lie a most revealing
measure of contemporary taste.

   Another key to popular taste may well reside in the indexes to
well-known periodicals and newspapers. For example, it is clearly
due to *someone*'s sense of the nature of literature (at least in America)
and the nature of its audience that the early indexers of the *New York
Times* omitted the category of book reviews altogether. This, despite
the fact that when the newspaper, and its index, began in 1852,
reviewing was in itself an extremely important activity, as witness
the flourishing condition of a whole class of journals termed
"Reviews." These included the *Contemporary, Democratic, Dublin,
Eclectic, Edinburgh, Fortnightly, International, North American, Quarterly,* and *Westminster Reviews,* all in full flower when the *Times* began.
Nevertheless, for six years, the *Times* indexers ignored the area of
book reviewing altogether. Then, in 1858, they began listing
references to literature under "Poetry and Poets" and "Writing and
Writers" as well as "Book Reviews." The focus here appears to be
more on the persons in connection with their productions than on the
works of literature being considered for their own sakes.

   There are a number of possible interpretations of these phenomena,
each of which deserves looking into. It is quite possible that the
readership of the reviews was understood to be different from that of the
newspapers, or that the function of each organ was seen differently.
That is, the immediate *news,* in the sense of significant occurrences in
the world about us, was one thing; significant *literature* in the form of
structured works to be perused in a thoughtful and leisurely fashion was
quite another, and each deserved or required somewhat different media
for its dissemination and analysis. Do the styles of reviewing, when
reviews do begin in the *Times,* for instance, bear out this supposition? Is
there a noticeable difference in the manner of reviewing in the daily
paper as compared to the periodical reviews?

   On this general subject of reviewing, a cursory check of the section
on newspapers and magazines in Volume 3 of the *Cambridge Bibliogra-*

phy of English Literature (CBEL) indicates that, if you were to plot a curve for the number of papers and magazines with the word "Review" occupying a prominent place in the title, you would discover a steady increase from one in 1750, through twelve in 1850, reaching a high of fifteen in 1860, and then leveling off to the turn of the century. And it is just about then, when the concept of "review" seems to have fully come of age, that we have, for the first time as a title, the phenomenon which called itself *The Review of Reviews.* Is this a reflection of an increasing amount of reading matter in response to increasing numbers of readers who, however, have a decreasing amount of time or ability or interest to devote? In other words, it might be fruitful to pursue the question: "Why at this time is it felt necessary or desirable to review the reviews, and why was the venture successful?"

Another interesting avenue of investigation is the attitude toward what we now refer to as "news" as reflected in the varieties of names affixed to news-dispensing organs. Again an examination of the very useful section in *CBEL* just referred to provides a fascinating range of soubriquets. Although certainly the name of a newspaper or magazine soon becomes so familiar as not to seem to mean anything in particular after it has been current for a relatively short time, the significant aspect is what the name meant, and therefore signified to the namer of the paper or journal, and thus what he expected his audience to understand by it when the term was being coined or freshly applied.

It would appear that one aspect of the newspapers' and magazines' function is being emphasized in such names as Advertiser (in the older sense of observer and informer), and Courier, the carrier of important news, repeated with an even greater sense of officialness, and therefore trustworthiness, in Herald, and· to a lesser degree in Messenger, diminishing to Traveler. A more passive and perhaps objective role is reflected in names such as Chronicle, Echo, Journal, Ledger, Magazine (i.e., storehouse), Mirror, Record, Register, and Report. These can be contrasted with those which give some sense of haste or at least official dignity, stature, or importance, such as Bulletin. Courant (i.e., running), Dispatch, Express, Gazette (with all of the authoritative connotations borrowed from the three official governmental "Gazettes" of Great Britain), Mail, Packet (the main boat bringing the latest intelligence), and Post (the carrier of important messages). Some of the names suggest either immediacy and topicality or the mechanisms by which the latest news can be transmitted: Age, Day, Morning, Week,

News (i.e., "of the new"), Sketch, Tattler, and Telegram, Telegraph, Telephone, and Telescope. Others emphasize the active role of the journal serving in lieu of some functionary: Adviser, Advocate, Censor, Champion, Director, Examiner, Guardian, Guide, Inquisitor, Leader, Monitor, Oracle, Pilot, Recorder, Referee, Reporter, Satirist, Selector, Sentinel, Spectator, Spy, and Umpire. A slightly different class adopts the names of individuals or things whose qualities are apparently admirable and thus suggest those qualities adhering to the paper or magazine: Citizen, Common Sense, Conservative, Constitution, Englishman, Freeholder, Freeman, Independent, Intelligence, John Bull, National, Patriot, People, Representative, Standard, Statesman, Truth, and Whig. It would be interesting to study when particular classes of terms seem especially popular and if there is any correlation between the generally "conservative" character of the class just listed and the temper of the times in which those organs were first named, and what correlates with the more intrusive characteristics of the class listed just before it. Another area to be questioned is that containing the terms which seem to define the scope of the organ's responsibilities or areas of coverage, such as Britannia, England, Globe, Life, Nation, Planet, Times, Town, and the World. But the most interesting, in many ways, are the two categories which reach back to the apparent significance of our classical heritage on the one hand and out to the connotations of metaphor on the other. The first includes Argus (the thousand-eyed), Atlas (holding the world), Mercury, Neptune and Sphynx. The second, mostly involved with "the light which is truth," includes Aurora and Aurora Borealis, Light, Luminary, Star, and the Sun.

Perhaps an equally fruitful examination might be made of these terms from the point of view of frequency, or density, at a given time in the nineteenth century. By count, the top seven (in order of frequency) are News, Times, Post, Chronicle, Mail, Gazette, and Express. Is there any significance to the preponderance of terms suggesting novelty over those connoting authoritative sanction? Have we tended to see our papers and magazines in a certain way, reflecting other unstated premises about the world we inhabit, unnoticed by us but enshrined in the names we give to them? It would be interesting to find out.

But we have spent more than enough time on this one area. Let us move on to other sources of investigation perhaps unnoticed but nevertheless available for our perusal.

When Edith Granger's *Index* first appeared in 1904, it contained, as is well known, citations to prose "recitations" as well as to poetry. Why were the two forms connected and why did the yoking persist for the next forty years? Or, perhaps, the question should be "Why did the connection persist for only forty years?" There must have been a clearer sense of poetry as aural, not so far removed from the set prose pieces then popular. Does dropping the recitations suggest an increased sense of the disparity between the two forms, a sense of the poem as *seen*? Is this the result of increased circulation of poetry in printed form, as well as the falling out of favor of the recitation? What equation can be made between the development of recording devices, the decline of the recitation, and the poem as sound; the compartmentalizing of "that to be heard" on a record (or tape), that to be seen in a book? If we take into account the normal time lag due to the natural conservatism of the average bibliography maker about including new elements in his or her listing, does the changed sense of the poem as something seen explain why a section on phonograph records was added in 1957 to the "Current Bibliography" in the *Keats-Shelley Journal?* It would seem that the addition of phonograph records to such a list, designed for those interested in the work of two important poets, indicates a desire to supplement the usual items on that list. Do we understand by this a supplementing of the critical articles and books (that is, the phonograph records of the poems contain "readings" which represent, by implication, interpretive comments), or are the records to be understood as supplementing *printed* editions of the poems? If the latter, this suggests that the printed poems are not thought of as being heard, but seen.

Related to what has already been suggested about changing attitudes toward poetry, an examination of the entries for "Poems" in the *Readers' Guide* between Volume 5 (1919–1921) and Volume 20 (March 1955–February 1957) reveals some interesting statistics.

For the volumes indicated, an estimate of the number of titles per column was made and a total was derived by multiplying that estimated average against the number of columns in each volume. Because the totals so arrived at referred to volumes covering different time periods, between three and five years, it was necessary to place the totals on a chronological graph to provide for even distribution over the years. The result is a graphic representation of a trend: beginning with an estimated 6,275 individual poems appearing in some popular periodicals between 1919 and the end of 1921, the graph rises to an astounding high of 8,254 in the period 1925–1928. The subsequent figures show a precipitous decline to mid-1936 (3,477). There is little significant change through mid-1944 (2,647), and after that there is a gradual rise to 4,071 poems as of early 1948 and a fairly stable plateau maintained thereafter—in the upper 3,000s. Why are there so many more poems being published in the popular periodicals in the 1920s, why is there such a dramatic drop in the 1930s, and what is the significance of the plateau effect since late 1936?

These same statistics might be set against those derived from *Biography Index*. That index has included a table of occupations with each of its listings since its beginnings in 1946. An examination of the "Authors" list reveals that there are ten columns of names in the volume for the four-year span between 1946 and 1949, whereas there are over fourteen columns in the volume for only two years, 1967–1968. The apparent increase in attention being paid to authors ought to be studied, perhaps in connection with the apparent falling off in interest in poetry. The question might be posed as to why, if the statistics are at all accurate, there is a decline of attention to poetry in the popular journals, but an increase of attention being paid the *lives* of writers. Is there a shift taking place from art to gossip?

Finally, to return briefly to that with which we started, entries in the *Readers' Guide*, that index could once again be utilized to study changing attitudes toward popular fiction and thus, one assumes, changing patterns in popular taste either as revealed in, or as influenced by, the changing fiction. Under that entry, FICTION, the *Guide* has, since its beginning in Volume 1 (1900–1904), listed articles on the subject, as well as a variety of connected matter in the appended "See also" listings, including areas such as Christmas fiction, detective stories, etc. Similarly, in *Book Review Digest,* subject indexes cover the contents from Volume 7 (1911) until the present. An analysis of the entries for such genres as "Essays," "Biography," or for works intended for young people variously described as "Books for Boys and Girls," "Children's Literature," and more recently "Juvenile Literature," might yield some interesting patterns revealing changes in taste in these areas. Particularly useful is the entry for "Fiction" which, because it has an elaborate subject breakdown, beginning with the index for Volume 12 (1916), constitutes a very detailed source for plotting the course of fictional trends over the last fifty years. Exactly the same things might well be done using such other, similar, tools as *Essay and General Literature Index.*

Without belaboring the point any further, it should be clear, from the variety of examples given, that there is more than enough material waiting to be discovered by the insightful researcher, material happily preserved in reference tools now to be turned to uses for which they were not originally designed. And in these "byproducts" of the indexer's toil may be found revealed new truths.

This article appeared originally in *RQ* 10 (Fall 1970), 9–14. Reprinted with permission.

INTERPRETING THE PAST: USING ARCHIVAL MATERIALS IN GROUP RESEARCH PROJECTS

Donald F. Larsson and Richard Pifer

The research paper is a perennial source of complaint in freshman composition courses. Aside from the basic problems students encounter in organization, expression, and documentation, it is difficult to impress upon students the important role that research and analytical thinking will play in their college and professional careers. The glut of papers on anorexia nervosa, marijuana, pornography, and other popular topics which the teacher acquires each semester even when done well betrays the students' reluctance or lack of motivation to use source material interpretively, analytically, and critically. Too often the students are content to relay information from secondary sources without coming to any fresh conclusions based on their own synthesis of these source materials. Similarly, few students ever go beyond the secondary literature to delve into the primary sources which would force just such a synthesis. In fact, students often are unaware of the many types of sources at their disposal.

One solution to this problem is to design class projects which, by their nature, expose students to primary source materials and force them to analyze the data and draw their own conclusions as to their meaning. By drawing on historical manuscript collections, which may be available locally, English composition students can tap a wealth of material unedited by others. When combined with background reading, primary sources can become a valuable curricular tool for practicing writing skills, formulating original conclusions, and developing an analytical approach to course materials. Such projects not only provide a needed change for students and teachers alike, but they open up a new type of resource for students and often result in refreshingly original papers.

In the spring of 1981, we attempted to provide three English composition classes with just such a change of pace. English composition at the University of Wisconsin–Eau Claire is a required course. Students may take either a five-credit, one-semester course (English 110) or a six-credit, two-semester sequence (English 101 and 102). One of the three classes taught by Don Larsson that spring was a section of 110, meeting five days a week with an enrollment of twenty-nine freshmen, and one sophomore, and the others were two sections of 102, meeting for 75 minutes twice and 50 minutes three times a week, respectively. The 102 sections consisted primarily of sophomores, although the enrollment included a few juniors and seniors. In either course, the student was expected to learn basic organizational skills (description, comparison, classification, and so on) and to write at least one documented research paper. As with any required composition course, the students represented a wide range of interests and abilities.

To meet these varied interests, spark an enthusiasm for writing, develop analytical skills and provide an exercise which would prepare the students for writing their individual research papers, Dr. Larsson—prompted by a suggestion by Rick Pifer, curator of the Area Research Center—turned to that center as a curricular resource. The Area Research Center is a regional manuscript depository connected with the State Historical Society of Wisconsin. It serves a nine-county region comprising most of the Chippewa Valley and houses collections relating to the lumber industry, settlement of northern Wisconsin, labor unions, business development, county government, and the court system. The records range from corporate financial documents to divorce records to private letters.

We designed an exercise which would prepare the students for writing their own research papers, and which would acquaint them with historical materials, such as those contained in the Area Research Center, as a future resource. We wanted the students to meet four goals: 1) to practice the skills (note-taking, incorporating quoted material, paraphrasing, footnoting, compiling a bibliography, editing, and rewriting) required for the individual research papers to be assigned following completion of this exercise; 2) to practice focusing diverse research materials on one particular topic and thesis; 3) to use primary materials which students might otherwise overlook or ignore; and 4) to work in a cooperative group experience, such as students might encounter later in their academic or professional careers. The final product of these projects was to be an oral report to the class, a written paper, and a bibliography of materials for possible further research.

For this project we chose four manuscript collections which varied greatly in content and focus, but which were all relatively small, easily comprehendible collections. The first collection consists of approximately a hundred letters written by Lucy Hastings, a pioneer woman who settled on the Wisconsin frontier in 1857. Her letters are particularly useful because she wrote clearly and without archaic language of her hopes and dreams for the future, of the religion which served her so well, and of her daily life. For a second collection we chose the diary of Orville Hinz, a World War II veteran who had served in the South Pacific. Although the entries are brief, they speak of the fear, tension, and endurance of men on a battlefront. This collection also includes a variety of materials, such as service newspapers and a few letters. The third collection consists of the personal papers of Benjamin Stucki, a teacher and Congregational missionary among the Winnebago of northern Wisconsin from about 1900 to the mid-1940s. While using his papers requires care, to the discerning reader they can open up a world of information on Native Americans in the first half of the twentieth century and on the practices of a missionary who spent most of his life with the Winnebago. The final collection used for this project is more complex than the others, but we expected it to appeal to students with interests in business, advertising, and Wisconsin settlement. This is the Wisconsin Colonization Company Collection, records of a company established to sell stripped lumber land in northern Wisconsin to immigrants, urban workers, and renting farmers. The collection contains a wealth of promotional materials which document the company's business methods, the clientele it wished to reach, and its advertising practices.

To prepare the students for group projects, a new experience for many of them, Dr. Larsson devoted several class sessions to discussing research techniques and paper writing, and provided the students with summaries of each collection and a set of questions to help them focus their attention on some of the major issues addressed by each collection. Students were asked to identify the backgrounds of the authors of the documents in question, the nature of the documents themselves, what the documents revealed or did not reveal about their authors, and what possible sources could be consulted for additional study on a related subject.

With this preparation, each class spent a session at the Area Research Center. This allowed Mr. Pifer to introduce the students to each collection, to describe the materials contained there, to elaborate on some of the main themes of the collections, and to provide the students with suggestions of complementary secondary sources they should read while preparing their papers. After the introduction the students had time to ask questions about each collection and to investigate briefly each collection firsthand. At the end of the class session they were asked to divide into groups according to which collection they wished to use. The result in each class was four relatively evenly divided groups, ranging—according to enrollment—from six to eight members each. Class time was set aside during the next few weeks in order to allow the groups to work together as a whole. Other class time was devoted to specific problems of the research paper, including footnoting and bibliographic formats.

At the end of four weeks, the 102 students gave their oral reports. Of the eight reports, four were satisfactory. Two others—one report on the Stucki Collection and one on the Hinz Collection—showed special effort and ingenuity. The Stucki report was thorough, balanced, and insightful about this missionary's efforts among the Native Americans with whom he worked. The Hinz group had shown unusual initiative by contacting Hinz himself. Their interview turned up new information that added useful background to the collection. It turned out that Hinz, rather than being just a radio operator as indicated in his diary, was actually a cryptographer in charge of relaying important and sensitive information. One interesting anecdote from Hinz revealed that he had nearly delayed and lost the Battle of the Coral Sea through a mistake in the interpretation of a message.

At the other end, two groups ran into serious difficulties in their reports. Another group working on the Stucki Collection had apparently entered the project with preconceptions and used the material at hand to justify their own stereotypes, concluding that "Stucki was a hypocrite." Even more serious than this oversimple conclusion was the fact that they had not used much in the way of concrete evidence to back up their assertion. Instead, they relied on hasty generalizations and facts and quotations taken out of context. The other major problem was more technical: one of the groups working with the Wisconsin Colonization Company had assigned the actual writing of the report to one of the weakest writers in the group. The report suffered from basic grammatical and organizational problems, and other members of the group were visibly embarrassed at having to turn it in. All groups were allowed to revise their projects once they had been read and commented on, and those two groups did make significant improvements, though the papers were still not so strong as they could, or should, have been.

Larsson's intent was to give copies of the revised reports to all class members to aid them as models while working on their own research papers. Although copies were eventually distributed, turnaround time proved too lengthy to be of much help in this regard. Following the projects' completion, students were given evaluation forms to fill out, in which they were asked to discuss the strengths and weaknesses of their projects and to suggest changes and improvements in various areas, such as length of time for the assignment, scope and clarity of the assignment, the extent of their own improvement in research skills, and the nature of the research groups.

The procedure described was repeated with the English 110 class following spring break. A few modifications were made at this point, even before evaluations from the other classes had come in. Description of the archival materials was made even more specific and many of the materials were copied and reduced in quantity for easier handling. The bibliographies, which had been the weakest portion of the first two sets of reports, were now required to be annotated. Since this class met five days a week, it was given only three weeks to complete the reports, but this time restriction did not seem to hinder progress (once again, class time was released for group work). Although none of the reports from this class showed the same quality as the best of those in 102, none of them displayed problems as severe as in the weakest 102 papers. Evaluation forms were also completed by this class.

The evaluations themselves cannot be considered completely valid responses since only about half of the students (thirteen out of thirty students in 110 and fifteen and sixteen out of twenty-five students in each of the 102 classes) bothered to respond. Still, those evaluations received were generally positive, particularly about the nature of the projects and the chance to find and use such original materials as those contained in the collections. Length of time, scope of project, and clarity of the assignment were all judged to be sufficient. The benefits of the project in terms of preparation for the individual research paper were considered to be mixed: the older students in the 102 classes who had already done a number of research papers in their classes did not find this aspect of the projects very helpful, while other students found varying degrees of usefulness according to how evenly work in their group had been distributed. Most students agreed that all persons in each group should participate in each part of the project, including, note-taking, writing, editing, and compiling the bibliography.

Predictably, the most complaints were about the nature of the group work. Inevitably, some students had done much more work than others. The one surprise was that the older 102 students, whom we expected to work together better on the basis of age and maturity, had more problems and objections than the freshman 110 students. Rather than age, the important factor seemed to be the frequency of class meetings, with the most positive results coming from the five-day-a-week 110 students and the most negative from the twice-a-week 102 students. None of the 110 students wanted the projects to be assigned individually, unlike a number of the 102 students. In all three classes, though, there were many calls for smaller groups—of two to four people. Other suggestions included formal consultations between the teacher and groups to monitor progress and redirect efforts as necessary. Some did feel more class time was needed for work together, especially in the 102 classes where students otherwise found problems in meeting. Some students also suggested that they be given more leeway in focusing their papers.

We plan to incorporate many of these suggestions as we continue these and similar projects in the future. It is clear that utilizing materials which have not been weeded and interpreted for them is a new and interesting experience for most undergraduates. This type of group work also seems well suited to preparing students for cooperative group work in their careers, but only if the groups are small, given specific directions, and closely monitored. In many cases, this was the first experience the students had had with group dynamics in a situation where they were expected to produce a final product, and special attention from the instructor is warranted to assured that the learning experience is profitable. One immediate step which we will take in the future is to limit the groups to no more than four persons each. Two advantages will result from such a change: the group size will be more workable, and there will be two groups per collection, thus establishing two groups within the class which are equally experienced with regard to a specific collection and which can act as critics for each other's work. Obviously, this would add a new twist to the assignment, for the students would have to think critically not only about their own work but about their partner group's work as well.

In discussing this project and the use of original source materials as a curricular tool with fellow faculty members we have noticed a certain reluctance to apply this type of project to underclass students, while there is a little more willingness to adapt it to upper-division courses. Our experience would seem to indicate that group projects of this sort may be most useful when applied to freshmen. The older students seem more set in the patterns they know and are often locked into an individualistic approach to such projects, while freshmen, though having less technical knowledge, are more open to innovative approaches. If cooperative work skills are an important part of the undergraduate learning experience, then there seems to be no time which is too soon to begin developing these skills. In addition, because the use of original source materials lends itself so well to developing a critical approach to one's subject material, there is no time which is too soon to make use of this valuable curricular resource.

One final lesson can be derived from our experiences: directions must be simple and clear. Undoubtedly, the experience of working with historical documents and of working in groups is new for most students. To avoid confusion and to prod students into thinking interpretively and critically, directions must explain exactly why the students are expected to undertake such an unusual project, what is expected of them, and how they should approach their subject material.

Such archival materials as those described here are one way of opening up students' perspectives on themselves and the world around them. We used these materials in an English writing class, but similar materials are applicable to many other disciplines as well. History classes can utilize historical documents to provide the students with writing experience and a taste of what professional historical research is like. Cultural geography classes can utilize collections of maps, diaries, letters, and census materials to develop an understanding of regional settlement patterns, urban growth, agricultural change, and cultural development. Feature writing classes can study court cases, corporate records, private correspondence, and photographs to enhance research skills and the ability to organize diverse pieces of information into a coherent historical article. The subject material will lend itself to many other disciplines as well: sociology, anthropology, political science, business history, and even accounting. One thing seems certain from our experiences: students enjoy working in new ways which enhance their writing, working, and thinking skills.

BIBLIOGRAPHY: MORE ON USING LIBRARIES AND LIBRARIANS

Block, Haskell M., and Sidney Mattis. "The Research Paper: A Cooperative Approach," *College English* 13 (Jan. 1952), 212–215. Suggests a program for teaching the research paper that brings teacher and librarian into a cooperative teaching relationship which solves students' specific problems more easily.

Blum, Mark E., and Stephen Spangehl. "Introducing the College Student to Academic Inquiry: An Individualized Course in Library Research Skills" (ERIC ED 152315). Presents a full bibliography, class schedule, and work sheets used by the authors when teaching three competencies of research: critical thinking, research methods to acquire knowledge, and methods of assessing use of library resources.

Ford, James. "The Research Loop: Helping Students Find Periodical Sources," *College Composition and Communication* 37 (May 1986), 223–227. A systematic method for finding subject-specific periodical sources *beyond Readers' Guide.*

Foster, Barbara. "Do-It-Yourself Videotape for Library Orientation Based on a Term Paper Project," *Wilson Library Bulletin* 48 (Feb. 1974), 476–481. Details how one teacher made her own library orientation video; comments help the teacher/librarian empathize with bewildered students approaching their first research topic.

Kennedy, James R., Thomas G. Kirk, and Gwendolyn A. Weaver. "Course-Related Library Instruction: A Case Study of the English and Biology Departments at Earlham College," *Drexel Library Quarterly* 7 (July/Oct. 1971), 277–297. Model of course-integrated library instruction in a small school; one of the most successful such programs. Four levels of instruction, from introduction and the freshman's first research paper assignment to introduction to the major, and, finally, the senior seminar project.

Pearson, Lennart. "What Has the Library Done for You Lately?" *Improving College and University Teaching* 26 (Fall 1978), 219–221. Offers ten ways librarians can help teachers ensure that library skills are "deliberately built into the curriculum."

Schmersahl, Carmen B. "Teaching Library Research: Process, Not Product," *Journal of Teaching Writing* 6 (Fall-Winter 1987), 231–238. Research should be treated as a recursive, generative process and incorporated into writing assignments throughout the term.

Trzyna, Thomas. "The Informational Structures of Disciplines: An Approach to Teaching Research" (ERIC ED 238004). Suggests more sophisticated research questions—"Who is likely to know this?"—that lead to source material.

Watt, James T., and Wade S. Hobbs. "Research and Report Writing: A Model of Their Inter-relationships," *ABCA Bulletin*, 42 (Sept. 1979), 22–25. After stating that identification of the problem and writing the report are the two focal points of any research, presents and explains a diamond-shaped research model which depicts the researcher's progress from defining the problem through preliminary and major research to the stages of consolidating and writing up the report.

Williams, Nancy. "Research as a Process," *Journal of Teaching Writing* 7 (Fall-Winter 1988), 193–204. Viewing research as a transactional process leads to improved reading, writing, and thinking.

Model Courses, Units, and Solutions to Specific
Problems

EXPLORING THE HERO CYCLE: A HEURISTIC FOR RESEARCH AND CRITICISM

Mimi R. Gladstein and Robert M. Esch

Heroism is a timely and timeless subject. Though ours has been characterized as an antiheroic age, an age "eager to define away heroism, or to dissolve it through analysis, psychological or sociological,"[1] there are indications that a shift in public attitudes is underway. If Hollywood is any indication of the tenor of the times, then heroes are definitely "in." Encouraged by the success of *Rocky I* and *Superman I,* a success exploited by their sequels, the movie industry has responded to audience enthusiasm and bombarded us with an assortment of heroes of all types. Transported into the future, we applaud the noble deeds of Luke Skywalker and Han Solo, as well as the intellectual and spiritual powers of Yoda; *Star Trek's* intrepid crew, older but no less daring, fearlessly battles the unknown. Contemporary cinematic heroes come in all categories: from magic makers like the somewhat befuddled Merlin in *Excalibur,* to magic seekers like the slightly shopworn but tirelessly brave archaeologist, Indiana Jones, searching for the lost ark of the covenant. Some heroes, however, are still in a learning process, like the sorcerer's apprentice Galen in *Dragonslayer.* Traditional heroes have also been revived and their stories given new treatments: Perseus' quest is the subject of *Clash of the Titans;* King Arthur's tragic tale is the substance of *Excalibur.* Comic books, long a source of popular culture heroes, have inspired screen figures like Conan, the larger-than-life heroic barbarian. A similar type of primitive hero appears in *The Beastmaster.* Both he and Conan battle the forces of darkness and ignorance. In *Tron,* however, the hero fights another kind of villain, technology gone berserk.

Students, as a large segment of the movie audience, respond naturally to these heroes. The subject of heroes and heroism has

185

proved effective in arousing the interest of freshman composition students when it is used as the theme for a semester of research and writing. This topic has the added advantage of encompassing both popular culture and academic subject matter. Understanding and developing theses about the heroic become the purpose of the semester's research. As most research begins with generalized reading on the subject, so grounding the study of the heroic in the context of mythology provides an appropriate beginning. The mythological context, for many reasons, not the least of which is its cross-disciplinary character, offers great diversity for writing projects.

Most students enter the class with naive assumptions about mythology. For them it is little more than a collection of stories about old gods and goddesses—fairy tales. They see no clear connection between current beliefs and what they define as "mythology." When they say, "That's a myth," they mean, "That's not true." Establishing a heuristic begins with the question "What is myth?"— a question that becomes the starting point in students' recognition of the relevance of myth to contemporary society. The answers emerge from preliminary lectures and a library assignment investigating definitions of "myth" and "archetype" and setting up ample boundaries and cross-references appropriate to the subject.

Several texts provide introductory reading matter. Richard Hughes surveys a variety of archetypes in his sections on the myths of Narcissus, Dionysus, Orpheus, and Christ in *The Lively Image*.[2] Bens and Baugh trace one myth in its chronological development in *Icarus*.[3] A text that is more directly to the point, David Leeming's *Mythology: The Voyage of the Hero*,[4] organizes a series of readings illustrating the stages of the Hero Cycle. Also, Harper and Row's "Sexual Identities" Media Series[5] has a helpful unit that examines the myths and archetypes of femininity and masculinity, in particular the heroine (seductress and angel) and the hero, whom it classifies in four chronological categories. From these various sources students can establish for themselves, or with the class as a whole, working definitions of "myth" and "archetype."

Once the subject has been restricted to the archetype of the hero, the class is ready to develop a more elaborate heuristic composed of such questions as: "What is a hero?" "Is there a pattern to a hero's life?" "Does the heroic differ in its applications to males and females?" The instructor and the students can initiate any number of relevant approaches. Questions about the heroic have the potential for stimulating research about the Hero Cycle or other patterns of heroic behavior.

At this point students can be sent to the library to read from a selected bibliography on the topic (see below), or the instructor may want to act as a resource person and distribute an abstracted study of the Hero Cycle (see Table I).[6] As an alternative strategy, students can go beyond the suggested bibliography to find discussions of the hero in contemporary journals or newspapers and compile a chart of their own criteria for heroism. For example, they might turn to such an unlikely source as *Penthouse* where Marilyn Stasio, annoyed by *Time*'s and *Newsweek*'s trivial standards for heroism, submits her own criteria: stature, independence, principles, purity, bravery, inspirational qualities, and universality.[7] Whether they imitate Stasio's standards or establish their own, students have alternatives to the Hero Cycle chart. They may abstract criteria from any number of such disparate discussions on heroism as appear in articles about the deaths of John Lennon or John Wayne, the return of the American hostages from Iran, or the reaction to the U.S. Olympic hockey team's triumph over the Soviet team.

Both the students' own charts and that outlined in Table I will require some elaboration; several class periods should be devoted to detailed discussion of terms. What does "universality" mean? What is implied by having two sets of parents? How does the group benefit from the hero's struggle? How can "stature" be defined in contemporary terms? Students may need to do supplementary reading to help them understand these concepts better.

Once the class members reach a consensus about the connotations of these terms, they are ready to choose an individual of particular interest to them and decide whether, or to what extent, he or she can be classified as a hero or heroine. The next step in formulating a heuristic is to ask, "Can _____ be defined as a hero?" The instructor may distribute a list of people whose lives students might want to study (see Table II). Or the class may expand the list with other seemingly appropriate names as candidates for heroism. If the students choose to follow the Hero Cycle chart, only the dead qualify, since stage V is part of the pattern. If they select a contemporary hero of a particular constituency, such as Ralph Nader, Gloria Steinem, or Phyllis

Schlafly, they will find that a chart of their own construction is more appropriate.

The assignment, then, is for students to evaluate their candidates for heroism by the criteria they choose to follow. For information about their heroes' lives, we normally encourage students to use no fewer than ten sources. Class discussions of definitions will help them realize that mythology encompasses a variety of narratives and that they should exploit this diversity in seeking out information about their particular hero. Useful sources might be poems, songs, television programs, jokes, or any number of art forms. Popular folk wisdom is also useful, such as the tales parents might have recounted about Paul Bunyan or Abraham Lincoln.

With their research completed, students are now ready to argue whether their particular heroes fit either the pattern of the Hero Cycle or contemporary criteria for heroes. The instructor has the option of making this assignment either a short paper or the traditional three-thousand-word research project. An initial short paper on a hero such as Conan might encourage the student to pursue a longer research paper on the comic book hero. In a more comprehensive paper students might well be drawing comparisons among several heroes. Such a title as "The Similarities of the Life Patterns of Benito Juarez and Prometheus" suggests how one student approached a comparative study of a mythical and historical hero. Another possibility is for the student to focus on one hero to pursue in other contexts, such as the political or historical. The George Washington of cherry-tree legend could be compared with the historical Washington. If the instructor chooses to use the shorter-paper format, then these papers can be enhanced by oral reports in which students share their findings with the class. Two, possibly more, reports can be presented within a class period. Class discussion follows in which the group tests the validity of each student's conclusions and perhaps inquires why certain information was included or omitted. In an oral presentation on Abraham Lincoln, one student cataloged a number of Lincoln's exceptional qualities: his development of powerful muscles and tremendous grip, his ability to sink a blade into a tree to a great depth, and his exceptional size—at least a foot taller than his peers. Yet in the presentation to the class the student made no connections between these remarkable features and the criteria of the

Hero Cycle. The class interpretations help show students how certain data may be qualified under specific categories outlined in the chart.

Students learn that all research data is evaluated through an individual frame of reference or perception that reflects the bias of the researcher, much in the same way that mythic narratives are transmitted through the point of view of a particular consciousness. Even the conclusions of Nobel Prize winner Linus Pauling about the preventive and curative powers of vitamin C differ significantly from those of other researchers. In a similar manner one student from her research on Geronimo pointed out that for many years, in traditional historical accounts, he was regarded as a bloodthirsty savage, but through revisionist history he has become the Napoleon of the Indians. She concludes:

> Geronimo's supernatural abilities as a soothsayer, as well as his rise to power by conquest and bravery, and his legendary exploits as an Apache leader serve to place him in the mold of the archetypal hero to some degree. In due time as the Indian myth and the white man's myth converge to form a new Geronimo legend, it would not be at all surprising to find him comfortably well within the bounds of criteria for the archetypal hero.

Students must, however, be encouraged to strive for as much objectivity as possible. Heroes need to be evaluated despite the prejudices of politics, religion, or nationality. In her report on Joseph Smith a student with obvious antipathy failed to appreciate some of the data. For example, she reported the story of Smith's fall from the second-story window of the jail in Carthage, Illinois, yet ignored the Mormon interpretation of the event. Mormon historians perceive Smith's actions as heroic—an attempt to divert the attention of his persecutors from his friends by purposefully drawing the mob's bullets to himself. The class was quick to note that the report also failed to mention Brigham Young, although the analogies among the Young/Smith, Joshua/Moses, and Peter/Jesus relationships were evident to them.

By contrast, another student discovered that Ho Chi Minh could be evaluated as a hero, despite the attempts of the Western media to portray his life in unglamorous terms. Through his research, this student came to realize how various perspectives interact, observing, "Ho gained his share of enemies in his lifetime and attempts were made to debunk his myth. Ho was labeled a 'Mongoloid Trotsky,' 'a tubercular agitator,' and 'goat bearded Communist' by the western press." Additionally, the student noted Ho's role in the decay of "the colonial myth of white supremacy and colored inferiority." He also learned that Ho is credited with initiating a new era in which many countries outside Asia overthrew their colonial masters.

As students hear one another's reports, they begin to recognize certain similarities among heroes from diverse cultures and times. The concept of archetype becomes clearer. A short theme based on inferences the students have drawn might follow discussion of class presentations. One student interested in medicine discussed the images of war and death-defying heroics in medical description. One of his sources argued, "The very term 'heart attack,' which involves the metaphor of a battle and promotes the taking on of the hero role, should be phased out."[8] As part of this process students learn note-taking techniques, weighing of evidence, and phrasing and testing a tentative thesis in preparation for an essay derived from what they discover. The research method becomes clearer to them as they individually and collectively gather information about heroes. The following example illustrates how a perceptive student, after listening to the class reports, which included such heroes as Moses, Hitler, John F. Kennedy, King Arthur, and Ho Chi Minh, gathered his own thoughts on social instability and the rise of national heroes:

> Heroes, however do not arise in every age in every culture. One must wonder if there is some unusual social factor which makes the appearance of a hero more likely. In *Galileo,* Bertolt Brecht suggests this when the character Galileo says, "Unhappy is the land that needs a hero." It seems to be true that a nation or tribe imperiled by its own disunity, misdirection, or an external threat often provides the context in which a hero presents himself.

After providing several illustrations of national chaos giving rise to a hero, he concluded, "A curious convergence of social needs and individual drive creates the legendary figures who are central to a country's history."

Obviously, the heuristics connected with this thematic approach stimulate a variety of writing assignments: the short and/or long research paper, a class report, an inductive theme. A critical essay is another possibility. We can assure the students that their knowledge of myth can help them evaluate their sources with confidence. A critical essay which judges the research, objectivity, and usefulness of one of their sources is yet another provocative assignment. The only limit to the options for writing projects growing out of this approach is the teacher's imagination.

NOTES

1. George Will, "Remembering a True Israeli Hero," *El Paso Times,* July 2, 1981, 4-A.
2. Richard Hughes, *The Lively Image* (Cambridge, Mass.: Winthrop, 1975).
3. John H. Bens and Douglas R. Baugh, *Icarus* (New York: Macmillan, 1970). See also John Vickery and J'nan M. Sellery, *The Scapegoat: Ritual and Literature* (Boston: Houghton Mifflin, 1972); James L. Sanderson and Irwin Gopnik, *Phaedra and Hippolytus* (Boston: Houghton Mifflin, 1966); and James L. Sanderson and Irwin Gopnik, *Medea* (Boston: Houghton Mifflin, 1967).
4. David Leeming, *Mythology: The Voyage of the Hero* (New York: Lippincott, 1973).
5. "Myths and Archetypes," in *Sexual Identities,* Media Series, unit 4 (New York: Harper and Row, 1976).
6. We are indebted to David Johnson, University of New Mexico, for the embryonic form of this chart, which has been updated and expanded.
7. Marilyn Stasio, "How to Become a Hero," *Penthouse* 11 (Aug. 1980), 45–46.
8. Stuart Bartle, "Denial of Cardiac Warnings," *Psychosomatics* 21 (Jan. 1980), 75.

The Hero Cycle: A Selected Bibliography

Auden, W. H. "The Quest Hero," collected in *Perspectives in Contemporary Criticism,* ed. Sheldon Grebstein. New York: Harper and Row, 1968.
Campbell, Joseph. *The Hero with a Thousand Faces.* 1949. Reprint. Cleveland: World Publishing Company, 1956.
Coffin, Tristram Potter, and Herrig Cohen, eds. *The Parade of Heroes.* Garden City, N.Y. Doubleday, 1978.
Frye, Northrop. *Anatomy of Criticism.* New York: Atheneum, 1969. Pp. 186–206.
Goodrich, Norma. *Myths of the Hero.* New York: Orion Press, 1962.
Kluckhohn, Clyde. "Recurrent Themes in Myths and Mythmaking." In *Myth and Mythmaking,* ed. Henry Murray. Boston: Beacon Press, 1968. (Kluckhohn uses Rank and Katherine Spencer's *Mythology and Values: An Analysis of Navaho Chantway Myths* to compare Old and New World hero myths.)
Leeming, David Adams. *Mythology: The Voyage of the Hero.* New York: Lippincott, 1973.
Murray, Gilbert. *Five Stages of Greek Religion.* New York: Doubleday Anchor Books, 1959.

Norman, Dorothy. *The Hero: Myth/Image/Symbol.* New York: World. 1969.

Raglan, Lord. *The Hero: A Study in Tradition, Myth and Drama.* 1936. Reprint. New York: Vintage Books, 1956.

Rank, Otto. *The Myth of the Birth of the Hero.* 1914. Reprint. New York: Vintage Books, 1959.

Table I. The Hero Cycle

Stages:	I. Prophecy & Birth	II. Infancy & Childhood	III. Maturation	IV. Ordeal & Victory	V. Return & Exaltation
Auden	*a special man: breeding or character*	*tests revealing hero; journey for precious object/person*	*battle for objects w/ guardians/obstacles*	*invaluable assistance from animal/ human*	*object possessed married person*
Campbell	*call to adventure*	*threshold crossing, battle, death, etc.*	*journey w/tests & helpers*	*nadir: ordeal, reward (marriage, apotheosis, boon)*	*return: flight, threshold again. arrival: restoration renewal elixir*
Frye	*birth: water associations; mysterious origin*	*innocent youth: pastoral, maternal*	*perilous journey*	*crucial struggle/ battle, victory*	*exaltation of the hero:reflective/idyllic culmination*
Goodrich	*unusual birth*	*childhood—isolated*	*initiation; long, perilous journey with trials*	*riddle solving; altruistic labors*	*aloneness*
Kluckhohn, Rank, & Spencer	*a special birth*	*separation from parents; help from animals*	*rivalry with family, kin*	*extraordinary adventures*	*heroic return to family; benefit to family & group*

	the miraculous conception	childhood initiation & divine signs	preparation; mediation & withdrawal, guest	death & the scapegoat	descent to the underworld; apotheosis resurrection, a new age initiated
Leeming					
Murray (the year king)	mixed parents; god/mortal; special birth	persecuted mother; saved by son; life threatened	savior from enemies/danger/death	sacrificial death; totemized	a new age initiated
Norman	movement toward dawn	forms of awakening (childhood)	symbolic contests (process of self-mastery)	tyrannical clinging to power	beyond combat—transformation
Raglan	virgin mother/unusual conception	life threatened; separation from parents; raised by foster parents	return/victory over kind/animal	becomes king; royal marriage	loses favor—death gains religious rank
Rank	prebirth problems: (a) of conception (b) prophecy of danger	distinguished royal parentage; escape by water (box, basket)	saved, suckled by animals, lowly folk	finds parents in "versatile" fashion	revenge on father acknowledgment; high rank & favor

Table II. The Hero Cycle

1. Achilles	21. Lincoln
2. King Arthur	22. Ho Chi Minh
3. Athena	23. Mohammed
4. Buddha	24. Moses
5. Paul Bunyan	25. Napoleon
6. Chiang Kai-shek	26. Oedipus
7. Conan	27. Osiris
8. Dionysus	28. Perseus
9. Francis of Assisi	29. Prometheus
10. Frodo	30. Quetzalcoatl
11. Genghis Khan	31. Robin Hood
12. Geronimo	32. Romulus
13. Hannibal	33. Joseph Smith
14. Heracles	34. Siegfried
15. Hitler	35. Superman
16. Isaac	36. Tarzan
17. Jason	37. Theseus
18. Jesus	38. Thor
19. Joan of Arc	39. Ulysses
20. John Kennedy	40. George Washington

FACT, TRANSITION, AND COMMENT: A PRACTICAL APPROACH TO RESEARCH PAPER WRITING

Greg Larkin

> There are 800,000 cattle in Utah. There are 1,000,000 sheep in Utah. It is predicted that 3,500,00 acres will be overgrazed in Utah by 1980. It is predicted that 1,500,000 acres of grazing land will be eroded. Utah has a serious overgrazing and erosion problem.

Every semester I find a number of students who have an intelligent thesis, well-researched notes, and a logical organization. Seemingly everything is going right, but when the paper comes in it isn't right because the student literally can't write. It's not a grammatical problem, for the sentences, although often choppy, are nonetheless correct. Nor is it a lack of intelligence, for the student has a clear and sensible line of reasoning. Writing like that quoted above is generated out of a combination of terror at the prospect of writing a research paper and a lack of any concrete sense of how to go about research paper writing. I would like to propose a simple model that even the most terrified and ill-prepared student can use to generate acceptably written research papers. This model, once mastered, is capable of nearly infinite variations, all of which will remain firmly grounded on the three basic principles of research paper writing (and in fact of all writing): fact, transition, and comment.

Let's assume that our intelligent but pen-shy student has successfully narrowed his or her research topic into a thesis, identified its inherent subparts, and taken copious notes on each subpart. Let's further assume that he or she has culled from these notes the most fitting and concrete supporting facts for each subpart of the paper, giving him or her at this point a logically ordered stack of note cards, something like this example:

Main Thesis: Utah has a serious overgrazing and erosion problem.
Support one: 800,000 cattle
Support two: 1,000,000 sheep
Support three: 3,500,000 overgrazed acres
Support four: 1,500,000 eroded acres of grazing land
Subthesis One. Eroded lands are more subject to costly floods
Support one: 1953 Springville flood
Support two: flooding is proportional to precipitation
Support three: floods start in small areas in canyon heads
Subthesis Two. Vegetation helps prevent erosion
Support one: Vegetation holds topsoil in place
Support two: Topsoil helps prevent erosion

This collection of logically ordered notes is the factual basis for the paper, the absolutely essential undergirding of support for the thesis. Most students can get this far on any halfway decent subject; but the facts, even when logically organized, do not speak for themselves. At this point, the student must use writing skills to make the facts support the thesis convincingly.

If the student is wise, or has good training from the teacher, he or she will have each one of the facts listed on its own individual card, so that at this point in the writing process, what the student has is a logically ordered stack of note cards, schematically represented thus.

1. Major thesis _____ Note card #1
   A. Subthesis One _____ Note card #2
      1. Support one _____ Note card #3
      2. Support two _____ Note card #4
      3. Support three _____ Note card #5
      4. Support four _____ Note card #6
   B. Subthesis Two _____ Note card #7
      1. Support one _____ Note card #8
      2. Support two _____ Note card #9
      3. Support three _____ Note card #10
   C. Subthesis Three _____ Note card #11
      1. Support one _____ Note card #12
      2. Support two _____ Note card #13

The student has now completed step one of the writing process, the factual level, and is ready for step two, the transitional level. The goal here is for the student, in his or her own words, to add a bridge of language connecting every adjacent pair of facts. In the schematic diagram, this step appears thus:

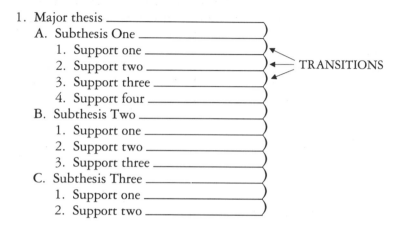

The paragraph which opened this paper might appear as follows after the transitions were added:

> Despite its relatively large size, Utah suffers from an over-population problem. The excess is not in people, but in animals. There are over 800,000 cattle in Utah, with an additional 1,000,000 sheep. The Utah Environmental Association predicts that 3,500,000 acres of Utah's land will be overgrazed by 1980. In addition, another 1,500,000 acres of grazing land will be eroded. The magnitude of these numbers suggests that Utah has a serious overgrazing and erosion problem.

The facts in this paragraph are identical to those in the original, factual-level paragraph. The difference is that, in the paragraph with transitions added, the reader is made overtly aware of the previously unstated but very important relationships among the facts. The paragraph without transitions is choppy and hard to read, even though its language is very simple. The paragraph with transitions flows smoothly and is thus easier to read, even though its language and sentence structure are actually more complicated than those in the first paragraph.

With the facts logically organized, and connected with smooth language bridges called transitions, the writer is now ready for the final step, the commentary. This critical step is also the most creative and the most challenging, for here the author, from his or her own mind, relates each fact back to the major thesis or the subthesis. These authorial comments go beyond the facts to make qualifications, elaborations, inferences, judgments, etc. In the comments, the author draws the conclusions that the careful ordering of facts and intelligent use of transitions allow him or her to make. Schematically, this third level, or commentary, looks like this:

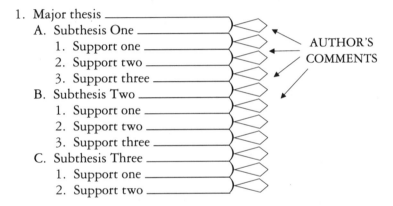

1. Major thesis
   A. Subthesis One
      1. Support one
      2. Support two
      3. Support three
   B. Subthesis Two
      1. Support one
      2. Support two
      3. Support three
   C. Subthesis Three
      1. Support one
      2. Support two

AUTHOR'S COMMENTS

The paragraph on Utah's overgrazing problem, with the author's comments added, might look like this:

> Contrary to popular opinion, Utah suffers from an overpopulation problem even though it is one of the larger states in terms of land area. Most of the people in Utah are crowded along the Wasatch Front, leaving the rest of the state relatively barren. The large barren areas in Utah are not a result of human overpopulation, but of animal overpopulation. There are over 800,000 cattle in Utah, and an additional 1,000,000 sheep. Some may be tempted to feel that most of Utah's land is only good for cattle and sheep, but the problem is not so simple as that. In fact, such laissez-faire attitudes have led the Utah Environmental Association to predict that 3,500,000 acres of Utah will be overgrazed by 1980. In addition, another

1,500,000 acres of grazing land will be eroded. The magnitude of these numbers suggests that Utah has a serious overgrazing and erosion problem, which cannot be solved by handing over large chunks of land to cattle and sheep.

In paragraphs like the one above, we find the kind of writing that should characterize all research papers: logically ordered facts, connected by smooth transitions, supporting the author's own intelligent commentary on the thesis. I have found that my students can understand what a research paper is supposed to be when they are taught to recognize these three levels in all research writing. To test their comprehension, I often give students a passage from a research paper and ask them to identify the facts by underlining them once, the transitions by underlining them twice, and the comments by underlining them three times. The following is a sample passage:

How does Shakespeare manage to keep the audience from

hooting at a statue "coming to life"? First of all, the statue

scene is only the last of a long series of parallel scenes based on

death in the first half of the play and life in the second half.

Almost every commentator has noted that the play is divided

into two halves, as Shakespeare makes clear with the line,

"Now bless thyself: thou met'st with things dying, I with

things new-born" (III, iii, 112–113).¹ The entire play breaks

into two parallel halves, Siemon observes, showing good and

evil exercising mutual restraints upon one another.² The first

half is all of deaths: Mamillius, Antigonus, Hermione, as well

as the deaths of love and family. In the second half Florizel

replaces Mamillius, Camillo replaces Antigonus, and Hermoine is reborn. Linking the two halves is the baby Perdita, lost in the first half, and found in the second. The pattern of death and loss in the first half creates in the audience a great need to see the evils righted and the injured people restored to felicity. C. L. Barber sees the play fulfilling this need by moving from experience of loss to recovery of the old family.[3] Beginning in act IV, love, joy, trust, hospitality, and good fellowship, in short all the human values that were lost at Leontes' court, are found again at the shepherd's cabin.[4] In other words, Shakespeare uses the overwhelming human tendency to look for and expect pattern. The more broken the pattern in the first half, the more powerful is the completion of the pattern in the second half. Conversely, the more completely the pattern is broken in the first half, the less likely it is that the pattern can be restored in the second half. Shakespeare solves his problem by making *The Winter's Tale* very frankly a fantastic tale. McFarland rightly concludes that the play combines tragic intensity with comic well-being at the cost of credibility.[5] Shakespeare plays this lack of credibility to the hilt, even going so far as to make a statue "come to life."

In passages such as this one, the footnotes are a giveaway that the material in that sentence must be factual, i.e., must have come from a note card rather than the student's own thinking. Therefore, I usually remove the footnote numbers for this exercise, and I find that if the transitions are well written, the students can quite easily distinguish the researched or borrowed comments (which are on the factual level because they are borrowed) from the original or authorial comments. If, with the footnote numbers deleted, the students cannot tell the differences between the factual (or borrowed level) and the original authorial commentary, we can almost always trace the problem to inadequate transitions; this in itself is a good lesson for the students to learn. An excellent lesson on plagiarism also fits in nicely here. To see a paragraph in which you can't tell the difference between borrowed and original commentary, simply read the paragraph on *The Winter's Tale,* deleting all sections with two underlines. To see plagiarism, simply delete the double underlined sections and all the footnote numbers.

With training, students can see these levels. However, recognition is one thing, but production is another. I have my students go through these three writing steps very mechanically at first, and then gradually, as they are able, allow them increasing freedom in their writing methods. Ultimately, it is having these three levels that counts, not precisely how they are arrived at.

A well-written research paper is one in which the author successfully controls his or her thesis throughout, so that the reader is always aware of how each point helps to establish the validity of the thesis. The second and equally crucial prerequisite is careful thought applied to the thesis over the space of several separate drafts of the paper. The three-step process of fact, transition, and comment simply gives a guiding hand to that careful thought, allowing the student to create three distinct drafts of the paper:

1. The facts organized into a series of logically ordered individual note cards.

2. Transitions added to a choppy collection of organized facts.

3. A flowing and organized factual paper supplemented by original comments of the author.

There is nothing magic about these three stages that go into a paper, but there is something almost magic about the effect of time on writing. In a sense, the three stages are simply a way of giving the writer time to think of the really important things that he or she has to say about the subject. Thus, the three stages move the writer's mind ever deeper into the subject matter. As writers go through the three steps, they learn more about their subjects. As they learn more, they become more capable of adding their own unique contributions, because they gain more insight. Good and original author's commentary, based on a firm foundation of logically ordered and smoothly connected facts, is the hallmark of good research writing.

COMBINING ENGLISH CLASSES: AN ALTERNATIVE APPROACH TO TEACHING THE RESEARCH PAPER

Elizabeth B. Griffey and Mary Sue Koeppel

Problem

As instructors in a large (89,000 students) urban community college with an open-door policy, we encountered difficulties teaching English Composition II—Research Writing—due to the wide diversity of writing skill levels that the open-door policy permits. The traditional lecture method provides only limited ways to meet these diverse individual needs: it is difficult to group for class instruction; all students are taught the same research skills at the same time and are expected to progress at the same rate. Furthermore, the typical lecture approach is impersonal and may prevent the instructor from knowing the specific skill needs of the students.

Solution

One solution to these problems has been our experiment with team teaching a composition course in the research paper. Team teaching, for us, consists of two English teachers combining two classes of English Composition II—Research Writing—into one and then sharing the planning, the teaching, and the evaluation. Neither instructor specializes in one aspect of the course, nor do the instructors identify with one particular group of students. This contrasts with other experiments in team teaching in writing across the curriculum which utilize an interdisciplinary approach (Fulwiler and Young). Such approaches have involved, for example, a team

205

from two disciplines, such as English and social science (Gillespie), English and psychology (Gentry and Touchton), and English and a technical subject (Thilsted), or a combination of English instructor and a research specialist.

Within our classroom, we instruct in two ways. We work with small groups giving explanations and providing materials, assignments, and evaluations of student work. We guide the collaborative learning among the peers in these groups.[1] A more important role of the teacher is to help the students understand, develop, and perfect their individual research writing. This is accomplished in conferences[2] which provide individualized instruction to each student at every step of the research and writing processes.

Course Content

When students enter this course, they must have completed successfully the Composition I course which instructs them in the process of developing undocumented essays. So we begin Composition II with a similar assignment: a nondocumented paper such as a definition essay, an opinion paper, or possibly an explanatory paper on a subject students may later wish to research. Once this paper is written, it can be used to compare with the research paper, that is, to show similarity in structures, but differences in style, tone, point of view, and, of course, documentation.

All the rest of the major assignments of the course require research. These major assignments are four short research papers; none is required to be any longer than 1,500 words, although most students' papers are longer. We believe with Renner and Lindemann that a sequence of short but progressively more complex assignments is more valuable and instructive to students than one involved paper.

The first of these four research assignments is a controlled research paper. For their sources, students use a collection of eighteen published articles in a sourcebook which they purchase. Our use of the sourcebook is not a new idea (Stone). It is, however, a very practical way to teach critical reading skills, note-taking, paraphrasing, summarizing, documentation, proper use of quotations, and the avoidance of plagiarism. We feel that using a sourcebook is to the advantage of the students because it removes from them the added burden of having to locate appropriate sources in a library while they are learning how to master the format of the research paper.

This controlled assignment is followed by another research paper on a subject of the student's choice. The major objective of this assignment is for the student to learn to locate, retrieve, and evaluate materials in a research library. In order to accomplish this objective, students must develop a working bibliography which shows that they have used a wide variety of sources, such as indexes to periodicals, indexes to major subject areas, indexes to editorials, the vertical files, audiovisual holdings, specialized reference books, etc. Students must then utilize a minimum number of these sources (four to five), but they often use many more in developing and supporting their theses. In the actual construction of their essays, students must follow the same procedures and practice the skills they learned while doing their controlled research papers.

The last research papers add a final dimension to the skills which students have already learned. That is, students are taught the structure of argumentative essays developed by reasons as well as by syllogistic reasoning. All the reasons as well as the premises in these argumentative papers must be supported by credible outside sources. At this point, students should have the facility to use the library to develop a bibliography, to evaluate sources, to incorporate these sources into a text, and to document them conventionally. Thus, our new dimension is a presentation of the principles of logical thinking, the traditional fallacies, and the principles of argumentation. At this point, then, students can no longer satisfy our assignments by submitting informative, researched reports; they must instead write thesis or proposal-type papers in which they take a stand on an issue or suggest a remedy for a problem. Thus, the more sophisticated of these research projects are saved for the end of the course.

Methodology: Self-Assessments and Grouping

Because we share the conviction that students have the innate ability to assess both their own skills and their most effective learning styles, we devised a Learning Inventory which we use for grouping students. By responding to this inventory, students are able to place themselves in appropriate groups which match their individual needs for teacher interaction, student interaction, motivation, and skill development.

In the first class meeting, students receive this inventory, a three-page questionnaire consisting of three sets of statements. Each set of statements is designed so that a student choosing an item in one set would not choose the comparable item in either of the other sets. These items include statements about the student's previous grades in English, personal ease with the composing process, self-confidence in writing, the student's reactions to working in a peer response group, the length of time necessary to do assignments, the need for deadlines, and the pleasure involved in writing. For example, an item concerning independence of learning is stated like this:

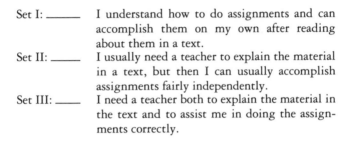

Set I: ——— I understand how to do assignments and can accomplish them on my own after reading about them in a text.

Set II: ——— I usually need a teacher to explain the material in a text, but then I can usually accomplish assignments fairly independently.

Set III: ——— I need a teacher both to explain the material in the text and to assist me in doing the assignments correctly.

Students are asked to read each of the three sets of statements and check any items which describe themselves. Then, after checking all of the pertinent items, they count the number of checks in each of the three sets. The set in which they have checked the most items will probably indicate their appropriate grouping for the class. However, in order to validate this choice, we also describe for the students the kind of teaching methodology which will be used with each group. For example, the students who have the most checks in Set III are advised: "This group will meet during each class period with a teacher, have specific deadline dates for each assignment, receive much individualized assistance from the teacher at each step of the research process, and receive complete explanations of each step involved in doing the research paper."[3]

Thus students have two bases for making their selection of a group: the results of their personal Learning Inventory and the description of learning methodology. Also, students are told that if, later, their self-placement seems inappropriate, they can place themselves in a different group. Such self-placement seems to be very effective since, for example, only two or three of fifty students typically placed themselves into new groups.

Objectives for all groups are the same—the requirements established for the course by the English department of the college. That is, students are required to learn research techniques and apply them to their own expository, argumentative, and persuasive writings. However, each group accomplishes these objectives in its own style. The group, for example, which requests much teacher-student interaction receives lectures on almost every major aspect of the research and composition process. These students also have a chance to discuss in small groups, do exercises, and meet individually with a teacher; they must meet specified deadlines set by the teachers. On the other hand, individuals who place themselves in the group which works independently set their own deadlines, meet in conferences with the teachers only when the students feel it is necessary, and may use class time to do research or to write. These are usually the "A" students. Another group has characteristics of both of these groups. This third group works somewhat independently but demands a good deal of explanation of research procedures as well as frequent critiques of their writings. This group receives lectures and explanations similar to those given the other group; however, these learners need fewer examples and exercises. Students work collaboratively in small groups both before and after meeting with an instructor. At any time, these students or the teachers may request conferences. Those students in this group who are unable to set their own deadlines must meet teacher-imposed deadlines. This group, the largest, is the most flexible from both the teachers' and students' point of view.

Methodology: Teaching Techniques

A typical class period might involve one instructor lecturing or discussing with one of the three groups while the other instructor is either working with another group or conducting short, individual conferences. During the course of the class period, the teacher conducting individual conferences might see as many as twenty students. Lectures and discussions with groups usually do not consume an entire class period. Thus, when these sessions are over, the teacher is free to conduct conferences or assist the students who are doing research in the library. On some days, depending upon the needs of the students, both teachers may be engaged in conferences. Some small groups of students may be working collaboratively, responding to peer writing. Learners who are not in a conference, lecture, or peer group will be working independently either writing or researching.

We recognize the usefulness of such traditional teaching techniques as lectures and collaborative peer work. But we are convinced that the single most important teaching technique in a writing course is the individual conference between the teacher and the student (Garrison, Koeppel, Murray, Simmons). During one of our conferences, a student submits a piece of writing (a proposition, a bibliography, note cards, a draft of some part of a research paper, even an entire draft). The discussion which ensues may have a twofold purpose since we believe in neither the totally teacher-centered conference nor the totally student-centered conference. Thus students may control a conference with questions which they originate and wish discussed. Or, on the other hand, students may bring work to be evaluated by the teacher; that is, the writers feel they have done the best they can do without further criticism and bring their own questions about their work for their teachers to answer. In both of these types of conferences, the students use the teachers as sounding boards. Gradually, the students are prepared to evaluate and make judgments about their own writings. This, we feel, is the ultimate advantage of the conference method: the students learn to evaluate and improve their own writing by an understanding of the very nature of the writing process.

Advantages

This alternate approach offers many advantages for the *students:*

1. the opportunity to assume responsibility for their own learning; that is, they must determine
   —how they will learn
   —when they will accomplish their specific objectives
   —when they will seek the teachers' advice and evaluation
   —when a paper is ready to be submitted for a grade
2. the opportunity to choose a methodology and learning environment suitable to the student's own learning style

3. the opportunity to receive critical appraisal during the research and writing processes rather than at the end
4. the opportunity, on an almost daily basis, to have the teacher point out how an individual writer (not a class) can improve individual writing
5. the opportunity to use the classroom as an active workshop rather than to sit constantly in the classroom as a spectator in a passive audience
6. the opportunity to use a teacher as a writing advisor rather than as just a lecturer and evaluator
7. the opportunity for early completion of the course for the students who have met the course requirements
8. the opportunity for students to reenroll in the class in a subsequent term in order to finish without the wasteful repetition of the course work already mastered.

This method also offers advantages for the *teachers:*

1. shared planning of the course
2. joint development of materials
3. shared grading and evaluation of the students' work
4. shared knowledge which allows each instructor to improve weak points
5. teacher interaction, the constant rubbing together of new ideas, which generates enthusiasm for the business of teaching

NOTES

1. See over a hundred collaborative-learning and peer-response activities in Mary Sue Koeppel, *Writing: Resources for Conferencing and Collaboration,* instructor's ed. (Englewood Cliffs: Prentice Hall, 1989), 1.37–1.45 and 1–3.41. Each chapter contains a special section of "Collaborative Learning Activities" designed to involve students in the writing process as peer learners, collaborative writers, or peer responders.
2. For further information about using the conference method in the teaching of writing, see Roger Garrison, "One to One Tutorial Instruction in Freshman Composition," *New Directions for Community Colleges* 2 (Spring 1974), 55–84; Koeppel, 1.27–1.36; Donald Murray, *A Writer Teaches Writing: A Practical Method of Teaching Composition,* 2nd ed. (Boston: Houghton Mifflin, 1985), 15–25.
3. For a complete copy of the personal Learning Inventory, write to Griffey/Koeppel, Communications Department, Florida Community College at Jacksonville, South Campus, 11901 Beach Boulevard, Jacksonville, Florida 32216-6624.

WORKS CITED

Fulwiler, Toby, and Art Young. *Programs That Work: Models and Methods for Writing Across the Curriculum.* Portsmouth: Boynton/Cook, 1990.

Garrison, Roger. "One to One Tutorial Instruction in Freshman Composition," *New Directions for Community Colleges* 2 (Spring 1974), 55–84.

Gentry, Robert B., and Reginald Touchton. Personal interview. May 19, 1991.

Gillespie, Joanne S. "Reliving the Depression: Integrating English and Social Studies," *English Journal* 79 (Oct. 1990), 64–69.

Koeppel, Mary Sue. *Writing: Resources for Conferencing and Collaboration.* Englewood Cliffs: Prentice Hall, 1989.

Lindemann, Erika. *A Rhetoric for Writing Teachers.* 2nd ed. New York: Oxford University Press, 1987.

Murray, Donald. *A Writer Teaches Writing: A Practical Method of Teaching Composition.* 2nd ed. Boston: Houghton Mifflin, 1985.

Renner, Dennis K. "Teaching the Research Assignment in the 1980's," *Clearing House* 54 (Sept. 1980), 19–23.

Simmons, Jo An, project director. *Testing the Effectiveness of the One to One Method of Teaching Composition: Improvement of Learning in English Project.*

Los Angeles: Los Angeles Community College District, Office of Educational Programs, 1979.

Stone, Edward. "Controlled Materials: A New Remedy for an Old Ailment," *Journal of General Education* 12 (Oct. 1959), 189–204.

Thilsted, Wanda M. "An Interdisciplinary Report Writing Course," *Technical Writing Teacher* 2 (Spring 1975), 1–3.

THE CASEBOOK AND THAT HAIRY DEVIL, RESEARCH WORK

Tommy Dodge

Now that Pandora's Box has been opened in the English class and the old demon grammar exorcised, the time has come to drive the wooden stake in the heart of another wild-eyed bogeyman who has intimidated English teachers since before the days of Dewey, the master sorcerer of the twentieth century. And that is the hairy devil called Research Work.

Many college teachers contend that the research paper should be left out of the high school English class entirely because, they say, it is just an exercise in *busywork*.

Students merely wait until the night before the paper is due, go through a stack of encyclopedias like termites through a two-by-four, copying, falsifying footnotes, and forging bibliographical entries.

The teacher is happy because the papers are neat (and fat), and the students are happy because they got their As without having to work—or think—and best of all, perhaps, they outmaneuvered the teacher.

Professors further maintain that even if these conditions were overcome by closer supervision the enterprise would still be difficult, because many high school libraries are grossly inadequate. Many contain only a smattering of the critical works and commentaries vital to research work. Some libraries do not even have a card catalog.

Don't Throw it Out

I disagree with the professors who would throw the research paper out of the high school, because all of their criticisms can be answered with the use of the casebook.

214

Casebooks are a whole library of commentary in a single volume and are designed especially for the students who are being introduced to the technicalities of research work.

They contain all the information the students need concerning footnoting, note carding, and paraphrasing. Some even include a sample research theme.

In addition to these instructions on mechanics, the casebooks are filled with essays, complete with source information—name of author, where originally published, title of book or periodical in which first published, date, and publishing company. Some even show the original page numbers in the margin.

Using this handy library-in-a-volume, students can easily seek out their information, assimilate it, organize it, and document it thoroughly, without suffering from the usual problems that constitute severe obstacles, even to the experienced researcher.

Perhaps the most convenient aspect of the casebook is that the teacher is sure that the students cannot outfox him—he has a copy of it himself, and the students know it. I always begin my instruction on the research paper with the admonition that I intend to check their every reference by looking it up in my casebook.

In addition, they are warned of a severe penalty for failure to footnote, for falsifying footnotes, and even for paraphrasing too closely.

Gratifying Results

The results are always gratifying. In the first place, there is no problem with students who are simply not capable of writing a research paper. The project is made optional by offering an alternative, such as a report on an author studied, or on some other subject chosen by the student.

The result is that the students who are incapable of writing a paper (and they know who they are) are anything but abashed by being left out, and go happily about the business of getting their report together.

Consequently, the A and B students, usually those who intend to go to college, are the ones who write the research paper. In case any of these decide to pursue their natural predilection for outsmarting the teacher by choosing the report, I always say that, although the project is optional, no one can make a higher grade than C who does not write the paper. No one has been brave enough to challenge me on this yet.

There are many casebooks available, none, unfortunately, specifically designed for the high school; but I have always used those for college students with great success.

Life on a Whaler, edited by Roland Bartel, fits in very well with the study of *Moby-Dick* in American literature. I have also used the casebook on Henry James' *The Turn of the Screw,* edited by Gerald Willen. We read the novel, which is included in the casebook, then wrote the research paper, using the many excellent essays in the casebook as sources.

Other casebooks available are *Johnson's London, London in Plague and Fire, Mr. Spectator's London, Dylan Thomas, Othello, Gulliver Among the Houyhnhnms,* and *Shakespeare's Sonnets.* These fit well in the English 4 class.

Some others for English 3: *Mark Twain's Picture of America; The Enigma of Poe; The Hawthorne Question; Ezra Pound; America Through Foreign Eyes, 1827–1842;* and *Modern America Through Foreign Eyes.*

Any of these may be ordered from the publisher or simply bought from a college bookstore, if one is nearby. I have done both. If the teacher is lucky, the school will buy them for him; if not, the students will have to pay for them or the teacher will have to find a way to get casebooks for his students.

When he does, he will be rewarded for his efforts. He will find that high school students can do more than he, and they themselves, thought was ever possible.

This article appeared originally in *Texas Outlook* 3 (Mar. 1969), 40–41. It is reprinted with permission.

CONTROLLED SOURCE RESEARCH

Philip M. Griffith

Author's Comment

In connection with the introduction, or review, of elementary research technique and documentation, the following exercise was devised and used many years before the new popular "controlled methods" approach was applied widely on the college freshman level. It may be assigned as a cooperative teacher-class project for classroom study, as an out-of-class assignment, or as an hour's test in documentation. A standard English handbook or approved style sheet (preferably the *MLA Style Sheet*) should be utilized. Teachers should, of course, devise their own "model" paragraph and rigidly adhere to the recommended style of documentation. This exercise has the advantage of not exhausting student interest, often the disadvantage of a longer casebook assignment.

Suppose that your research paper is concerned with the early career of Andrew Jackson. You have assembled in your notes the following quotations, all of which treat the controversial problem of Jackson's birthplace.

1. Write the paragraph dealing with Jackson's birthplace, utilizing the materials below.
2. Document with correct footnotes. Observe that the sources given below are complete, but incorrectly arranged, punctuated, and capitalized.
3. Compile this part of the bibliography.
   a. Chicago, lewis publishing company, 1941, Archibald henderson, volume II, *North Carolina, the old north state and the new,* pages 42–43.

217

For many years Andrew Jackson believed and repeatedly stated that he was a native of South Carolina. For example, on August 11, 1824, in reply to a query as to the place of his birth, Jackson wrote to James H. Witherspoon of Lancaster, South Carolina: "I was born in South Carolina, as I have been told, at the plantation whereon James Crawford lived, about 1 mile from the Carolina road (crossing) of the Waxhaw creek. . . ."

James D. Craig in 1828 sent all the original affidavits (of those present at or having family-neighborhood knowledge of the birthplace of Jackson) to George Nevills of Ohio, chairman of a Jackson committee. These affidavits evidently came to Jackson's notice, and convinced him that he was born in the George McKemey house, present Union County, North Carolina, the exact spot being located by a boulder just 407 yards east of the eight-mile state line between North and South Carolina which runs due north and south.

b. *The life of andrew jackson,* new york, John spencer Bassett, Macmillan company, 1925, pages 5–6.

The exact spot at which Jackson was born has become a subject of controversy. By a tradition which lingered in the Leslie branch of the family the event was said to have occurred at the house of George McKemey. When the mother, so the story runs, journeyed from her abode to her sister's home, she stopped for a visit at the home of McKemey, and here labor came upon her. But when she was able to travel she continued her journey: and thus it came about that people thought the Crawford home welcomed into the world the future President.

c. Marquis James, 1938, *The Life of Andrew Jackson,* Bobbs-Merrill Company, New York, page 10.

Elizabeth (Jackson) and her boys slept that night at the home of one of Mrs. Jackson's sisters, one would think Jane Crawford, whose house was nearest by two miles and the best provided for the reception of guests. Before sunrise a few mornings later "at the plantation whereon James Crawford lived . . . on the 15th of March in the year 1767," Elizabeth Jackson's third son was born. Such is General Jackson's own Statement as to the place of his birth. In the opinion of the present reviewer it is the best evidence available bearing on the issue though several of his biographers have accepted an elaborate and interesting tradition that he was born at George McKemey's. In any event Elizabeth named the baby Andrew, carried him to be baptized in Waxhaw Church and took up her permanent abode under the Crawford roof.

d. Dictionary of American biography, Thomas P. Abernethy, volume XI, "Andrew Jackson," 1932, page 526.

JACKSON, ANDREW (Mar. 15, 1767—June 8, 1845), seventh president of the United States, was born in the lean backwoods settlement of the Waxhaw in South Carolina.

This article originally appeared in *Exercise Exchange* 9 (Apr. 1962), 13–15. Reprinted with permission.

MEXICAN-AMERICAN FOLKLORE: AN APPROACH TO THE RESEARCH PAPER

Jan Seale

The freshman research project has always been, at least in my teaching, a clumsy beast to handle. Where does one begin to teach students that there is a reason for this creature, that hours of patient handling are required with the animal, that a student will be stronger for wrestling with it, and that, although it is submitted at roundup time in a clean and docile state, it will not necessarily be branded with a large *A*?

One of my more successful attempts to deal with the research project has been suggesting that students do their papers on subjects of local folklore. I should pause here to say that although it's possible to find other ethnic groups with folkloric elements in the Rio Grande Valley of Texas, it's obvious that the bulk of folk practices, legends and beliefs is of Mexican origin or has to do in some way with our region's proximity to Mexico. And so, when I say local folklore, I will be talking mainly about Mexican and Mexican-American lore.

I usually begin the research project by suggesting to the class that our area is rich in folklore but poor in recorders of it. I tell them that they as college students can be a liaison between the world of beliefs and practices of the folk and the world of scholarly categorizing and preservation of these things. I point out that any freshman in the United States can write a paper on marijuana, abortion, or mental retardation—all subjects which have been worked to exhaustion—but very few can write with freshness and authority on *mal de ojo,* the Los Ebanos crossing or medicinal herbs in the Rio Grande Valley of Texas. Usually, when I begin to talk about the possibilities for this subject, the class extrovert will volunteer a story from his or her family. The taboo broken, the stories pour out: "My grandmother says . . .," "I know this old man . . .," "When I was a child . . ."

So much for the motivation. There remains only the student who comes in private after class to ask incredulously, "You mean I could interview my grandmother in Reynosa and put what she believes in a research paper for English?"

"Yes," I reply, "with certain qualifications which I will spell out at the next class meeting."

And thus we are launched. The next step is to help them settle on a particular subject. When I first began teaching the folklore paper, I allowed students to write on common subjects, such as *curanderismo* and *mal de ojo*. Later, I began to discourage these as single topics because I found they were much too broad for a freshman paper. As one student wrote in one of those early, unwieldy papers, "The number of beliefs surrounding the evil eye almost matches the number of those who believe in it." If the student really desires to write on *curanderismo*, I ask him or her to limit it to one particular kind, such as the *partera*, or midwife. Likewise, if the student is interested in *mal de ojo*, the subject must be limited to something such as *mal de ojo* cures affected by the use of eggs, or *mal de ojo* interpreted as electrical energy.

A further consideration in helping the student decide on a topic is the availability of materials. This is more important than ever if students are writing on folklore topics because the library resources are likely to be much more limited. The more I teach the folklore research paper, the better I become at guessing whether the student will find suitable library sources. Sometimes though it remains a shot in the dark, and I try to warn the student that original research can just as well lead down dead-end streets as up thrilling secret passageways.

For the bibliography, I ask the student to use a minimum of ten sources for a 2,000-word paper, these being divided as far as possible in this way: two periodicals, one reference book, two book-length studies, and five interviews.

The student needs some help in interviewing unless he or she has studied journalism in high school. I ask students to draw up lists of questions they plan to put to their informants, and we sometimes discuss these before they go out. Students need to be reminded that what is often a "superstition" to them is a "belief" to their informants. I counsel them to think through very carefully beforehand the terms they will use in asking their questions. Otherwise, the informant may feel ridiculed or threatened and simply refuse to give any information.

The recorded interview is a good place to teach some skill in handling direct and indirect quotes. If I get to see the rough draft, I suggest revision for better balance when it appears there are whole pages of verbatim reportage, or conversely, a terse, understated summary. Students frequently have trouble organizing the results of their interviews. They see the interviews as narratives and should be discouraged from recording them in their papers as a string of anecdotes. I ask them to categorize the viewpoints gained from the interviews according to the material they are working with and not according to the chronology of the interviews or the personalities of the informants.

Some students lack imagination in dealing with details surrounding the interviews. They need to be encouraged to report some details about the informants, such as age, appearance, manner, and surroundings, if these things have bearing on the information being gathered. Here is an example from a student paper of skillful handling of details: "According to Mrs. Antonia Negrete, who is a mother of ten, living in a rural area, home remedies and herbs that are found in her backyard are very helpful to her because with so many children, taking them to the doctor frequently will make her husband be working only for medical bills."

Unfortunately, the idea of interviewing people is taken by some students to mean a substitute for hours in the library. This notion must be quickly countered in an early class discussion by the instructor's emphasizing the folklore paper as a combination of field research and scholarly library work. Then the heat is on to prove that the student can, indeed, find something in the library about the subject. At this point, I would like to give some idea of the range of library materials that may be drawn on, at the same time suggesting three possibilities for developing the student's chosen topic.

In one kind of paper, the student attempts to catalog the variations of a belief or legend prevalent in the area. The object is to show that such a belief does still exist, that it has many variants, and that it is propagated and altered even today. Here the student's research job is one of verification and classification. A variation on this approach is the discussion of a place with folkloric interest. One student did a paper of this type last year, gathering the various legends about an old cross on a hilltop at Santa Cruz in Starr County, Texas. One valuable source for this kind of research is area newspapers. Students are often surprised to find in our college library the *McAllen Monitor* and the *Brownsville Herald* on microfilm. Small city libraries throughout the Rio Grande Valley contain rather good vertical files on local subjects, a definite argument for teaching the local folklore research paper at a commuter college. For any given region, there are usually general reference books useful for this approach—in our case such ones as *Folk Life and Folklore of the Mexican Border* by Adeline Dinger[1] and *The Lower Rio Grande Valley of Texas* by the Stambaughs.[2] If the research paper is begun early enough in the semester, interlibrary loans prove fruitful.

A second approach might be a comparison of a practice or belief current in Mexican-American culture along the border to that same practice as it is or was interpreted in the interior of Mexico, in the other Central American countries, or in South America. I received an excellent paper on myths about the menses from a premedical student who compared the stories she uncovered from native mountain girls near her home in Nicaragua with those she found here along the border. In this approach, students often exercise their bilingual skills by reading from sources in Spanish. Persons doing comparative research might also use such works as *A Treasury of Mexican Folkways* by Frances Toor,[3] and *The Types of the Folktale in Cuba, Puerto Rico, the Dominican Republic, and Spanish South America.*[4]

A third tack toward the folklore subject could be to take some local folklore topic and show how it corresponds to similar practices in other areas throughout the world. Mature students who want to do this kind of paper should be directed to work with the definitive Stith Thompson *Motif-Index of Folk-Literature,*[5] a work which attempts to classify the elements in folktales and legends according to kind and to give examples of variations from throughout the world. Some students have had good luck using Sir James George Frazier's *The Golden Bough*[6] for comparative analyses.

Sometimes a student will combine all three approaches in one paper. The success of this paper depends on the magnitude of the chosen topic, the availability of information, and the organizational skills of the student.

Some general observations, now, about teaching the folklore paper: I feel it is unwise to make the writing of a folklore paper mandatory for an entire class. In our particular case, the library would be strained to serve thirty or sixty students, all doing research on local folklore. Also, some students will naturally have greater advantages over others in securing information—those who have relatives in

Mexico, those who speak Spanish, and those who have available transportation to sources. And, regretfully, it is better not to make the folklore subject mandatory because a few students interpret such an assignment as an attempt to make them pay homage to a culture against which they are prejudiced. These students can be either Anglo-Americans with inbred suspicions, or they may be Mexican-Americans who, for a variety of reasons, wish to suppress their heritage. At any rate, I find it best not to make any assumptions about who will want to write a paper on Mexican-American folklore.

This brings up the subject of objectivity in handling the material. Frequently students are troubled about their own positions on the beliefs, superstitions, and practices of their families; this confusion is often reflected in their papers. Home at night to the established and workable values of a household rich in folklore, back the next morning to academia with its scientific approach to phenomena—it is no wonder that they write papers which begin in an objective way: "There are many legends here in the Rio Grande Valley of Texas about miracles worked by the Virgin of Guadalupe," and end subjectively: "The Virgin has helped me every time I have prayed to her."

In cases like this, I never argue with the student about the belief in question nor do I lower the grade if the opinion is not mine. What I do is ask the writer to delete his or her own cause-and-effect theory from the paper, allowing the work to be a record of information gained and not an argument for the validity of the belief or practice.

I think it's especially important in the folklore paper to keep the viewpoint problem in proper perspective. Occasional slips in logic shouldn't be considered so serious as they might be in other subjects, simply because much folklore is not logical. Students—emotionally, culturally, familially involved in it as they are—are going to have problems with the objective viewpoint. I am not condoning papers based on personal feeling and emotion; I am condoning the instructor's not being horror-struck when these elements find their way into a first draft.

One rather peculiar disadvantage of the folklore paper is often found in the student's inability to do any creative thinking on researching a subject, for the reason that he or she is too familiar with it. The student has lived so much a part of this folklore that there is a failure to recognize it for its investigative possibilities. Not all students weather this problem so well as Rosalinda Garcia did.

Rosalinda came to my office several days after we had begun work on the research paper, complaining that she had been unable to think of anything to write on. It was a dry day for me, too, so I relied on an old pedagogical stall: I asked what her hobbies were.

"Cooking and sewing," she replied. Although fascinating papers of folklore might be written on either, now there were two of us too close to the possible subject.

I tried again. "Where do you live, Rosalinda?"

"In a little town named Los Ebanos on the river," she said. "It's really dead."

Now we were getting somewhere. I asked her to tell me about the hand-drawn ferry at Los Ebanos. She admitted she had never thought anything about it. It was part of her life, as common as a brother or a tortilla. I asked if she knew of anyone in Los Ebanos who could tell her some stories about the crossing. She thought that maybe her mother knew someone. She went away, not excited, but at least committed to a paper on legends about the Los Ebanos crossing.

Several weeks passed. Papers were turned in, and I was delighted to see that possibly household chores had taken a back seat to the Los Ebanos crossing. Here was a student discussing confidently the legends of Los Ebanos springing from events like Zachary Taylor's invasion of Mexico from there in 1846 or the recovery of five hundred head of cattle stolen from Richard King in 1874.

I'm very glad I happened to ask Rosalinda that day where she lived. As a result of that paper, I think she is a little prouder of being Rosalinda Garcia of Los Ebanos, Texas. I saw Rosalinda the other day—appropriately enough at the card catalog in the library. She told me she was a senior. She had obviously been expanding new horizons.

Incidentally, a glance at Rosalinda's bibliography reveals that a paper done on a local subject does not preclude a good workout in the library. Her list includes a pamphlet from the centennial celebration of the organization of Midalgo County, *Tip-O-Texas* magazine, Carrol Norquest's book on Rio Grande wetbacks, the Stambaughs' history of the Lower Rio Grande, the Texas Forest Service's *Famous Trees of Texas,* several columns by Frank X. Tolbert in the *Dallas News,* and Walter Prescott Webb's history of the Texas Rangers.

Closely related to the problem of being too deep in the cultural forest to recognize the fruitful trees is the one of lack of imagination. I have already touched on this in connection with the interview but I should like to say just a little more about it as it concerns the whole subject of folklore. Folklore research requires a certain amount of lust after the facts, a derring-do, some vision of what might be out there awaiting record and interpretation. The firsthandedness of it all scares the prosaic-minded student. Some students, like Reynaldo, never quite get the hang of it.

Reynaldo needed a topic, so I suggested he write a paper on the *ojo de venado,* or deer's eye. Two weeks later he showed up saying, "I've got it." Thinking he meant he had his paper written, I complimented him for having it in early. "No," he said. "I don't have the paper written; I mean I've got an *ojo de venado,"* and with that, he fished it from his pocket and laid it in my hand.

"There's nothing to tell about it," he said forlornly. "It's just a good luck charm." No amount of prodding on my part could make Reynaldo see the *ojo de venado* as anything but an amulet.

I suggested another subject or two but he was a blank on these as well. Maybe Reynaldo could not have settled on any subject in the wide world for a research paper, but I'm inclined to think that my suggestion that the *ojo de venado* could be *written* about threw him into a state of wonderment over the sanity of English teachers.

There are two possible aids I know of for eager but unimaginative folklorists. One is a thorough class discussion of the range of folklore subjects—from homeopathic magic of the *bruja* to the use of the folk remedy aloe vera for treating burn patients at sophisticated medical installations around the country. The other is an examination, preferably by use of the opaque projector, of an A paper based on a folklore subject.

What are the humanistic implications of the research paper written on a folklore theme? It has been my observation that folklore papers are easier on the student than papers dealing with current issues of Mexican-American life, papers for instance, on the United Farm Workers, bilingual education, or the problems of the migrant worker. I think this is because it is difficult for the freshman—any freshman—to write objectively in areas where he or she has a high personal stake. Folklore as a theme subject retains all the ethnic interest and cultural pride that social issues carry but without the baggage of unhappy experiences or difficult emotions to work through.

I think of the folklore paper as an instrument of affirmation. It has been a particularly good thing for students who are straddling two worlds, unable to decide on which foot to put their weight. It gives them a respectable, meaningful, moderate way to say they are proud of themselves and their past. It gives them a chance to make a definite contribution to the preservation of the fabric of a rich culture. It is, in the end, a way to integrate living and learning.

NOTES

1. *Folk Life and Folklore of the Mexican Border* (Edinburg, Tex.: Hidalgo County Historical Museum, 1972).
2. Lee Stambaugh and Lillian J. Stambaugh, *The Lower Rio Grande Valley of Texas* (Austin, Tex.: Jenkins, San Felipe Press, 1974).
3. *A Treasury of Mexican Folkways* (New York: Crown, 1947).
4. Terrence Leslie Hansen, *The Types of the Folktale in Cuba, Puerto Rico, the Dominican Republic, and Spanish South America* (Berkeley: University of California Press, 1957).
5. *Motif-Index of Folk-Literature* (Bloomington: Indiana University Press, 1955–1958).
6. *The Golden Bough,* 3rd ed. (New York: Macmillan, 1951).

TEACHING MINORITY AND DISADVANTAGED UNIVERSITY FRESHMEN TO WRITE A RESEARCH PAPER: TOWARD A MULTICULTURAL MODEL

Sara Zimmerman Steinman

Just as Mina Shaughnessy found, when she was writing *Errors and Expectations,* that "little has as yet been written about the problems and progress of basic writing students,"[1] so have I found few studies written about the problems and progress of ethnic minority students or of culturally, economically, and educationally disadvantaged students (hereafter referred to as M/D students). More specifically, the literature reveals few articles that are directly about teaching the research paper to M/D students; other articles are relevant by analogy: they discuss research problems or student attitudes like those of M/D students.

For example, Soll's paper, "Writing an Original Research Paper Involves an Ability to Perform,"[2] suggests a Moffett-inspired[3] program for teaching the research paper to students in open-admissions schools. She sends students into the "real world" to observe and interview, with the eventual goal of demonstrating to them that their experience and knowledge can be treated in an academic style.

Seale's approach in "Mexican-American Folklore: An Approach to the Research Paper"[4] is similar to Soll's; she also suggests interviews and use of firsthand knowledge and echoes Soll's concern that the students realize the value of their previous experience and knowledge. "It is, in the end," Seale writes, "a way to integrate living and learning." In her course, Mexican-American students are asked to write papers on Mexican-American folklore, and are told that as college students they "can become a liaison between the world of beliefs and practices of the folk and the world of scholarly categorizing and preservation of these things."[5] Seale's statement can be seen as simplistic: a university does more than categorize and preserve data; it analyzes before it categorizes, for example, and disseminates as well as preserves. Nevertheless, her identification of the students' role as liaison between beliefs/practices and scholarly categorizing/ preservation is extremely helpful. Seale assists the students in their role as liaison by teaching them how to categorize raw data (interviews, observations) by using the inductive method, though she does not use this logical term.

Although he is not concerned with research paper writing, Frank Bonham's lively narrative "The Temporary Expert: Field Research as Literary Life Support"[6] is even more convincing. In justifying the gathering of raw data, Bonham cites many personal experiences that have led to published books and articles. For example, as a college student interested in social problems, he spent a night in a flophouse on Los Angeles's skid row, and made surreptitious notes leading to a magazine article. "Not very deep research, nor wide, but stimulating," he says.[7]

I am not advocating that research paper writers sleep anywhere but in their own beds; Bonham's advice, after all, is directed to writers of fiction. I am advocating that the same recording of experience that Bonham uses to write stories can be used to write research papers. He includes an explicit explanation of why and how note cards are kept.[8]

Foster's narrative report, "Do-It-Yourself Videotape for Library Orientation Based on a Term Paper Project,"[9] provides a detailed how-to for anyone interested in developing the best possible library orientation for ethnic minority and culturally/economically disadvantaged students. Like Seale and Soll, she recognizes the gap between the M/D students' personal experiences and academic expectations.

White and Franklin found a way to involve previously turned-off M/D students in learning basic college skills: use of the lab approach.

> Lessons on writing the research paper extended throughout five (5) out of fifteen (15) class sessions. During these sessions students are taught how to set up a bibliography and footnotes, how to select and research a proposed topic and how to begin the first draft of their papers.[10]

Like Soll and Seale, White and Franklin regard personal experience and observation as the "stuff" of research papers.

There would seem, then, to be a consensus: teachers of M/D students writing research papers need not only to teach basic skills, such as how to set up a bibliography; above all, we must convince students of the academic value of their previous experiences and knowledge by having them integrate that experience and knowledge into their papers.

However, since it is the purpose of this paper to suggest a definitive model of a research paper course that would address M/D students' needs, I would like more systematically to examine those needs before drawing any conclusions. For one thing, I am not satisfied that students can integrate personal experience unless they understand inductive logic and the need to process experience to find a thesis. While attempting to make the research project easier for M/D students by advising them to use their own experience, we may actually be making the project more difficult, unless we explain how to go about it.

For example, students in composition courses practice writing narratives and then the theme-at-the-top 500-word essay. At UW-Milwaukee and many other universities, English 101 students are taught to formulate a deductive thesis and support it. Rarely are they taught to do the inductive opposite: "List your personal experience and make judgments about your life," or "Interview fifty people and tabulate results." Yet, when we ask them in English 102 to base all or part of their research papers on personal experience, we ask them to observe, synthesize, and categorize before they write anything.

It seems ironic that in a study unrelated to M/D teaching, Colleen Marshall[11] suggests a method for teaching the research paper that is apparently *easier* than those suggested for M/D students: the student writes an opinion paper, the instructor treats it as a rough draft and suggests refinements, and then the student finds support for those opinions. There is clearly less need to observe, synthesize, and categorize in this kind of documented paper.

But what Marshall's approach lacks for the M/D student is that bridge between personal experience and academic success. A model is needed that not only encourages students to use personal experience, but also teaches the students the need—and how—to assimilate that experience.

In teaching research paper writing to Educational Opportunity classes at UW-Milwaukee, I find it helpful to analyze the tasks according to jargon describing the learning process borrowed from educational psychologists: input, processing, and output.[12] In order for students to evaluate their needs at any given point, I provide this chart:

Input	Processing	Output
improving basic skills	choosing a topic	producing final
participating in library	formulating a thesis	draft
orientation	making definitive outline	proofreading
reading Bazerman[13]	synthesizing	
learning formats	categorizing	
taking preliminary notes	assimilating	
making preliminary out-	writing preliminary drafts,	
line	including integration of	
learning documenting	personal experience	
and footnoting	paraphrasing	
	summarizing	

I discuss with them the objectivity of items under "Input." My students frequently point out that there is nothing on that list that could not be self-taught; plenty of how-to-write-the-research-paper texts are sold in university bookstores. However, because "synthesizing" and "assimilating" are abstract terms, the "Process" column is more difficult to understand; indeed, not many how-to books explain how to synthesize and assimilate. We as teachers and scholars know that we assimilate information, synthesize it, sometimes by writing it down in preliminary form and often by *verbalizing*. We talk. We talk to our spouses, our colleagues, our pets, our mentors, and to ourselves. To assist my students in assimilation and synthesis of material and with the other elements of process, I provide plenty of class opportunity to work in groups of two or three. At this processing stage it is not plagiarism if a student helps another to find a way for information on a note card to become assimilated into a paper. In fact, it is a triumph in that it makes both students feel good. While they have not needed so much assistance in writing personal-experience narratives in previous courses, they do need assistance when inserting parts of that experience into logically organized research papers.[14]

At this point a refinement and addition to the above consensus is in order:

1. It goes without saying that teachers of M/D students need to teach, or provide materials for self-teaching and testing of, the items listed under "Input."

2. Teachers of M/D students should dedicate much of their class time to peer-support assimilating and synthesizing activities; see "Processing."

3. Teachers of M/D students should encourage use of personal knowledge, because that use bridges the gap between nonacademic personal ethos and academia.

Seale's approach to no. 3 seems near perfect (student as liaison between personal belief and practice, and scholarly categorizer). At UW-Milwaukee we must offer more variety of topic than does Seale, whose student population is primarily Mexican-American. In my Department of Education Opportunity English 102 sections, I therefore suggest multiethnic/multicultural topics, our population representing not only Mexican-Americans, but also blacks and Native Americans. As an urban university, we serve in addition students of Greek, Italian, and East European heritage who are the first in their families to attend university and who frequently enter the university through Educational Opportunity's doors.

In attempts to foster an acceptance of cultural plurality, and to provide topic ideas, I invite guest speakers from the immediate campus to present various cultural points of view. A recent semesters' list included Keewaydinoquay, Anthropology Professor and Native American; Michael Mikós, Slavics Professor and Polish-American; Suleyman Kurter, Department of Educational Opportunity Academic Advisor and Turkish-American; and Ventura Castañeda, Department of Educational Opportunity Administrator and Mexican-American.

In these presentations of specific topics drawing on personal experience, students hear models of *assimilated* personal experience or concerns; that is, the speakers use their experience or concerns as anecdotal or nonnarrative support for a thesis. With the guest's permission, the lecture is videotaped and placed on reserve in the library for repeated viewings.

For example, Castañeda discusses "The Education of Juan Rodriquez," a fictitious but nonetheless very real child of migrant workers who, for many reasons and no fault of his own, receives an inferior education as he is uprooted from his Texas school to move to Wisconsin early every spring and is returned to Texas at least a month after school starts every fall. Neither a child of migrant laborers nor a migrant laborer himself, Castañeda nevertheless speaks with convincing emotion: he once directed a program for migrant children in Wisconsin and felt their frustrations. He decries the lack of coordinated education for the children as well as the lack of cooperation among local, state, and federal agencies. Castañeda has inspired a number of students to write about migrant problems. For the students not interested in this topic for their research papers, the talk provides a model of personal experience assimilated and presented as evidence supporting a clear, convincing thesis.

Also speaking with conviction, Professor Michael Mikós traces the historical development of the Solidarity movement. Mikós, who was born in Warsaw, mentions prominent Polish figures who had close ties to America and who are of special interest to students interested in Polish-American relations. One such figure was Thaddeus Kosciusko, Polish patriot and soldier who came to American in 1776, fought with the revolutionary army, and became an aide to General Washington. He returned to Poland where he led a revolutionary movement to regain Polish independence. His will granted his sizable estate in America to black Americans. As Mikós notes, "This was at the end of the eighteenth century when the notion of freedom of black people was not even discussed." Although Kosciusko is well known in Milwaukee—there is a large park bearing his name—students show surprise at this cross-cultural link between the Polish patriot and black landownership. Several students of a recent semester wrote papers that clearly have been inspired by Professor Mikós's talk. For example, one student of Polish ethnic origin who plans a career in law researched the fate of those lands Kosciusko willed to blacks.

No topics are assigned to students. Through my encouraging them to use their own experience, through hearing speakers, and through discussing topics from past semesters, students rarely delay in deciding what they want to write about. One class period is devoted to a roundtable discussion of their topic ideas. They are strongly encouraged to choose multicultural/multiethnic topics, but I do not insist that they write about topics relevant to their own ethnic origins if they are not inclined to do so. Intolerance of their interest in another ethnic group or culture would be in itself destructive of the multicultural plurality and acceptance I nurture in this model.

Several other items in the processing column that I will cover here include formulating a working thesis, assimilating personal experience, making an outline, and writing the preliminary draft. Readers will note some similarities to and overlap with research paper approaches mentioned above. What I offer here is the UW-Milwaukee Department of Educational Opportunity model which encompasses those approaches and addresses M/D students' needs more directly.

Formulating a Working Thesis and Assimilating Personal Experience

A question works best as a working thesis because it assists students in synthesizing such materials as their own experience, interviews, historical narratives, and secondary sources. For example, Theresa Jones's[15] working thesis was "What is the state of black elderly health care in Milwaukee?" With that question in mind, Jones began to prepare the paper by analyzing relevant experiences, interviewing health care professionals, and summarizing published sources. Similarly, Nuzhet Quareshi's working thesis question was "What is the expected role of Muslim women in the United States?" Quareshi, who came from Pakistan as a child, also combined personal experience, interviews, and secondary sources in a research paper project that originated with this kind of inductive questioning. After a few weeks of research, Jones and Quareshi formulated their deductive thesis statements:

> Jones: Black elderly in Milwaukee receive inadequate health care for several reasons: inadequate information, too little money, and inaccessibility.

> Quareshi: Muslim women in the U.S. are expected somehow to blend (and find a compromise between) ancient Islamic doctrine and modern western customs.

Support during this thesis-forming stage comes from two sources: the instructor and the classroom peers. Students suggest their working thesis statements while in one-to-one conference with me; then, soon after, concurrent with a preliminary library search, they discuss them with the class in a roundtable discussion. Sometimes at this stage, students warn one another about possible flaws in the deductive statements that they seem about to make. They sometimes ask, for example, "Are you sure you're not stacking the evidence?" More often, students will offer one another support: "I'm really interested in that"; "I know someone you can talk to"; "I saw a citation in the *Social Sciences Index* of 1980 that will help you."

Jones's and Quareshi's topics were typical of those who integrated personal experience in their papers. Recently I asked two other students, Ida Wisniewski and Suzanne Crouch, who had previously taken DEO English 102, if they remembered why they had chosen their topics, "Contributions Made by the Oneida Nation to the Iroquois League," and "History of Italian Migration to Milwaukee." Each responded in a way that indicates her own, perhaps subconscious, attempts to bridge the gap between nonacademic personal ethos and academia:

> Crouch: I wanted to write something about my Italian immigrant uncle, Mario Magna, and his life in the old Third Ward (Milwaukee's old Italian neighborhood) and to show him as part of a whole movement.

> Wisniewski: I am three-quarters Oneida Indian in the first place. I came to the university to learn more about Native Americans, about my ethnic heritage. But I couldn't find anything about Oneidas! All of the Native Americans were treated as one group. I was so disappointed and decided that if I was going to learn anything, I'd have to research it myself!

And so she did. The result is a paper that notably contributes to the literature about the Oneida tribe. In an ambiance that encourages cultural plurality and ethnic acceptance, such contributions as Wisniewski's are natural reflections of students' enthusiasm, of peer and instructor support—especially in the process phase—and of hard work.

Making an Outline and Writing the Preliminary Draft

Because students' previous writing assignments usually have been 500-word and not 2,500- and 3,000-word essays, I require that they divide the support for the thesis into four parts, each of which they then develop in 500 or 600 words. The deadline for part 1 is in week 7, or two weeks after students and peers develop the working theses and preliminary outlines. Successive parts are due in weeks 9, 11, and 13.

Support during this outlining and preliminary draft-writing stage comes from small groups of peers and from the class as a whole. Groups of two or three discuss the outlines: Is there any overlap? Is each section relevant to the topic and to the other sections? Is the order logical? Then, before the first section is due, students formulate a "checklist for evaluation of research papers." I guide and assist them by encouraging brainstorming, listing their impulsive remarks on the board, suggesting additions and corrections. A recent semester's checklist is three typed pages long, includes three main sections— "overall coherence," "correct mechanics" and "correct documentation"—and provides boxes to check if the evaluation is of a preliminary section or of the final paper. There are "yes" and "no" boxes beside each question and an inch of space between each question for comments.

The students then use these checklists to evaluate not only one another's preliminary drafts, but the final paper as well. They do not assign grades; my assistant and I read each paper and evaluation checklist before we do so. We have noticed that the continuous repetition of the checklist exercise acts as a kind of drill, for even as students are evaluating other students' papers, they are reviewing individual criteria of general areas they consider important: coherence, documentation, and mechanics.

Conclusion

Our Department of Educational Opportunity model at UW-Milwaukee provides more assistance to the M/D student than some of the models discussed above provide. Our model does this in part by providing opportunities for students to produce 500-word assignments which become part of a longer paper, hear lectures representing a multitude of cultures and approaches, and work closely with peers in the assimilation and evaluation phases.

How can we further assist M/D students writing research papers? Certainly there is a need to develop additional methods for teaching the "Process" phase. There is also a need for studies showing correlations, I would hope positive correlations, between special course approaches and achievement.

NOTES

1. Mina P. Shaughnessy, *Errors and Expectations: A Guide for the Teacher of Basic Writing* (New York: Oxford University Press, 1977), 298.
2. Lila Soll, *Writing an Original Research Paper Involves an Ability to Perform* (ERIC ED 140331), 2.
3. Soll cites James Moffett's *A Student Centered Language Arts Program* (Boston: Houghton Mifflin, 1968).
4. Jan Seale, *Mexican-American Folklore: An Approach to the Research Paper* (ERIC ED 135012).
5. Seale, 2.
6. Frank Bonham, "The Temporary Expert: Field Research as Literary Life Support," *Language Arts* 58 (1981), 799–804.
7. Bonham, 800.
8. Bonham, 802.
9. Barbara Foster, "Do-It-Yourself Videotape for Library Orientation Based on a Term Paper Project," *Wilson Library Bulletin* 48 (1974), 476–481.
10. Judith C. White and Harry I. Franklin, *Freshman Seminar at Malcolm-King: Harlem College Extension—A Tool for Providing Emotional Support* (ERIC ED 117287), 21.
11. Colleen Marshall, "A System for Teaching College Freshmen to Write a Research Paper," *College English* 40 (1978), 87–89.
12. See, for example, the discussion of these terms in a study by John H. Krouse and Helen J. Krouse, "Toward a Multimodal Theory of Academic Underachievement," *Educational Psychologist* 16 (1981), 157. I am indebted to my colleague Louise Lapine for her suggestion that I explore the Krouses' theories.
13. Charles Bazerman, *The Informed Writer* (Boston: Houghton Mifflin, 1981). As a Department of Educational Opportunity English 102 lecturer, I am responsible for meeting both the English department's requirements and my students' special needs. I have, therefore, fit the multicultural approach and materials around the English department's sixteen-week syllabus, which is based largely on Bazerman's text and these assignments: paraphrase, summary, analysis, book review, comparison of sources, and research paper.
14. For guidance in developing warm-up exercises for teaching M/D students how to process materials, we should, perhaps, look first to Susan Miller's text, *Writing: Process and Product* (Cambridge, Mass.: Winthrop Publishers, 1976). I am thinking in particular of the section, "Getting Things Down: What to Do with Your Hands," 71–81.
15. This student asked not to be identified by her real name.

THE RESEARCH PAPER AND THE FUTURE: A SOLUTION

Gweneth Schwab

One of the classic problems in basic composition is the thesis statement. Those students who understand the nature of a thesis statement, whether instinctively or intellectually, usually not only survive their freshman experience but actually "succeed" by one standard or another. But unfortunately, most students follow the examples and patterns provided by faithful composition instructors without truly understanding the principles involved. They often get by with fuzzy theses until a more advanced course with an assigned research paper causes them renewed anguish over a basic concept they usually feel they should have already mastered. (The instructors' feelings need not be commented upon.)

The lack of perception of a good thesis results in a report which offers at worst what James Lester calls "a recital of investigations without the commentary that is the ultimate purpose of all research writing"[1] and at best a collection of authoritative reference material without any of the formed judgments and opinions which it was meant to support. My experience in teaching the research paper led me near despair because no matter how I instructed my students as to the purpose of evaluation and critical judgment, I still continued to receive reports: collections of paragraphs, often coherent, often unified, always well documented, but rarely the conclusive results of judgments born of sound research.

The problem, then, is how to encourage students to evaluate, speculate perhaps, form a conclusion, and demonstrate that conclusion in a paper.

It was my students' fascination with the technology of this decade (computers, kidney machines, Skylabs) plus their great and growing interest in science fiction which caused me to limit their choice of research paper subjects to "the future," with the stipulation that the thesis statement be in the future tense and that one-third to one-half of the paper deal with development of that thesis in the future. In other words, background material, although necessary, is not allowed to take over the paper.

Most students respond favorably, as they can choose *anything* that fits the subject limitation. Over half the students proceed in the direction of their disciplines. This prevents the assignment from seeming as artificial as it can under other circumstances; the students investigate either areas they really care about or areas which another instructor (not the beleaguered writing instructor) tells them they should care about. A sociology major may write a paper about the future of the family; a physics major may explore his fascination with solar energy in a paper forecasting its use in the future; or a psychology major may maintain that computer-assisted education will not, as some believe, seriously hamper the important *human* development of the child.

An unexpected bonus occurs with subjects which look to the future. The card catalog, to which most college freshmen have already been introduced, becomes less useful than more current index sources. Not only do students immerse themselves in *Readers' Guide, Social Sciences and Humanities Index,* and *Biological and Agricultural Index,* but many also plunge into *Congressional Informational Services* and *American Statistical Index.* With the future before them, more students also turn to primary as well as secondary sources. They interview, survey, and count.

Once the students begin their investigations, apprehension grows. Most feel inadequate to the job of prophet and fear that they will be wrong. At this stage they need to be reassured that after adequate research they *will* be able to speak authoritatively. I reinforce this by using terms such as "expert" or "mini-expert" when referring to the student beginning to form conclusions.

The thesis statements focus the generalizations about the future and take on cutting edges. One student examines the peril of passenger trains to conclude that "recent developments in the rail passenger industry have given it a foundation upon which it can build to become an integral part of the transportation complex in the future United States."[2] Another, after examining the lower classes' educational failures, asserts: "In order to provide education for these trapped, underprivileged people, in addition to providing the means, the type of education, its techniques, and public opinion about it will have to change."[3] Still another analyzed higher education, contending that

> the future will bring an increased relevancy to the curricula and environment of colleges and universities which has not been evidenced in traditional instruction and which is essential if these institutions are to adequately serve our expanding society.[4]

The following thesis perhaps best reveals the lack of constraint possible by the end of the research. "The world will find unity, and will find it in the foreseeable future."[5] These statements reflect the absence of report characteristics and the presence of a well-formed, arguable conclusion.

Not only are the theses improved, but with the disappearance of artificiality from the research paper, many students feel free to experiment stylistically as they have never done before. Despite the restrictive nature of such rules as the tense of the thesis statement and the relative space given to background material, many students utilize some clever techniques and present their conclusions creatively.

Students begin to make use of complicated metaphors and complex analogies. One student writing about pentecostalism in the Anglican church introduces the paper with the images conjured up by the word "firestorm" and describes "another type of firestorm [which] has been gaining force in the last twenty years or so, and while it is not as outwardly terrifying as the explosion of a bomb, its effect has been nonetheless spectacular to those touched by its influence."[6] Since the first Pentecost was marked by tongues of fire (also the title of the paper) the fire image is appropriate. To mark the transition from the introductory section backward in time to a historical discussion, the student's "fired up" imagination created this sentence: "The Anglicans as a whole have never been a fiery lot (with the possible exception of Henry VIII, who was more inclined towards temper tantrums rather than religious fervor)."[7]

A tinderbox, a few firebugs, and "a vapor of smoke" appear elsewhere in the paper.

Students illustrate unusual concepts more readily and are able to do this naturally and sometimes humorously. In an aside, one paper about population prediction defines a *parent* as "one who uses the rhythm method."[8] And one paper dealing with the future of advertising explains the technique of association:

> Of course, National Distillers is not the only one trying this approach; many other distillers and importers are using drinks like this one [the Frazier] and associating them with their brand names to gain a position in the liquor market, which can only be described as "fluid."[9]

Students take examples from "Star Trek" episodes, the bionics industry, comic books, science fiction, reading, the news, and recent research accomplishments on campus. Communicating becomes a result of their whole environment, not just the card catalog. The language in many papers becomes picturesque:

> Nevertheless, [the idea of a united world] is an idea that dies hard. We are talking of a concept nearly as old as man himself: an idea that flourished a beard when Alexander the Great was still in diapers. But it did not die with Alexander, nor did it die with any of the emperors after him; with Charlemagne, Napoleon, or even Hitler. Nor is it dead even today, though it has gone into hiding for lack of fashionability, and one has to turn over a few bushels and brush away some nationalistic cobwebs in order to find it.[10]

Few writing instructors would complain of the texture of this paper.

One fascinating paper is written in the past tense—as if the year were 2000. It analyzes by way of "historical survey" and is titled, "Looking Back: The Green Revolution." It begins profoundly: "The trouble with the world is people. And the joy, too." It recaptures the consternation of the seventies over the population explosion before the beginning of the great discoveries in agriculture which marked the Green Revolution from 1970–2000. The paper presents the major contributing groups and the direction of population control and agricultural balance in well-organized and quite human terms, escaping clinical sterility partly through that first introductory statement. It concludes in summary fashion:

> Since the beginning in the late seventies the Green Revolution has made great steps towards solving the hunger problem. Americans have worked hand-in-hand, as breeders develop . . . as scientists contribute . . . and as farmers practice . . . This is

only a start toward the solution to feeding the more and more people the future is to bring. Agriculture will not be able to cease its never ending quest to feed the people of the world, for the trouble with the world is people. And the joy, too.[11]

These are, of course, only a few of many such fine papers which have come since my futuristic approach began. What had been a dreary and tedious writing task for the students, to be equaled and surpassed only by the dreariness and tedium which usually accompanied the grading, has turned into enthusiastic research and writing and happy anticipation and grading. The future is bright.

NOTES

1. James D. Lester, *Writing Research Papers: A Complete Guide* (Glenview, Ill.: Scott Foresman, 1971), 1–2.
2. Thomas F. Nichols, "Passenger Trains Today?" Research paper submitted for English 60: Exposition, November 1972, ii.
3. Richard McLean, "The Boost of Education for the Poor," Research paper submitted for English 60: Exposition, November 1972, ii.
4. John E. Adams, "Academic Relevancy in the Future," Research paper submitted for English 60: Exposition, November 1972, ii.
5. Louis Luth, "On a United World," Research paper submitted for English 60: Exposition, October 1972, ii.
6. Melissa R. Watson, "Tongues of Fire: The Holy Spirit in the Anglican Church," Research paper submitted for English 60: Exposition, November 1972, ii.
7. Watson, 2.
8. Alexis Swoboda, "Contraception," Research paper submitted for English 60: Exposition, Spring 1972, 5.
9. Michael Ragan, "The Future of Effective Advertising," Research paper submitted for English 60: Exposition, November 1972, 7–8.
10. Luth, 1.
11. Robert Barnes, "Looking Back: The Green Revolution," Research paper submitted for English 60: Exposition, November 1972, 12.

A WORK-SHEET APPROACH TO THE RESEARCH PAPER

Ellen Strenski

The complex set of skills required to write a research paper must be taught separately and in some sequence. Textbook information, even the excellent new *MLA Style Sheet*, for instance, does not provide this structured guidance. For most freshman college students, many of whom have never written one in high school, a research paper is a mystery.

So they need to be taught, which means that we instructors need to isolate and explain the necessary skills and then, most importantly, give students practice in mastering each, *one at a time*, before proceeding. Otherwise the research paper handed in will be a hit-and-miss disappointment reinforcing bad habits, and we will be forced unfairly to penalize students for those mistakes which, after all, are only a necessary part of learning. Merely presenting passive students with examples of correct footnotes, etc., may clarify principles, but does little to insure that students will be able to put them into practice correctly on their own.

Therefore, instructors must devise preparatory exercises and assignments. The suggested work sheets that follow have been developed over the last five years at Mohegan Community College. They have worked well as part of a unit, spread over about ten weeks and interspersed with other assignments, within a semester of freshman composition. They have the added benefits of lowering student fear of the research paper assignment and of all that goes with that reduced anxiety: eliminating procrastination and plagiarism and, if completed, almost guaranteeing a passable research paper.

Students are told that these work sheets, although not graded, are compulsory. The instructor will correct mistakes on the work sheets and return them quickly; students must keep the returned work sheets and hand them back in to the instructor with their completed research paper on the due date. With the completed research paper, in a manila folder given to them for that purpose, they will also be handing in their note cards, bibliography cards, a book review of one of their book sources according to required specifications, and a signed, dated copy of the following checklist, which is given to them at the end of the unit along with the manila folder.

English 111   name_____
Research Paper
Checklist to accompany research paper

___ The paper is at least 1,000 words in length.
___ It includes information from at least five sources.
___ The introductory paragraph identifies the thesis statement and gives a bird's-eye view of what is to come.
___ Information from the five sources has been integrated so that the organization of the paper reflects my understanding of the subject.
___ I have put most of the information into my own words.
___ Quotation marks have been used around any words, phrases, or sentences that are copied exactly from a source.
___ All quotations are footnoted.
___ Paraphrases of facts and opinions from sources are footnoted.
___ Footnotes and bibliography follow, *MLA Style Sheet* form
___ All corrected work sheets are included
___ Bibliography cards are included
___ Note cards are included
___ Book review is included

This paper is *completely* or *essentially* (circle one) my own work

I wish to acknowledge help from the following people
(Explain who helped you do what, such as proofread, type, find sources)

Signed _____
Date _____

The instructor begins by explaining what a research paper is and what this unit involves. At this point the instructor has a somewhat hidden agenda with two main objectives: 1) to clarify many common misconceptions and 2) to allow students to express their own uneasiness by getting them to talk about research papers they did previously, problems they encountered, research papers they may be working on presently, and problems they anticipate. Just voicing these concerns diffuses much of the hostility students invariably bring to this assignment, with the result that they feel encouraged and willing to cooperate. The main misconceptions that need to be addressed are variations on 1) writing a research paper is impossible or requires magical skills, or 2) a research paper is a totally different kind of assignment, which is not true for any student who has already written a book report and an essay.

The first work sheet, "Using Encyclopedias," is handed to students as homework after a demonstration of making a bibliography card for an encyclopedia and an explanation of the importance of this step to refresh one's memory, to inform, to suggest interesting problems on which a thesis might be based, to recommend additional readings, or identify main sources of information in the field. Although students need to consult only one up-to-date encyclopedia in order to complete this first work sheet, they are urged to use at least two in order to compare approaches. They are also encouraged, for practice, to try to find and use one of the specialized encyclopedias for this work sheet. At this point, in order to complete the work sheet, students must pick a provisional topic. Each work sheet fits on one ditto stencil, with material on it spaced so there is room for students to answer or complete or respond as required.

English 111   name_____

Research Paper Work Sheet #1   topic _____

Using Encyclopedias

Part One: Find an article on your subject in any encyclopedia in the library.

1. Is there an author of this article?

2. If there is an author, who is it?

3. What is the exact title of this article? Fill in below:

4. What is the exact and complete title of the encyclopedia you are using?

---

5. When was this edition published? _____

Part Two: In the space below make a complete bibliography card for this article.

This first work sheet, now corrected, is returned to the student in the next class, and the instructor moves on to the next step: recording card catalog and index information on bibliography cards. This is demonstrated in class, with a trip to the library if necessary. At the end of this class, work sheet #2 is distributed for homework.

English 111   name _____
Research Paper Work Sheet #2   topic _____
Card Catalog and Index Informa-
tion to Bibliography Card

1. Using bibliography card format, list the appropriate information for one book in our library on Franklin D. Roosevelt.

2. Using *Readers' Guide to Periodical Literature,* copy EXACTLY one reference to an article on safety belts. Keep the abbreviations just as they are.

3. Now translate the above information into a bibliography card including author, title, magazine, volume, date, and page(s).

4. Using *Social Sciences* and/or *Humanities Index,* prepare a correct bibliography card for each of the following subjects:
   A. Voter Registration
   B. Television Commercials

In the next class, once the second corrected work sheet is returned, the instructor can hand out #3 and go on to something else in the course not explicitly related to research papers (such as writing summaries and reconstructing outlines, which fits very usefully here).

English 111   name _____
Research Paper Work Sheet #3   topic _____
Bibliography Cards

Using correct bibliography card format, list the appropriate information for FIVE possible sources for your research paper. Make sure you find both books and articles.

With work sheet #3 in hand, the instructor moves on to the next step, an absolutely essential preliminary for taking notes, which is reading (a chapter in a book or an article) for the main idea. Again, principles are explained and illustrated in class, and work sheet #4 is handed out for homework.

English 111   name _____
Research Paper Work Sheet #4   topic _____
Reading for the Main Ideas

1. Using correct bibliography card format, list the appropriate information for ONE of the ARTICLES (or one chapter in a book) you need for your research paper.

2. Complete this sentence (fill in THREE things):
   The thesis of " _____ " (name of article)
   by _____ (author)

   is that............
   ....
   ....

3. Complete this sentence: The *purpose* of this article is to _____

4. The major topics covered in this article are:

5. Supporting details in this article include:

Once the corrected work sheet #4 is handed back, the instructor can explain and illustrate note-taking, using the blackboard to show students how ideas in a passage can be recorded in different ways according to proper note card format. The critical problem for most students at this stage is they can paraphrase properly. At the end of this class, work sheet #5 is given out to be worked on at home or in the library.

English 111   name _____
Research Paper Work Sheet #5   topic _____
Taking Notes

Pick an important paragraph from one article, or from one chapter in a book, which you intend to use for your research paper.

1. Write a note card in the space below QUOTING your paragraph, or a good part of it, verbatim. Use ellipses if you omit any words. Conform to proper note card format: indicate the source, the page number(s), and an appropriate subject heading.

2. Write a note card in the space below PARAPHRASING the SAME paragraph that you quoted above in #1.

3. Write a note card on the back of this sheet combining a paraphrase of and a quotation from your paragraph.

The next step in writing a research paper is outlining, and that means grouping note cards. So, once the fifth work sheet is corrected and returned, outlining can be discussed and illustrated and work sheet #6 distributed.

English 111   name _____
Research Paper Work Sheet #6   topic _____
Outline
(Grouping Your Note Cards)

1. Your thesis statement (central idea):

2. List as many questions as you can addressed to your generalization (thesis statement) above. It will be your responsibility to answer them, later, for instance in the conclusion to your research paper.

3. Outline of major headings and minor supporting details for your paper (sequence of ideas and balanced relationship of ideas). Continue on back.

The seventh work sheet is given out at the next class.

English 111   name _____
Research Paper Work Sheet #7   topic _____
Documentation

Part One:

1. Make a footnote to your first reference to page 23 of the book *Red Wolves and Black Bears* by Edward Hoagland. It was published in 1976 by Random House in New York.

2. Make a footnote for a subsequent reference to pages 78 and 79 in Hoagland's book.

3. Make a footnote for a reference to an article " 'Adult Ed'—The Ultimate Goal" by Benjamin DeMott, published in the September 20 issue of *Saturday Review* in 1975.

4. Make a footnote for a reference to an article called "News as Purposive Behavior" by H. Moloch and M. Lester in the February 1974 issue of *American Sociological Review,* volume 39, covering pages 101 to 104.

5. Make a footnote for a reference to an article on "Wolf" in the *Encyclopedia Americana* in the 1976 edition. The article was written by Tracy I. Storer.

Part Two: List, as in a proper bibliography, complete references to the magazine articles and books referred to above.

Finally, work sheet #8 starts students on a draft of the paper itself and requires a title.

English 111   name _____
Research Paper Work Sheet #8   TITLE OF PAPER_____
Introductory Paragraph

Write your first paragraph below. This will include a statement of your thesis (central idea), and will indicate your procedure without naming yourself. The rest of the first paragraph will provide a context for that thesis statement, by explaining why the subject is important and worth examining in the paper, by asking focusing questions, introducing a key concept or definition, isolating reasons, explanations, etc. It will justify the whole undertaking and give the reader a bird's-eye view of what is to come (main ideas and heading from the outline.)

On the due date, the instructor brings into class a large cardboard box for all these bulging manila folders, and a blank sign-up schedule for individual conferences which will preempt classes for the following two weeks. At the conference, the instructor returns the folder with the graded research paper and goes over anything that did not seem quite correct or clear. The whole point is to make sure that the next time the student must write a research paper for another course, then quite independently, it will be successful.

Reading and grading all this work may seem like an impossible undertaking for an instructor, but it is not. Most of the annoying mechanical and proofreading mistakes, as well as more serious problems of logical organization, have already been cleared up at the work sheet stage. The most burdensome task is to read the student's note cards to see how appropriate they are to the announced topic or thesis and how well they have been integrated into the paper. However, the satisfaction of seeing a competent, tangible product at the end of this unit holds true for both student and instructor, and the instructor can be pleased with the good job of teaching, as well as all the student's effort, which it represents.

The concepts in this paper were used in the development of Ellen Strenski and Madge Manfred, *The Research Paper Workbook* (New York: Longman, 1981).

FRESHMAN HISTORIES: A BASIC RESEARCH ASSIGNMENT

William F. Woods

No sane freshman wants to write a research paper. The things are compiled during end-of-semester crunch, and furthermore, students tend to feel that their papers aren't real research. Lawyers, literary critics, newspaper reporters have a duty to their subjects, if not always a passion for them; but most freshmen, at least, have yet to develop that sense of purpose. Ultimately, they slip out from under the task, stringing together short ideas and long quotes, and then adding some footnotes for the "research" part of it. Clearly, this product and the high-pressure, low-yield situations that produce it are not what the teacher wants. Still, we don't want to abandon the research assignment. We want to improve it—find ways to get students digging, not just shoveling; writing, not merely typing. With this goal in mind, some of us at Wichita State University developed an assignment we called "Researching the Day You Were Born." The results were favorable, in that the students said the papers weren't too long or hard to write, and they obviously enjoyed showing off the specimens they dug up from those quaint old times, the 1950s. From our point of view, the assignment was worthwhile because it gave the students a short, circumscribed, but intensive exercise in research methods. Also, having defined in advance the length of the papers and the approach we wanted the students to use, we found it easier at every stage of the writing to make concrete suggestions, and to explain why such changes were necessary.

In planning this assignment, we had assumed that a short, focused paper would be a handier teaching tool than the longer writing project, and we suspected that students would remember just enough about their personal origins that they might want to know more. We also needed a controlled assignment that would encourage careful use

251

of a limited number of sources, partly because the assignment had to double as a short, practical library research unit to back up our library orientation program. Finally, we were thinking about the paper as an essay assignment: an exercise that would require the student to synthesize various kinds of material and relate it to a central idea—in this case, the significance of the day when the student was born.

The result of our planning was a description of a three-page paper that would characterize the time when the student first came into the world. Students were expected to demonstrate the significance of the major events that took place that day, or if necessary, during the week between the preceding Monday and the following Sunday. In addition, they were to suggest the atmosphere and the color of that period by bringing in references to the customs, the fashions, the advertising, the economy, and the acts and opinions of famous people. In essence, we asked the student to write a miniature history of the day of his or her birth; as a historian, he or she would try to show the reader what the world was like then, and why that day might be worth our attention as a small yet significant part of our history.

Before we introduced the assignment to our classes, we worked out a research outline, an overview of the tasks involved in writing the paper. It went something like this: 1) The first step is to collect the data, and this involves consulting newspapers, magazines, and other records of the time, and recording details that seem important, or perhaps just interesting. 2) As the student proceeds with his note-taking, he or she should be trying to discover the main theme of the paper. Deciding on a theme is the most difficult step for most people, but it is crucial, because the impact of these short papers depends upon the rapid emergence of some kind of pattern in the events described. 3) Once the main theme has been chosen, the writer needs to start thinking of an overall structure for the paper which will help to emphasize that theme. 4) Then he or she can begin to select and put into order those details which will form the body of the paper. This selection is partly determined by the theme, naturally, but the student is also concerned with the continuity, coherence, and significance of his or her historical sketch as he or she forges it into a narration. 5) Last, there are the mechanics of the notes and bibliography, and the questions of format, including the possibility of graphics to accompany the text. This research outline is nothing new, of course, but we found that it helped the students to use a standard procedure as a frame for the following techniques, which are especially useful in writing these brief histories:

Sources. Typically, the student's first question about this paper concerns the number of sources he or she has to look up. This is an impertinent question, in a sense, but it's aimed in the right direction. The sources are the life of these papers, and the sooner they are discussed, the better for the students. We discovered that most people have enough material for a good essay if they consult a total of seven sources from these two categories:

Four basic sources from:
New York Times; Times (London); local newspapers, if any; *Time; Newsweek; U.S. News and World Report; Life; Look; Saturday Evening Post; World Almanac;* etc.

Three others from:
Harper's; Saturday Review; Argosy; True; Vogue; Redbook; Ladies' Home Journal; Popular Mechanics; Foreign Affairs; etc.

In the newspapers and news magazines, students will find convenient summaries of the main events of the time, while the popular magazines contain the peripheral detail necessary for showing what life was like some twenty years ago. In practice, we found that most students drew their primary material from one newspaper and a couple of magazines, relying on the other sources for the odd fact or illustration.

Theme and Structure. Before we actually sent our classes off to the stacks, we gave them general instructions on how to discover a theme or guiding idea which would keep them from being swamped by their reading. One way to provide the paper with such a theme is to focus on a few main events that occurred on or near the date in question, and let those events characterize the period. Then a certain amount of amplifying detail—customs, fashions, gossip and so forth—can be brought in by analogy, or perhaps by contrast, to suggest the atmosphere of the times. The following example shows how one student focused his paper on the events of one week during Eisenhower's administration. The lead paragraph of the essay announces the events, and its concluding paragraph provides a sense of closure by summarizing the same events in retrospect:

The week was that of January 19, 1957. Newly re-elected President Dwight Eisenhower was proposing a 72 billion dollar budget for the year 1957–1958. He was also touring the Great Plains states that had been stricken by drought. On the international scene, the United States government was making the crucial decision of whether or not to send aid to the Middle East. And on that date, in Plainsville, Kansas, I was born.

* * *

Though I may have been the main attraction for my family that week, the world's eyes were on U.S. President Eisenhower as he began his new term in office. There were important decisions to be made concerning U.S. affairs both at home and abroad. The determination of the new budget aid for drought-stricken states, and aid to the Middle East rested with President Eisenhower and those under him.

Another way to structure this research paper is to choose a theme or dominant impression suggested by the events of that week, and then show how the other material is related to it. Such a theme might be a writer's feeling that when he was born, our nation, or even the world, was going through some very hard times. Here is the lead paragraph from a paper organized in this way:

I was born amidst turmoil. Not only the turmoil of labor, but the birth-pangs of a world violently struggling in its womb that week of September 21, 1958. On the small island of Quemoy, just off the coast of China, the old regime of Nationalist Chinese fought against the awakening Red Chinese giant. We were not without our own troubles in the U.S., for while our unknowing children were hula-hooping their way to new world records, the high schools of Little Rock stood empty rather than admit a single black student.

A simple, yet practical way to structure the paper is to choose one or more famous people in the news, and present what they said and did as characteristic of the times. The following paragraphs are the introduction and conclusion of a paper written in this way:

My father and mother knew the names well. They had read for years of Joseph McCarthy, Douglas MacArthur and Harry Truman. But during the week of October 17, 1949, I was blissfully unaware of these names. I had just been born that

Monday, and to me, my mother was more important than McCarthy, MacArthur or Truman.

* * *

What happened to McCarthy? He was censured by the Senate and died in 1956. What happened to MacArthur? He left the army, wrote his memoirs and died in 1969. What happened to Truman? He left the Whitte House, wrote his memoirs and died in 1970. What happened to me? I am a student at Wichita State University, and I am compiling my memoirs.

Selection of Material. Beyond the problem of structuring these essays lies the question of how to select, combine, and present the material so as to emphasize the theme. To put it a little more grandly, the students need ways of suggesting the historical significance of the time of their birth—an idea that may require some explaining. For some people, history suggests a string of momentous crises; others may imagine it simply as a record of everything that happened—all the facts. Consequently, it is worth spending some time to demonstrate that the significance of one's birth date has to be *created* by the writer. "Significance" arises from the coherence of the events as the historian renders them, the continuity of the events described, the explanation of cause and effect relationships between events, and finally the way in which those past events foreshadowed, or prepared for what would happen later on:

1) Once he or she has established the theme and laid out the structure of the essay, the writer must shape the narrative so that it presents a coherent picture, or more accurately, series of pictures. One needs to show that the several different aspects of each situation are related, because they express a main trend or tendency of the period. A coherent idea of a national problem, for instance, can be built up by showing that the same kinds of events occurred in separate areas of the country about the same time. One student used this simple device to create a brief sketch of the racial conflicts of the late fifties:

> On the homefront things were just as tense. In 1958 racial discrimination was rampant throughout the south, just as it had been 100 years before—"In Memphis . . . six negroes who wandered into a public zoo were chased out because it was not their designated day to see the animals." Under the threat of forced integration the Little Rock school board asked the

> Supreme Court to "indicate a path away from the bedlam,
> turmoil and chaos" that was sure to result. They asked for either
> a two and one half year delay of integration or a solution to "the
> threat of renewed violence." The situation was equally as bad in
> Virginia where a federal judge accused politicians of inciting
> hostility to the integration of Virginia's public schools. Al-
> though the Supreme Court unanimously rejected the appeals
> for the delay of integration, the governors of Virginia and
> Arkansas defied the Court and continued their opposition of
> racial integration.

In contrast, if the student is unaware or neglectful of this convention
we call coherence, he or she may bring together several episodes
which are superficially connected to a main situation, but have no
essential relationship to one another. The following paragraph by
another student shows how such apparent relationships can lack any
real coherence:

> President Eisenhower was in the news spotlight all week. He
> began his week in New York City, commemorating Columbus
> Day by laying a wreath in Columbus Circle. He also attended a
> cornerstone-laying at the Interchurch Center for the Protestant
> and Orthodox denominations. President Eisenhower returned
> to Washington, D.C., leading the list of diplomats that paid
> final tribute to Pope Pius XII, who was buried earlier in the
> week in Rome. "Ike" spent the last part of his week celebrating
> his sixty-eighth birthday. He visited his boyhood home and
> toured the Eisenhower museum in Abilene, Kansas.

2) Continuity is another main criterion for writing these short
histories. To begin with, the narrative has to be placed in the context
of its times. A brief phrase like "during the last part of the Korean
war" is easy enough to slip into the introductory paragraph, and it
draws little attention to itself. Leave out that kind of orienting
phrase, however, and nothing in the paper sounds quite right.

Of course the principle of continuity applies to more than just lead
paragraphs and paragraph markers. Within the individual sections of
the paper the reader needs to retain his or her sense of the order of
events. Here, instead of framing the incidents, the writer tries to
show how they fit into a larger pattern, or process. One way to
suggest this continuity is to use a storyteller's technique and supply
some narrative links, as this student did in describing the course of
the day when she was born:

> Although my day began at about 9:55 a.m., most people had
> begun their Friday hours before. Businessmen had fastidiously
> combed their hair with Top Brass moisturizing hair dressing—
> the wet head was certainly not dead. Children were just starting
> a new school term, and they were eager to show old friends the
> new tricks they had learned on their $1.95 hula hoops. In Little
> Rock, black high school students were wondering if they would
> even be allowed to learn at all. Housewives were off on
> shopping excursions to buy the latest fashion in dresses—
> empire waistlines, shaggy fabrics, and shorter hemlines. NASA
> officials were biting their nails, trying to explain why the first
> U.S. satellite to orbit the moon exploded after seventy-seven
> seconds of flight. And everyone—across the nation, across the
> world—was worried about waking up to a third world war.

3) In these brief histories it is hardly possible for the writers to
speculate at length about the causes of the events or attitudes they are
describing. Nevertheless, with a phrase or two hinting at the reasons
things happened as they did, they can add considerable depth to their
short essays. Here is one example: "With the Russian launching of
Sputnik, scientific studies became more important in the schools. This
could be seen in the article featured in the May 10 issue of the *Saturday
Evening Post,* 'Should Your Child Be a Scientist?' " Even this passing
reference to *Sputnik* is enough to suggest how minor events in American
education had their roots in a national preoccupation with the cold war.

4) Finally, the writers of these histories should give some thought
to the consequences of the events they have selected. An event may be
significant not only because it is related to a main trend (coherence)
or to other current events (continuity) or to prior events, but also
because it foreshadows important events which were to take place in
the future. As with the discussion of causes, a little said will go a long
way. But observations about the predictive nature of events are
valuable because they demonstrate the links between the events of
the past and our own lives in the present—one of the basic reasons for
writing any history. Here is a concluding paragraph which indicates
what are, in one student's opinion, some current trends that have
been carried over from the fifties: ‸

> It seemed, despite all the turmoil, that nothing was actually
> accomplished that week. Events kept spinning around like
> those innumerable hula-hoops, and like them, too, never got
> anywhere. At the end of the week, Little Rock's schools were

still closed, and would not open for another year. The trouble in Quemoy dragged on without solution, and lingers today, the future of Taiwan unresolved. Only our fads changed. Or did they? Those hoops are back, and the same familiar shows are re-run on T.V. Only I am different today, 18 years since my birth that week in September.

Format and Mechanical Details. The results of this freshman research—the manuscript turned in for credit—can take several forms. If the teacher wants the paper to be a library project or research exercise, it need only be an informal essay of three or four pages, like the ones which supplied these quotations. For more advanced students, or for research assignments that require a more sophisticated investigation of the week the student was born, the papers can be longer, drawing upon a greater variety of sources. Whatever the case, each paper should be accompanied by separate notes and bibliography that conform to a style manual selected by the teacher.

The nice thing about holding these papers to a set length and format is that it opens up the possibility of publishing an anthology; the class can combine their essays to make a short book with title page, table of contents, index, and the essays themselves, each followed by its own notes and bibliography. This can be an amusing project, and it has the added benefit of allowing each student to complete one of the basic tasks necessary to assembling a book. For example, one or more people can be assigned to 1) binding, design of cover, title page; 2) table of contents, numbering of pages; 3) editing and proofreading; 4) index; 5) printing (typing, duplicating, mimeographing, etc.); 6) illustrating. Other divisions are possible. The point is that by designing a book of essays, the students form a better idea of what a book is, just as by writing "freshman histories," they begin to develop a historical sense—an awareness of how history is written, and how our own times may be seen within the context of history.

NOTES

1. My colleagues Nancy Burns and Roy Campbell both worked on this assignment and developed some of the materials we now use in teaching it.

SUGGESTED READING

Becker, Carl L. *Everyman His Own Historian: Essays on History and Politics* (New York: F.S. Crofts, 1935).

CAREER RESEARCH—A MULTI-DISCIPLINE APPROACH

Gwen Dungy, Mary Sigler, Jane Bergman and Elaine Blatt

"Give me a fish, and I will eat for today; teach me to fish, and I will eat for the rest of my life." This ancient proverb is the underlying philosophy behind the research project assigned in English composition classes at St. Louis Community College at Meramec.

Few students enrolled in community college English composition classes have been asked to do extensive research; most have never investigated a topic more fully than looking it up in an encyclopedia. They are therefore frightened at the prospect of writing a research paper. We've found that teaching students to research their own career choices eases these fears. The assignment introduces them to the satisfaction of being able to find out information for themselves and apply it to their own lives.

Choosing Jobs According to Gender

It is particularly important that students improve their research skills. It is also important that they use these skills to investigate career opportunities and critically evaluate what these career opportunities can offer them. A recent study, found in *Community College Frontiers,* profiles major findings among male and female instructors at the two-year college.[1] Of the total sample of 1,493 instructors, two-thirds were males. Other data indicated that more women (10 percent) than men (6 percent) were working on their master's degrees. Fewer women (20 percent), however, than men (26 percent) were working on their doctorates. Women were found chiefly in the teaching fields of art, foreign languages, and literature rather than in

260

the more male-oriented fields of philosophy, law/government, history, engineering, and such technical fields as forestry.

These patterns reflect the propensity of men and women to choose their jobs according to their gender. One woman student in her career research paper gave similar reasons for wanting to be an art teacher: "An art teacher has to be interested in others' problems, especially those of her students. People have always been running to me with their problems, and I have always been compassionate and patient with them. . . . Art teaching would suit my life-style and the way I want to live. I intend to get married sometime; I don't know when."

Part of the career choice problem is that college course offerings and course content still tend to reinforce career decisions on the basis of traditional sex roles. Students who are taught research skills will not be confined by traditional sex-role definitions when searching for direction. Further competency in decision making will increase the likelihood that men and women will continue to earn advanced degrees and will seek out occupations according to their interests and skills, rather than settle for an "appropriate" job for their sex. Furthermore, the infusion of career education concepts into existing college programs is a solution to the present dualism between liberal arts and vocational training.

The Sally Syndrome

We have developed a project that we feel will be valuable in guiding students to less traditional, more rewarding job positions. This development was largely due to the manifestation of a common syndrome in a student we shall call "Sally." Sally is characteristic of today's women. Twenty-nine and unskilled, she attended a traditional advanced composition class at the St. Louis Community College at Meramec. Newly divorced, she is part of the growing number of households headed by females, a number that increased 30 percent between 1970 and 1975.[2] According to a recent Census Bureau report, 13 percent of all American families are now headed by single, separated, divorced, or widowed women.[3]

Sally was the ideal student, interested and verbally oriented. Sitting in the front row, she added her experienced voice to every classroom discussion. But in a private postmortem, she confessed that the traditional college research project had little to do with the realities of her life—supporting her children, examining various job occupations, improving her dwindling self-image and financial status. It was obvious she was far too bright to stand behind the counter of Woolworth's. She could easily handle a management position, but first she needed "empowerment," a "process in which the goal and acknowledged result is that the student becomes stronger and more in control of his or her own life."[4]

Steps Toward Empowerment

Teaching research in relation to a project as vital as career goals is a giant step toward empowering students to use the tool of decision making. In *A Practical Manual For Job-Hunters and Career Changes: What Color Is Your Parachute?*, Richard Nelson Bolles begins his article by quoting the ancient proverb which began our article. Teaching research in an English composition class rather than teaching writing alone is an attempt to teach a student "to fish." This personalized research approach empowers the student to repeat the process whenever he or she needs to make a decision.

The decision-making process could be pictured as in the accompanying diagram.

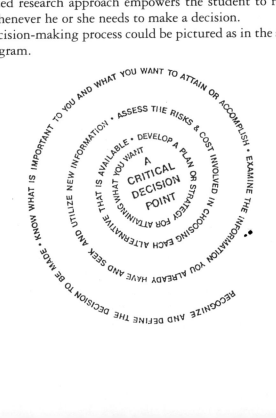

Any career development process goes through the same decision-making steps.

The research/library report is an investigative project which asks the student to analyze and evaluate a future career choice. The first step, recognizing and defining a decision, is achieved in the assignment of the project.

The Strong-Campbell Interest Inventory test which has the longest history of any psychological test in widespread use today, is administered to each student before the research begins. This allows time for computer analyses of the tests. The resulting data will help to define priorities, the second step of the decision diagram. The test provides the results for both sexes on the profile form. The profile contains 6 general occupational themes, 23 basic interest scales, and 124 occupational scales. The scores are presented so that each student can compare his or her score with general reference groups and with reference groups of his or her own sex.

The results of the inventory provide direction and several possibilities which the students may investigate further. Each student receives a computer printout of career alternatives, ordered according to the basic interest scales recorded on the Strong-Campbell Interest Inventory. This helps the student eliminate certain choices from the search. Of course, the Strong-Campbell Interest Inventory is only one source of information.The data provide a valuable tool to guide further research. However, because a student may overestimate the importance of certain information in the Strong-Campbell Interest Inventory results, he or she may then need the assistance of a counselor.

Using the Career Information Center

At the St. Louis Community College at Meramec, the English department employs the services of the Career Information Center, a part of the counseling office. The Career Information Center was created to be the center of career decision-making activities. It provides information on degree requirements, transfer options, and occupations. The six Holland occupational themes are used, which are the same themes on the Strong-Campbell Interest Inventory: artistic, conventional, enterprising, investigative, realistic, and social.

After helping to interpret the Strong-Campbell Interest Inventory, a counselor can suggest ways that a student can use the inventory to guide the search in the Career Information Center. If a student needs additional assistance or just wants to talk over tentative plans, he or she may schedule further individual appointments with a counselor or educational advisor. The counselor gives personal attention to each student's goals and aptitudes and may suggest other options, other aspects of the decision, and new sources of information.

The center became a valuable resource for some students. By spending just a little time looking under the various categories keyed to the Strong-Campbell Interest Inventory, students found information about a number of occupations. One student said, "The Career Information Center gave me exact directives as to what would be expected of me in my field. Much of the information that I used in writing my paper came from the Career Information Center." Another student said, "I didn't just look up the one I wanted to be, but I compared it with some other jobs I was sort of interested in." By knowing the center exists, students can use it many times to investigate a variety of occupations. They are now able to make knowledgeable choices.

Searching Out Specifics

Having acquired a basic knowledge of specific interest areas from the Strong-Campbell Interest Inventory and the Career Information Center, each student is then asked to research a career choice to find out if that decision will indeed be beneficial. Emphasis is placed on the need for specific, concrete information about the occupation: job openings in the field, wages, opportunities for advancement, etc.

One helpful reference in the Career Information Center is the *Occupational Outlook Handbook,* published every other year by the Department of Labor. In the table of contents, jobs are listed in clusters under major headings, such as "Office Occupations," "Education and Related Occupations," and "Health Occupations." The index is useful when looking up a specific job. It lists the occupations alphabetically and includes page numbers where additional information can be found. For each occupation, the handbook gives information on the nature of the work, places of employment, training required, employment outlook, earnings, and sources of additional information.

The college reference librarians have also compiled career materials. They augment these materials by teaching students how to use the library as a decision-making resource.

Gaining Insight Through Interviews

In addition to the use of more traditional research materials, each student is required to interview at least one person in the chosen field. This process helps the student become aware of the qualities which provide expertise in a career field. On a class day preceding the scheduled interview, the student can draw up a list of questions to ask the interviewee. Since the student has a list of probing questions when the interview begins, he or she is ready to look at and listen to the interviewee thoughtfully. Following the interview, it is easy to help the student evaluate the quality of the interview as a research source. Through this entire procedure the students have learned the standards for a valid piece of research. The interview is an excellent research tool because the interviewee not only provides practical information on the subject but also acts as a role model for the student.

Students were enthusiastic about this aspect of the project. One student remarked: "Perhaps the most informative part of my research project was the interview. I went to a hospital, observed, questioned, and learned much about the therapeutic fields which is what my paper was discussing. It gave me an insight into the kind of surroundings and kind of work I may be doing. It also provided another way to get information without your nose in a book all the time." On an even more practical level, one student wrote that he learned "all kinds of things about getting a job in my field and I even got a lead on a prospective employer." One interviewee offered a student a job as a result of the interview.

Breaking Socialization Patterns

One aspect of the career research project which may be frustrating to the instructor is that both men and women may tend to investigate the same traditional fields their older brothers and sisters might have chosen ten years ago. The instructor, however, must not interfere with these decisions because the purpose of the project is to enable students to make their own choices, and some of the choices will be better thought out and more realistic than others. However, with the skills gained in the career research paper, students will be able to investigate further opportunities.

Teaching, home economics, nursing, social work, and English and art education still ranked highest among women's career choices in our classes. These conventional choices were usually made according to the traditional reasoning. A woman who chose to investigate teaching considered the nine-month working year an advantage for a woman "especially if she is a mother" because "it would allow her to be with her children during the summer."

Even if women do not choose their careers for the convenience of meeting family responsibilities, they may choose a career because of personal characteristics usually identified as feminine: tactfulness, patience, caring, warmth, cheerfulness, nurturing. Because her scores on the Strong-Campbell Interest Inventory test listed the qualities of self-confidence, cheerful attitude, sociable personality, concern with welfare of others, and the ability to sell, one woman concluded she "had the qualifications required to be a good nurse."

Although many do not stray from their socialization patterns, a few students will choose to investigate nontraditional fields. One woman, for example, chose food management in a large corporation. She writes, "At 19 years of age, I know few other girls with such an opportunity for advancement. McDonald's is a rapidly growing business, and female managers are in demand. Few other businesses offer such interesting careers as McDonald's. It is sad to see so many people think of a job at McDonald's as only a temporary stepping stone to a better career. 'Are you still working at McDonald's?' is the question that is thrown up to me rather frequently. Yet I am enjoying my job, working around school hours, being paid for going to school, and making over $10,000 in gross income per year—not to mention paid vacation, meeting new and interesting people and excellent chances for promotion. . . . McDonald's truly offers a challenging, interesting, and rewarding career ahead of me."

Goals and Achievements

The goal of this research/library report paper is not an abstract one. In addition to learning research and writing skills, it is believed that the subject matter is invaluable to the students' futures. Since the project has a built-in motivation factor, the problems that plague traditional topics of research papers—plagiarism and purchase of professionally written papers—are avoided.

The benefits for the students are obvious. For the instructor, one of the most rewarding aspects of the assignment is the positive feedback about the research experience. One student evaluated the paper this way: "The career research paper . . . gave me insight into the career of physical therapy, which is what I would like to do. It was much more valuable to me than an ordinary research paper because I could put the research to good use instead of just researching something that I had no further use for." Another student commented: "I was usually too busy with school to get too deeply into deciding on a career, but this paper gave me the chance to really check up on my choices." Typical of the undecided student who benefited from the research was this comment: "I'm glad we used our career goals as the topic. I was changing and very confused. The Strong-Campbell Interest Inventory test caused me to look into a different field. . . . Now I know what I want to do and I'm excited about starting school for this program."

Students learn from their research that there are many aspects to a career, both good and bad. Armed with that knowledge, they are better able to choose rewarding careers as they grow and change. The main goal for the project, however, is to make research skills available to students and to interest them in learning more about themselves and their futures. By the time they have finished the many steps in the project, these students have been empowered. They have been taught to fish, and thus have more control over their lives.

This article appeared originally in *Community College Frontiers* 7 (Fall 1978), 15–19. Reprinted by permission of the publisher, Sangamon State University, Springfield, Illinois.

REFERENCES

1. Florence B. Brawer, "Women in Community Colleges," *Community College Frontiers* 5, no. 3 (Spring 1977), 19.
2. U.S. Bureau of Census, *Current Population Report,* Series P-23, no. 50.

3. U.S. Bureau of Census, *Current Population Report,* series P-20, nos. 28 and 291.

4. Richard Nelson Bolles, "The Essential Marks of Effective Counseling in the 1970s," keynote address delivered at the National Career Counseling and Placement Institute at the University of California, Los Angeles, 1973, 5.

5. H. B. Gelatt et al., *Decisions and Outcomes* (New York: College Entrance Examination Board, 1973), 7.

OUTSIDE THE LIBRARY: THE INTERVIEW PROFILE AS A MODEL FOR RESEARCH

William F. Woods

Few students enter a writing class ready to write a research paper. Even if they know how to take notes and organize them, they seldom understand what it means to work on a research problem. Research is really a process, a sustained inquiry that involves a sense of purpose, a knowledge of method, some intuition, and most importantly, a framework of ideas within which the inquiry can take place. Our academic disciplines exist for this very purpose of framing questions for scholars. But most students do not possess such a framework; unable to see the contextual outlines of a subject, they feel threatened by it and, like good conservatives, avoid spending time on a project that might lead nowhere.

Our job as teachers, then, is to show students how to explore new subjects by building on the knowledge they already possess. If we can help them identify and develop their present conceptual and investigative skills, they can proceed to refine their techniques as they apply them to a variety of materials. One way to help students exercise their basic research skills is to assign a profile essay based on one or more interviews. In essence, an interview is a dialogue between the researcher and another person. As such, it is not unlike the interchange, or "dialectic" that scholars carry on with their data; in both cases, the researcher is engaging in that process of question and answer, probing and evaluating that forms any kind of inquiry. But since the purpose of these interviews is to prepare for writing a character sketch, students can also apply their existing social skills in questioning the person and drawing conclusions from what they have heard. In short, by interviewing a person and then using the information for writing up a profile, students are going through the basic steps necessary to research; later on, this informal research exercise can be used as a paradigm for explaining how to carry out a formal process of inquiry in preparation for writing a standard research report.

Getting students ready for conducting an interview means showing them how to do the necessary groundwork before that first meeting with the subject. Generally, the interviewer is expected to choose the subject, and so the first question is—Who? Then there are the mechanics of setting up the meeting, taking notes, and the problem of what in the world to talk about. My own instructions to the students go something like this:

1. Choosing a subject. The best way is to start with people you know. Friends of the family or people at work make your job easier because you already know a great deal about them, and you are familiar with their surroundings. Better yet, these people also know you, and will probably volunteer information about themselves that you didn't even think of asking. But if the subject is not an acquaintance, it pays to find out something about that person in advance. If the interview will focus on the person's job, find out about the company and its employees. You can collect this background information by asking around, or by spending a couple of hours reading magazines in the library (for example, if you are interviewing a nurse, look through some issues of *Nursing* or *Nursing Forum*).The main thing is to get a general sense of what your subject's job is like before you ask him or her about it. In a formal research paper, this preliminary background search is called establishing the context of the study.

2. Setting up the interview. For some interviews, an appointment is absolutely necessary. For instance, when one of my students interviewed the City Manager of Wichita, Kansas, she had to make an appointment two weeks ahead of time. But calling paid off; the Manager gave her a full half hour, and she was able to ask some involved questions about the city's government. Setting up the meeting ahead of time also makes it easier to find the person in his or her characteristic surroundings. As a general rule, a person's home or place of work tells us a good deal about his or her life; and after all, that's the main purpose of a profile. One last note on appointments; if the first meeting is held at the person's convenience, it may be possible to ask for a second interview. Depending on the length of the paper and the complexity of the subject matter, this second discussion might be crucial.

3. Taking notes. Most people don't mind if an interviewer records the discussion on a pad, and if it's hard to keep up with the flow, one

can always switch to a kind of reporter's shorthand, writing down only the key words and phrases. Of course there's nothing like a tape recorder for getting down exactly what the person said. Yet some people are made nervous by a whirring machine, and furthermore, in order to edit the material effectively, you have to transcribe it, and the tedium of this job is indescribable to someone who has never done it. Ultimately, the particular nature of the interview will help decide which method to use. But a good basic strategy is to record as much as possible, and then sit down directly after the interview and fill in the missing parts before they fade from memory.

4. The sheet of prepared questions. There are several reasons for bringing prepared questions to the interview. First, the person may not feel like talking that day, and unless you are very well informed, you may find it hard to invent good questions on the spot. Second, your time with the person is limited; if you aren't able to steer the discussion away from small talk, you may find yourself walking away from the interview with only a few general remarks, instead of the person's real ideas and opinions. It is simply unwise, therefore, to go to an interview without at least some brief notes on what you want the person to talk about. These prepared questions should accomplish two basic objectives:

a) Identify the person's basis of authority. Your first questions should prepare the ground for the rest of the discussion by establishing the person's identity and relationship to his or her surroundings. For example, if the person sells chickens to fast food restaurants, as did the subject of one student's interview, you want to find out how long he has sold poultry, where and when he sells it, and how successfully. It makes a difference, in other words, whether you're getting the opinions of a big-city poultry dealer, or someone who sells a few chickens on Saturdays.

b) Get a clear picture of the person's ideas. You can't really know what the person will say before it comes out in the discussion, but you can and should prepare yourself to follow up on the ideas and opinions when they emerge. And if the person doesn't volunteer a point of view, it's your job to ask about it, to suggest ways for the person to talk about his or her ideas; for example, you can ask the person to analyze a problem, explain the causes of a situation, or trace the history of a career. Often, the person will use a special phrase or expression which seems to sum up a point of view; try to record the exact wording of such key phrases, and make some notes to yourself on how the phrase was meant. One student used this technique when he interviewed a bum on East Douglas, Wichita's skid row. The student pulled out a tape recorder, but the bum pushed it away, saying "When you're comen offa wine drunk, you don't wanna talk inta one of those things." Luckily, the student had a good ear for language, and reproduced the comment from memory.

In the foregoing section, I have discussed how the interviewer chooses a person to interview, forms a sense of the person's background, and finally prepares some questions which can be used in the interview. These steps correspond roughly to the beginning stages of a research project, where the investigator senses a problematic situation, or conflict in the data, then states the problem by specifying what *kinds* of things have to be known in order to explain the conflict, and finally devises a set of questions with which to explore the problem. These leading (or "heuristic") questions provide new information and new perspectives on the problem, thereby preparing the investigator to formulate a hypothesis. The same function is performed by the interviewer's questions (both the prepared ones and others which arise spontaneously) when they are put to work during the interview: using these questions, the interviewer tries to open up perspectives into the person's character, situation and attitudes—material which later makes it possible to create a vivid, rounded, meaningful account of that person's life experience.

The next step in the process of inquiry, as in interviewing, is to arrive at a hypothesis, or meaningful statement about the subject. Unfortunately, there is no rule we can follow, either to formulate a hypothesis about a problem, or to derive a meaningful statement about the subject of an interview. Still, there are some general guidelines. In problem solving, an investigator tries to match known concepts with the problem situation, hoping to explain the new pattern as a transformation or variation of an old one. In writing up an interview, we can employ another kind of pattern as a matrix, or mold, in an attempt to give a meaningful shape to the new information produced by our questions. This "pattern" can be expressed as five main objectives:

1. Arriving on the scene. Writing a profile is like writing a narrative: one describes an interaction between two people, provides a setting for that action, and devises ways of bringing the readers into this scene at the beginning and leading them out of it at the end. Here we are concerned with the beginning. The main function of the

opening paragraphs is to help the reader become accustomed to looking over the writer's shoulder, so to speak. Perhaps the easiest way for the writer to do this is simply to describe his or her own entry onto the scene—the arrival at the person's home or the drive out to the job. One student, who was interviewing a local astrologer, produced the following introduction:

> Astrology is defined in the dictionary as a *pseudo science* but to Mildred Schuler it is "the basic science" and I wouldn't want to argue the point with this local astrologer. She has been charting, studying and interpreting the heavenly bodies for fifty years and is a staunch believer that "education is knowledge of astrology." I was anxious to meet this Astrological Authority, although I had no idea what type of person to expect when I knocked at the door at the little white cottage in East Wichita. I half-anticipated a jewelry-laden, cosmetic-masked and veiled lady but instead the woman that asked me into her home could have been my own grandmother, dear, sweet grandmother, complete in blue gingham sundress. (Beverly Danly)

2. Conveying a sense of the character. In this last passage, the writer surprises us with an astrologer in a gingham sundress, but by now, of course, we already know that Mildred Schuler is "a staunch believer that 'education is knowledge of astrology.' " Indeed, the heart of any interview is this sense of the subject's character, which emerges from overt comments by the writer, from the person's anecdotes and opinions, and even from oblique hints like this brief description of two dogs:

> At 1:15 I turned into the driveway and was promptly greeted by two German Shepherds barking furiously. However, by the time I had stopped the car, they were both standing on their hind legs looking in the driver's window and wagging their tails. This was my welcome to the home of Beth-Anne Chard, who greeted me at the door and warmly accepted me into her home. (Shirley Leftwich)

Perhaps the most common technique for conveying character, however, is the direct description of what the person *does* during the interview. This running description keeps us from losing our sense of the person's presence in the scene; it might also be called a "narrative line" because it holds the interview together, providing a frame for the anecdotes and background information which take up the discussion. Here is one example of how the writer can convey the person's character, while at the same time introducing matters for discussion:

> We sat down on the floor in the hall, and she pulled a cigarette out of her tiny purse and lit it. Deciding that the best choice would be to ignore it, I began by asking her why she had to go to court in the first place.
>
> "Shoplifting" was her answer and given with a really "cute" smile. I am sure that the look on my face belied my answer of "Oh yeah." I was mortified. She looked very young, so I asked her how old she was. She told me that she was eleven years old and that she had done about everything, including stabbing her cat with a fork. (Dana Decker)

3. The cargo of information. Aside from the fascination of glimpsing the quality of another person's life, the profile's main source of power is its promise of information—the facts, the inside story, the distilled wisdom of a person's life and work, if you will. As Aristotle tells us, however, the trick is to mingle instruction with delight—in this case, to make sure the new material retains the flavor of the experiences and the outlook peculiar to that person. Probably the most effective way to introduce this substantive material is simply to record the person's anecdotes. People find it natural to explain matters by telling stories about themselves and others (the rhetorical term is *exempla*, or "parables"), and as long as the narrative line, or sense of scene is maintained, the writer can build a strong profile from such tales. The following anecdote is from an interview with a gravedigger:

> Sandy soil is another obstacle for gravediggers near Williams, Indiana—situated along White River. With an ornery, little-boy expression on his face, Fout recalled an incident involving that soil. "I had instructed this preacher not to stand too close to the open gravesite 'cause I hadn't reinforced the edges. As he pronounced the benediction and poised his right arm over the casket his body leaned forward and disappeared into the grave. I had to chuckle to myself," Fout recalled. (Linda Jones)

Anecdotes are not the only method of conveying information about the character's job or primary interests, of course. For short periods, the writer can step in and relate the pertinent facts directly to the reader. The only requirements are that the information should add to our understanding of the person involved, and that these facts generate their own interest. Here is such an informative section from the same interview with Fout the gravedigger:

> A new era arrived in 1957 when Fout incorporated the use of a mechanical digger. Opposed to many, like myself, who might have thought this to mean the end of hard labor, the device is far from the answer to all manual tasks. Hand digging is done in the final stage of every grave to ensure exactness—the bottom must be perfectly level. A carpenter's level is used for this purpose. In the closing of a grave the machinery is useless and the human back solely supports the process. A wooden paddle is used to edge the dirt in and around the sides of the vault, then a hand tamp, weighing approximately 11 lbs. is used to pack the blanket of earth over the sealed tomb. (Linda Jones)

4. The time dimension. Supplying information about a job or other experience opens up one sort of perspective, or "dimension" for the reader, but a further dimension can be added by drawing out the relationship between the person's past experience and his or her present conditions. Call it the time dimension, a sense of history, or just "roots"—the effect is the same: the reader begins to see a meaningful pattern in the person's life as it develops over a period of years. It is just this sense of purpose in a life, and perhaps even more, the fulfillment and clarification of a purpose, that arises from the best profiles, and allows them to make a statement worthy of the person they describe. Here is such a statement about Jim Banks, a mechanic:

> "I don't know how I got started," he added. "I have been a mechanic around the country most of my life, the past 25 or 30 years, and I just decided that I wanted an old car. So in 1955, I bought a Model T Ford and restored it, and I've been buying and restoring ever since."
>
> As Jim has pointed out, restoring can sometimes be expensive and is always time consuming, but the final result is worth the effort. It is gratifying to take a rusty, broken down piece of junk, and through diligent, hard work, turn it into a masterpiece. "It's like saving a piece of history," Jim Banks said quietly, "and if we don't do it, they'll be gone forever. They won't be coming back." (Jerry Glessner)

This "statement" the interviewer makes about the person's life is best described as supplying a perspective in time, but really it is more like the fundamental theme of the interview, drawing strength from all the other parts. For unless the writer's treatment of the person's character and occupation have prepared us for our long retrospective look, we won't get the desired sense of inevitability as we see the person arriving finally at his or her present condition after years of effort. This sense of a basic pattern emerging in a person's life is probably the most difficult effect for an interviewer to achieve. Nevertheless, by trying to achieve it, writers cease to be mere takers of notes and become *interpreters* of experience, on a par with research workers, whose hypotheses, or new statements about the facts, are simply another kind of interpretation.

5. Leaving the interview. Ending a profile presents the same problems as ending a piece of fiction: one has to avoid the "bump" when the reader falls out of the story on the last page. It is possible simply to end with the person's answer to the last question, but if the writer has maintained throughout a sense of scene, or interaction between the two people, it is best to give their discussion a sense of closure. One way to do this is to show the interviewer leaving the scene, glancing back on it, or thinking about it in order to give the reader a way of holding the interview in memory. Here is the way Linda Jones ended her interview with Fout:

> Then, quite unexpectedly, my interviewed subject took off his frayed brim grey hat and shaking my hand tightly, said, "Thank-you, Mizz Jones. You've made my day!" I glanced in the rear view mirror as I waited for a break in the traffic to enter the street. Fout was still leaning against the service gate, his hat still dangling from his hand.

In summary, the chief advantages of the interview profile as an introductory research assignment are: 1) It brings the writer directly into contact with the material, and 2) It puts to use the writer's life-long training in carrying out question-and-answer routines, sifting the evidence, and drawing conclusions about the motives, experience and personality of the other person. The teacher's task is then to guide the students in applying these skills by providing general guidelines like those suggested above, and by pointing out analogies between the process of interviewing and the process of inquiry which they will be practicing in the future.

RESEARCH OUTSIDE THE LIBRARY: LEARNING A FIELD

Thomas N. Trzyna

Several recent articles have re-assessed the goals of research writing, and there appears to be a consensus that if research writing is to be taught at all, assignments should call for more than the assembly of information collected in a library.[1] Some texts now provide sections on interviewing, but students need to learn how to identify and use sources of information outside the library. An interviewing strategy is useless without a strategy for identifying contacts. This essay proposes two methods for gathering information outside the library, methods that help students to understand the full context in which research activities are carried out. I will also offer theoretical support for the methods and give an example of their application.

So-called "research papers" are often mere assemblies of barely related facts. This situation is hardly surprising, because the basic premise of much library research training—that information is available on students' topics—is misleading. It is *not* possible to find information about many interesting topics because no one else is writing about precisely those topics; if a student carefully frames a research question, chances are great that the library will be able to provide articles only about related issues, not about the central question. In such a case, if the student wants to find out what experts think about his (or her) own topic, the student must talk to the experts themselves. Too often, when a student is unable to find information that bears directly on a well-conceived topic, the teacher responds by helping the student to change to a different topic. If our job is to teach research skills, though, we should be able to help students find information on what interests them, not on something second best. Interviewing methods can help students get past this fundamental limitation of library collections.

277

Libraries are limited in two other ways that are relevant in this context. First, all library materials are dated. The articles in this month's journals were probably in an editor's hands several months before, on the writer's desk several months or years before that, and based on information or experiments still older. Interviewing is a method for finding information that is current today, information that will be in print next month or next year. Second, all library collections are limited. Even the largest libraries do not subscribe to all the updating services, specialty newsletters, and trade journals. Some important trade publications are not easily available to libraries even when libraries want them.

People, of course, are the ultimate source of information: people and their organizations. Before discussing how the right people can be located, however, it is worth considering another reason why people are generally better sources than articles and books. Articles do not provide their own contexts. Some essays, it is true, open with a review of a debate or include bibliographies of current literature, but often this information is presented at a level that does not allow a beginner to understand the questions that are being asked, the issues that are at stake, or the applications of what might seem to be trivial theoretical or empirical details. In many fields, unless a student catches on to the content of the current controversies, that student will be unable to interpret the published data accurately. For example, suppose a student writes a paper on the future of nuclear power and uses only materials published by the Nuclear Regulatory Commission and a major power company. The resulting paper might be factually correct, yet it is likely that the interpretation of the facts will be altogether favorable to nuclear power. Unless the student understands that nuclear power is a subject on which sides are being taken—and that the Nuclear Regulatory Commission is likely to be on a particular side of the debate—the student will not adequately interpret her sources.

The philosopher Stephen Pepper draw a useful distinction between data (discrete facts) and danda (facts about the structure of information in a field).[2] For example, knowing a discrete fact like the weight of an electron is not useful information unless you know about the particle theory of matter. Similarly, knowing some authority's estimate of the probability that the radioactive matter in a nuclear power plant will melt down is not useful unless you know who made the calculation for what agency, under what pressures or circumstances, and so on. In short, facts are not enough. Knowledge of the context of facts is necessary if facts are to be interpreted properly, and people and organizations are the best sources of information about controversies in a field, theories current in a discipline, sources most frequently consulted by researchers in the discipline, and other contextual "danda."

What teaching strategies follow from these observations? Students should be encouraged to use professional help, to get experts to reflect on students' own topics. After all, it's a natural impulse to ask someone else for help. The first method for identifying experts includes posing three questions. 1) Who is likely to know about this? If I am writing a paper on Victorian literature, should I ask the librarian for help? Or might I talk either to my own professor or to another professor of Victorian studies, perhaps a faculty member in a different but related discipline? 2) Where is this information likely to come from? Would nuclear power be an issue of interest to state or local governments? If so, what sort of agency would deal with it? Whom should I call? 3) Who would pay to have this information gathered? This question is an intensified version of the second question. If I want to write about the feasibility of electric cars, would *Popular Mechanics* pay for this research? Or might a major automobile manufacturer be interested enough to have commissioned a study?

These three questions are aids to invention, but they will not produce much unless the student has categories of information sources to work with—ideas about where information actually comes from in this society. The remainder of this paper attempts to provide 1) a general introduction to the kinds of organizations that can be found in *any* field, 2) an explanation of how to find the names of organizations in specific fields, and 3) an example of how organizational information about a field can be used to identify controversies and competing approaches. Because I have a general (not discipline specific) research writing class in mind, I have chosen to use a major public issue, nuclear power, for my example. The contribution of organizations to American research and government has long been neglected, except on a few issues, such as national defense. Some foundations and extra-governmental organizations—such as the national conferences of governors and legislators—have an enormous impact on legislation, the flow of ideas, and our futures. Yet, as Joan Roeloff recently pointed out, "there are probably more critical studies of foundation garments than of the massive institutions 'overpinning' our society."[3] Those who teach research should also be aware of the political structure of information sources in the United States.

Table I lists sixteen types of organizations that publish information in most fields. A short list of typical publication methods is presented under each type of organization. Many of the documents produced by corporations, lobbies, and other organizations are available to the public, yet they are not listed in traditional references or found in libraries either because they are not widely published or because they are not marketed for library collections. These publications are available only from members of associations, corporation offices, government officials, and so on. To put this point another way, much of the information that gets into libraries comes from only eight of the sources listed in Table I: large trade publishers, academic publishers, and government agencies. The other eight types of sources are tapped by libraries only in limited ways if at all.

Table II presents a list of print materials and methods that can be used to learn about entire fields of study, specific organizations, particular researchers, and specialized or limited-distribution publications. Some of the guides and directories listed in Table II are available only if you know something about the organizations in a field. Membership lists, for example, are seldom widely distributed. Most of the other resources are available even in small libraries, yet only a few of these are normally introduced by chapters or texts on library research.

To carry out an effective search, students should use a few directories or initial interviews to locate an expert who can provide an overview of organizations and current controversies in a given field, as well as components on specific topics or research questions. A detailed discussion of the information in Tables I and II would take several chapters; an example can convey something of how the methods work. Table III shows how Table I can be filled out for a specific field, nuclear power research. Table III was compiled in less than an hour with data from only one source of information about organizations, *The Nuclear Power Issue: A Guide to Who's Doing What in the U.S. and Abroad.*[4] This guide provides much more information than can be condensed in the table, including names, addresses, profiles of organizations, and information about publications. Guides to specific fields are available for energy, the environment (several), human rights (at least two), population control, hunger, the world water supply, prison reform, the media, women's issues, transportation, several regions of the country, manufacturers, banks, and many other fields. With the help of these materials, students can find useful persons to contact in any urban area and many rural areas.

What can be learned from one of these indexes or directories? From Table III it is easy not only to pick out people and groups to write or call, but also to draw many useful inferences about the field of nuclear power, such as the following simple observations. Nuclear power is probably not a field crowded with independent inventors. It is an issue of concern to the federal government more than a local or regional matter. Large corporations are active in the field, as are their associations and lobbies. The issue is highly polarized, as a glance at this short list of lobbies demonstrates: Alliance for Survival, the John Birch Society, the American Friends Service Committee. University research centers are spread throughout the country, so that experts should be readily available.

Moreover, after looking at a chart like this, students should understand why some materials—such as popular magazines—are not usually appropriate sources of information for an extended research project. Popular materials are not part of the discipline, which can be defined as a self-limiting group of researchers, organizations, and specialized publications. Given an awareness of the agents and agencies in a discipline, students can be taught to ask, "Where can I find a local expert in this field?" If a local specialist can be found, the student can then ask questions about recent trends, current debates, other experts and organizations, and the location of print information, especially types of documents that cannot be found in academic or civic libraries.

This approach to research is not intended to replace the traditional bibliographic approach, but to supplement and enrich that method by enabling students 1) to gain rapid access to more current information than is sometimes available in libraries, and 2) to gather contextual information that will help them to interpret the data they collect. This method helps students to use interviews, telephone calls, and letters of inquiry in gathering their data, and it also frees them to attempt prospective as well as retrospective research. The approach outlined here emphasizes institutional connections in order to make the point that locating a scholar or an organization and understanding its place in the context of a discipline can be as useful as finding a good review article or a select bibliography.

Composition classes or classes in research writing do not have time
to review the bibliographic materials and research methods appropriate to more than one or two disciplines; time can be found, however,
to acquaint students with the types of organizations that exist in all
disciplines and to supplement traditional bibliographic training
with an introduction to the print resources that help professionals to
find each other and share their expertise. Instruction in this method
takes only a few hours, and in most urban areas students will be able
to find experts or organizational contacts who are willing to be of
assistance. Advanced students can be made aware that several long
distance telephone calls to scholars in their fields will cost about as
much as a computer data search and might produce more useful and
more focused results.

NOTES

1. Richard L. Larson, "The 'Research Paper' in the Writing Course: A
   Non-Form of Writing," *College English,* 44 (December, 1982), 811–816;
   Robert A. Schwegler and Linda K. Shamoon, "The Aims of the Research
   Paper," *College English* 44 (December, 1982), 812–824; James E. Ford
   and Dennis R. Perry. "Research Paper Instruction in the Undergraduate
   Writing Program," *College English* 44 (December, 1982), 825–831;
   Thomas Trzyna, "Research Writing: A Review of the Handbooks with
   Some Suggestions," *College Composition and Communication,* 34 (May,
   1983), 202–207. I am indebted throughout this paper to the California
   Institute of Public Affairs, which provided me with copies of many
   specialized reference works.
2. Stephen C. Pepper, *World Hypotheses: A Study in Evidence* (Berkeley:
   University of California Press, 1942 [rpt. 1966]), passim.
3. "Results of Scholarly Research That Were Reported Last Week,"
   Chronicle of Higher Education, 7 September 1983, pp. 5–6.
4. Kimberly J. Mueller, *The Nuclear Power Issue: A Guide to Who's Doing
   What in the U.S. and Abroad* (Claremont, CA: California Institute of
   Public Affairs, 1981).

Table I
Types of Organizations and Their Methods of Publication

1. *Inventors, Small Firms*
   internal reports
   patents, news reports
2. *Corporations*
   internal reports
   proposals
   publications for sale
   patents
3. *Small Publishers*
   reference books
   catalogues
   specialty newsletters
4. *Large Publishers*
   trade lists
   internal publications
   journal management offices
5. *Lobbies/Professional Associations*
   membership publications
   trade publications
   convention reports
   position papers
6. *Charities/Churches*
   newsletters,
   newspapers, annual reports,
   magazines
   commission reports
7. *Foundations*
   publishing offices
   annual reports
   catalogues
   information offices
   project reports
8. *Think Tanks*
   (Rand, SRI, MITRE, etc.)
   internal reports
   articles, books
   publications for sale

9. *University Departments*
   internal reports
   articles, books,
   funded research reports
10. *University Research Centers*
    journals
    monograph series
11. *Federal Government*
    all forms of reports, books, min-
    utes, newspapers, catalogues,
    data bases, contract reports,
    information centers, specialized
    libraries, research centers
12. *State Governments*
    similar to federal government in
    range and complexity
13. *Local Governments*
    reports, newspapers, newsletters,
    manuals, minutes
14. *Extra-Governmental and Quasi-
    Governmental Agencies*
    (see Federal Manual for defini-
    tion; e.g., Academy for Contem-
    porary Problems, U.S. City
    Managers Association, Confer-
    ence of State Legislatures) re-
    ports, newsletters, books,
    information offices, conference
    proceedings, suggested legisla-
    tion
15. *Regional Governments*
    (e.g., regional water, transit, and
    power agencies) reports, annual
    reports, membership lists
16. *International Government*
    (e.g., United National Agencies,
    Treaty Associations, Common
    Market, World Court, etc.) range
    of publication methods similar
    to U.S. Federal Government

Table II
Methods of Access to Organizational Information

1. Patent Office, regional patent depositories	15. Government Manuals, Yearbooks, Legislative Directories
2. Letters of Inquiry	16. State, Local, and Regional Directories
3. Survey forms	
4. Membership lists, separately bound or in journals	17. Industry Directories, in journals or as separately bound publications
5. Directories of Research in Progress, often available as special indexes, notes in periodicals, or through notices of grant awards.	18. Telephone Books, Government (all levels), special group (e.g., U.S. Thai Telephone Directory), telephone company
6. Directories of Trade Associations	19. Directories of Conventions and Convention Proceedings
7. Directories of Research Centers	
8. Indexes and Abstracts	20. Indexes of In-House Presentations (e.g. Bell Labs Directory)
9. Publication Lists and catalogues	
10. Citation Indexes	21. Data Bases (e.g., Medline, or large systems such as DIALOG, ORBIT, BRS)
11. Directories of Persons	
12. Professional networks	
13. National Technical Information Service (U.S. Department of Commerce)	22. Library Networks: OCLC, Washington Library Network.
14. National Referral Service (Library of Congress)	23. Special Library Directories
	24. Directories of Fields (see Table III for an example)

Table III
A Preliminary Classification of Organizations Active in the
Field of Nuclear Power Research

(All data in this chart are taken from *The Nuclear Power Issue: A Guide to Who's Doing What in the U.S. and Abroad,* edited by Kimberly J. Mueller [Claremont, California: California Institute of Public Affairs, 1981].)

Inventors
  none located
Small Firms
  none located
Corporations
  Tennessee Valley Authority
  Alabama Power Company
  Pacific Gas and Electric
  Southern California Edison
  (many others; total of 72 power plants
  in operation in United States)
Small Publishers
  large number of local newsletters,
  generally anti-nuclear power
Large Publishers
  Nuclear News
  Nuclear Standards News
  Nuclear Export Monitor
  News Digest of Nuclear Hazards
Lobbies/Churches
  American Nuclear Energy Council
  Atomic Industrial Forum, Inc.
  Union of Concerned Scientists
  Abalone Alliance
  American Power Committee (John
    Birch Society)
  Committee for Nuclear Responsibility
  Clergy and Laity Concerned
  (several hundred such groups listed in
    this reference)
Professional Associations
  American Nuclear Society
  American Physical Society
  American Medical Association
  American Bar Association
  many others
Foundations
  Center for Development Policy
  National Academy of Sciences
  Scientists Institute for Public Information

Think Tanks
  Rand Corporation
  Battelle
University Departments
  University of Michigan; University of
  Iowa; University of California, San
  Diego; UCLA; Kansas State University; Louisiana State University; MIT;
  Oregon State University; Texas
  A&M; University of California,
  Berkeley; many others
Federal Government (U.S.)
  General Accounting Office
  President's Commission on Three
  Mile Island, Council on Environmental Quality, Department of Defense, Department of Energy (many
  offices), Nuclear Regulatory Commission, many offices in other cabinet
  level agencies
National Governments
  France, United Kingdom, U.S.S.R.,
  India, many others
State Governments
  Agencies in all 50 states.
Local Governments
  No local agencies located
Regional Governments
  Five regions of the Nuclear Regulatory Commission, other multistate
  consortia.
International Agencies
  International Atomic Energy Agency
  International Commission on Radiological Protection

PLAGIARISM AND DOCUMENTATION: A SELF-INSTRUCTIONAL LESSON

Beverly Lyon Clark

Instructions: Cover the right side of each page with a piece of paper. As you answer each question, move the piece of paper to see if your answer agrees with mine.

Plagiarism is dishonesty. It's theft. It means stealing someone else's ideas or words and pretending that they're your own.

Yet often researchers develop their best ideas by puzzling over others' theories and opinions. You simply need to acknowledge what these people have said—in a footnote or its equivalent.

Deciding when to document your source takes some practice. First, let's work on general principles. You probably know most of them already.

1. Should you document your source (provide a footnote or otherwise indicate your source) when you directly quote what an author has said?

1. Yes, of course! You're clearly using someone else's words.

2. Should you document your source when you paraphrase what the author has said (that is, you put the author's ideas into your own words)?

2. Yes. You may not be using someone else's words, but you are using his or her ideas.

3. Should you document your source when you mention a commonly known fact or figure?

3. No, it's not necessary.

4. Should you document your source when you mention an unusual fact or figure?

4. Yes. If it's unusual—if it's something, for instance, that your source discovered—then you should document that discovery.

5. Should you document your source when you mention the results of other people's experiments?

5. Yes. If someone has discovered something by performing an experiment, then he or she should certainly receive credit.

Thus quotations, ideas, experiments, and not-commonly-known facts and figures require documentation.

Still you need to make difficult decisions. When, for instance, is a fact or figure commonly known? You need to exercise judgment.

Let's practice that judgment right now. Decide which of the following statements require documentation.

1. Columbus sighted America in 1492.

1. No, of course not. This fact is commonly known.

2. The per capita national debt has grown from $61.06 in 1870 to more than $9,600.

2. Yes. Specific statistics, not generally known, require documentation. (My source is the 1989 *World Almanac and Book of Facts.*)

3. The population of the United States is now well over two hundred million.

3. No. This fact is generally known by the well educated. Furthermore, it's just an approximation. An exact figure, however, and especially one that your source specifically calculated (for example, with statistical projection techniques), would usually require documentation.

4. Wilhelm C. Roentgen, the discover of X rays, won the first Nobel Prize in physics.

4. No, probably not. You may not have known this fact, but you could readily find it in a reference book, and it would be considered generally known.

5. John Stuart Mill lived from 1806 to 1873.

5. No. You may not have known this fact, but you can readily find it in a reference book, and it would be considered generally known. Furthermore, there's no controversy about these dates. If there were, then you might use documentation to indicate which authority you are following.

6. John Stuart Mill probably had an IQ of 190.

6. Yes. This fact is not generally known nor readily available. (I got it from *The Book of Lists.*) Furthermore, some researcher is responsible for calculating Mill's IQ (he lived

before IQ tests were developed), and that researcher deserves credit.

7. Milgram found that most people are surprisingly susceptible to the influence of scientific authority: they will follow orders even when they think they are inflicting pain.

7. You've given some documentation in the sentence—by naming Stanley Milgram—but you should include more. You need to give him credit for his experiment.

8. At least one critic has suggested that Lewis Carroll's Alice is symbolically a phallus, as she expands and contracts.

8. Yes. For one thing, the idea is sufficiently striking and unusual that it should be attributed to a particular critic. For another thing, the phrase "At least one critic" suggests that you have a specific critic in mind (in this case, Martin Grotjahn), and thus you should name him. In general, whenever you say, "As studies show" or "One researcher disagrees" or the like, you should document the studies and researchers.

9. The original Alice was Alice Liddell, to whom Carroll told stories as he rowed with her and her sisters and Robinson Duckworth on the Isis.

9. Documentation here depends on context. You probably do not need to document the statement—especially not if you're writing entirely about Carroll. You may not have known these details before you started doing research, but they are generally known to critics of Carroll.

Let me suggest, though, two situations when you might need to document this information. One would be if you were challenging the facts—if you had come up with different facts. Then you would need to trace the information in sentence no. 9 back to its original source—back to Carroll's diaries (and you would need very strong evidence to refute what he says in his diary).

Another situation when you might want to document this sentence would be in a paper treating, say, ten different authors and how they were inspired to compose their works. Then you would not assume that your reader is knowledgeable about each author and would need to document the facts about each.

10. Investigation of the original manuscript recently revealed that Carroll first ended with a sketch of Alice Liddell, but then he pasted a photograph over the sketch.

10. Whose investigation revealed this discovery? You need to give Morton Cohen credit.

Now you should have some idea of when you need to document facts, figures, discoveries, ideas.

Documenting quotations is simpler—every quotation should be documented. But quotations, too, require judgment. You need to decide when to quote in the first place. Let's go over some ground rules.

Decide whether the following statements are true or false.

1. Whether you quote or paraphrase, whenever you use an individual's ideas you should document your source.

   1. True, of course!

2. Lots of long quotations show that you have done lots of reading.

   2. False. Lots of long quotations suggest that you're too lazy to organize your own ideas—you're relying too heavily on others'. If you include quotations, it's generally better to use short ones, just enough to support your points, not to make those points and structure your paper for you.

3. An occasional long quotation may be appropriate—when, for instance, you're going to analyze the wording or logic of the passage in detail.

   3. True. If you're going to analyze the passage in detail, referring, for instance, to specific words in specific sentences, you may need to provide the reader with a context. You can include a long quotation to make the reader's work easier—not to make your own easier.

4. Quotations should correspond word for word with the source, omissions indicated with ellipses (. . .) and additions with brackets ([]).

   4. True. Be sure that you omit and add words not to misrepresent the author but only to fit his or her words into your sentences. For example, suppose you want to quote from this sentence:

      "When *I* use a word," Humpty Dumpty said, in rather a scornful tone, "it means just what I choose it to mean—neither more nor less."

You might write one of the following:

As Humpty Dumpty says, "When *I* use a word, . . . it means just what I choose it to mean—neither more nor less."

Humpty Dumpty claims that in his use of a word "it means just what [he] choose[s] it to mean— neither more nor less."

5. Quotations are usually self-explanatory: you don't usually need to explain them.

5. False. Quotations should illustrate your points, not explain them for you. You need to do the explaining yourself, and you need to provide clear contexts for the quotations.

6. You may want to quote a passage when it expresses something dramatically or vividly, or when you want to lend authority to what you say.

6. True. If you're writing about the civil rights movement, for instance, you may well want to quote Martin Luther King's statements in support of your own. His "I Have a Dream" speech also makes vivid use of language.

7. Papers on literature often use more quotations than papers in the social or natural sciences.

7. True. In part the practice of incorporating more quotations is simply customary to the discipline. But in addition, the evidence for the

points you're making in a literary paper is the words of the text.

8. Paraphrasing simply requires changing a few words—then a passage is in your own words.

8. False—absolutely not! Paraphrasing requires more than just changing a word here and there—most of the words and also the sentence structure need to be your own. A good rule of thumb: as soon as you've written three words in a row that are identical with three consecutive words in your source, you're doing more than paraphrasing— you're quoting.

Now let's suppose that you're writing a paper on why people choose the names that they do, sometimes for their children, sometimes for themselves. You come across the following passage, in Studs Terkel's interview with Roberta Victor:

You never used your own name in hustling. I used a different name practically every week. If you got busted, it was more difficult for them to find out who you really were. The role one plays when hustling has nothing to do with who you are. It's only fitting and proper you take another name.

There were certain

names that were in great demand. Every second hustler had the name Kim or Tracy or Stacy and a couple others that were in vogue. These were all young women from seventeen to twenty-five, and we picked these very non-ethnic-oriented WASP names, rich names.

Let's suppose you've decided to paraphase parts of this passage.

Which of the following is an acceptable paraphrase?

1. Many prostitutes used the name Kim or Tracy or Stacy or others that were in vogue.

1. Unacceptable. Notice how close the wording is to that of the source: "the name Kim or Tracy or Stacy" and "others that were in vogue." The writer has not put the ideas into her own words. One technique is to turn the book over on your desk and then, without looking at the original wording, to write your own version.

2. Many prostitutes adopted upper-class names such as Stacy.

2. Acceptable. The statement uses ideas from the interview with Roberta Victor and mentions one of her examples, but the wording is different.

Sentence no. 2 is an acceptable paraphrase—but now let me ask another question. Does it need to be documented?

Of course it does. The ideas are clearly not your own. You need to acknowledge Studs Terkel's investigative research. You're also using one of the examples ("Stacy") that Roberta Victor mentions.

Thus, if you paraphrase Terkel and Victor's information, you need to give them credit. As with quoting, paraphrasing requires acknowledgment.

Suppose that you decide to quote from the passage to lend authority to your statement (Roberta Victor is probably more of an authority on hustling than you are) and to catch the flavor of her speech.

Which of the following phrases might you want to use?

A. "all young women from seventeen to twenty-five"
B. "very non-ethnic-oriented WASP names, rich names"
C. "certain names . . . were in great demand"

I would choose B. The other phrases give less of the flavor of her speech. B also makes a good supporting example. Quotations should usually support rather than replace your own statements—and thus C would not be a good choice, for it is a general statement, something that you should state in your own words.

Let's now go over the format for documenting your sources. I'll go over two common modes here: the Modern Language Association (MLA) format for papers in the humanities, and the American Psychological Association (APA) format for papers in the sciences.

According to both MLA and APA guidelines, you indicate the source of your information parenthetically within the text. The MLA would have you indicate the author and the page number, as in the following examples:

One critic claimed . . . (Grotjahn 40).

Grotjahn claimed . . . (40).

The APA would have you indicate the author and the date, as in the following:

One researcher (Grotjahn, 1947) found . . .

Grotjahn (1947) found . . .

Then at the end of the paper you should list the works you cite in your bibliography. The following are examples of bibliographic entries using MLA format:

Grotjahn, Martin. "About the Symbolization of Alice in Wonderland." *American Imago* 4 (1947): 32–41.

Maimon, Elaine, et al. *Writing in the Arts and Sciences.* Cambridge: Winthrop, 1981.

Terkel, Studs. "Roberta Victor." *Working: People Talk About What They Do All Day and How They Feel About What They Do.* New York: Pantheon, 1975. Rpt. in *The Nor-*

ton Reader: An Anthology of Expository Prose. Ed. Arthur M. Eastman, et al. 4th ed. New York: Norton, 1977. 580–89.

Using these examples as guides, write bibliographic entries for the following:

1. Warren Weaver's article entitled "Lewis Carroll, Mathematician," which appeared in *Scientific American* in 1956, volume number 194, on pages 116–28.

   Weaver, Warren. "Lewis Carroll, Mathematician." *Scientific American* 194 (1956): 116–28.

2. A novel called *A Wizard of Earthsea* by Ursula K. LeGuin, published in 1968 by Parnassus in Berkeley, California.

   LeGuin, Ursula K. *A Wizard of Earthsea.*BerkeleyParnassus,1968.

Now here are two examples using APA format:

Grotjahn, M. About the symbolization of Alice in Wonderland. *American Imago,* 1947, *4,* 32–41.

Maimon, E. P.; Belcher, G. L.; Hearɪ., G. W.; Nodine, B. F.; and O'Connor, F. W. *Writing in the Arts and Sciences,* Cambridge; Winthrop, 1981.

Using these examples as guides, write the Weaver and LeGuin entries according to the APA format.

Weaver, W. Lewis Carroll, mathematician. *Scientific American* 1956, *194,* 116–28.

LeGuin, U. K. *A wizard of Earthsea.* Berkeley: Parnassus, 1968.

CITING BORROWED MATERIAL

Katherine Burton

Author's Comment

Since students unversed in research often use the words of a source without acknowledgment when they have no intention of plagiarizing, I base an exercise on a single short passage which is before us all, preferably a passage with which we are all so familiar that even a single word from the source rings a bell in our minds. The students at first think that there is nothing new to be said about such a passage, but the range in their results shows them the infinite possibilities in paraphrase and comment.

Exercise

1. Hand out duplicated slips containing the last sentence of Lincoln's Gettysburg Address:

> It is rather for us to be here dedicated to the great task remaining before us—that from these honored dead we take increased devotion to that cause for which they gave the last full measure of devotion; that we here highly resolve that these dead shall not have died in vain; that this nation, under God, shall have a new birth of freedom; and that government of the people, by the people, for the people, shall not perish from the earth.

2. Discuss the importance of quoting exactly, checking back to the source, what paraphrasing is, etc. Read a loose paraphrase in class too quickly for the sample to stay fixed in the students' minds:

Lincoln concluded by pointing out the necessity of the dedication of the people rather than of the place. He reminded his
hearers that the dead whom they honored had given full final
devotion to a cause; the survivors should not do less, but should
resolve firmly that the freedom for which the soldiers had died
should be maintained in a people's government, a kind of
government—he implied—in danger of perishing unless saved
by firm resolution.

3. Ask students to write their own paraphrases with suitable
acknowledgment of Lincoln's contribution to what they produce.
Calling on various students to read their passages aloud will lead to as
much discussion as desired on whether certain points made in the
paraphrases are actually there in the original passage.

4. The isolation of particular points, using Lincoln's own words,
is relatively easy. The students may call them out in quick success-
ion instead of writing them down: "As Lincoln realized, the great
task still remained." This leads to the point that it may still be
necessary to acknowledge his paraphrasing even though a passage is
fairly far removed from the source. We paused for the class to write
samples:

Lincoln never forgot that the nation, much as it had accomplished by its own efforts in a terrible struggle, was still a
nation under God, that it should not be cocksure and irrelig-
ious, but even in its high idealism must remember that it was
only under God that its high hopes were to be fulfilled.

The conception of democratic government which Lincoln set
forth was of a people's government of, by, and for the people, as
his rhetorical phrases made so emphatic.

As Lincoln implied in the conclusion to his Gettysburg
Address, American democracy was the one great free government of the nineteenth century. If democracy failed here, it
perished from the whole earth, he said in his final words.

This section in which only part of the material in the passage is used
gives the teacher a chance to discuss relevancy as well as the
differences between "said" and "implied" (for instance) and the
whole matter of fairness to the source. But the teacher will have to
watch the clock to get through no. 5 in the first class hour.

5. Students should be asked next to make single points in their own words:

> As Lincoln points out, the dedication was not to be of the place, but of the people who came to view it.

> Lincoln knew well that the place would lose its importance if it didn't inspire the people.

> Lincoln set up the dead as an inspiration to the devotion of the people.

6. The preceding exercises have built up to assigning a completely independent comment on the passage to be done before the next class hour. If any quotation or paraphrase is used, it should be subordinated to thought of the students' own. Discussion of results led to the matter of being true to the spirit of the original. We talked about which was the better of the two following passages:

> Lincoln's turning of the dedication from the place to the people must have profoundly stirred his audience. Awed by the historic battlefield, they must have trembled to feel that the real importance was in themselves, not in the ground on which they stood. To use modern jargon, it was audience participation of a sort all the more thrilling because it was utterly unexpected, and Lincoln had proved himself a great master of ceremonies, all the greater in that he most certainly had no thought of himself as he stood there.

> Lincoln here seems to be attracted by the two themes of birth and death. He first dwells on the past, on those who died for their country; he presents the hopelessness of the feeling that perhaps they died in vain and implores the living to look to them and their actions for inspiration.Then he turns to birth, figuratively used, a new birth of freedom, a chance to start again, a new promise of hope for the country. Here is the goal to which the people may aspire. Death and the past, birth and the future—and those who are between them, in the present, must receive inspiration from the one and strive toward the other.

Comparison of the two passages brought up, incidentally, such questions as whether the speech was, in fact, well received, whether the war was over at the time the speech was made, what the occasion was, who was there (whether there had been special arrangements to bring relatives of those who had died there), etc. We didn't try to answer most of these questions, but left the matter at the general realization that to write even this short comment on a short familiar passage as well as possible would take some research, that it would easily grow into a miniature source theme, that most academic work does, and that this is why the source theme techniques are so much emphasized in English classes.

NOTE-TAKING FOR A DOCUMENTED PAPER

Mary B. Deaton

Author's Comment:

After instructions on the form of note cards—that recommended by the text in use or the instructor's preference—the following class exercise will provide practice and serve as basis for analysis of common problems.

Exercise:

The passage quoted below is from pages 104–106 of a book entitled *Lord Bacon and Sir Walter Raleigh*. The author's name is Macvey Napier. The book was published in Cambridge, England, by Macmillan and Company, in 1853.
1. Take a note for a paper which is to present the character of Sir Walter Raleigh.
2. Take a note for a paper on famous naval battles.
3. Make a note card for a theme on Sir Walter Raleigh's literary style.
4. Make a note card for a paper on Sir Richard Grenville.
5. Make a note card for a paper which is to discuss the literary style of the 1850s—assuming this passage to be a fair sample.
6. Make a bibliography card for the information provided on the source of the quotation.

> The mind dwells with satisfaction on such bright spots in
> Raleigh's ambitious and troubled career, where his native
> generosity, unobstructed by any adverse feeling, exerts itself in

acts entitling him to our approbation and esteem. He had another opportunity of showing the friendliness of his disposition, and his congenial admiration of superior merit, as well in arms as in letters, by the account which he published in 1591, of the sea-fight at the Azores, maintained for fifteen hours in a single ship, commanded by Admiral Sir Richard Grenville, against a Spanish fleet of fifty-three sail, manned with ten thousand men! His description of the action, in which the enemy's numerous fleet formed a circle around the ship of the heroic Admiral, who, pierced with mortal wounds, continued to fight her till her ammunition was exhausted, when he commanded the master-gunner, a kindred spirit, to sink her, 'that nothing might remain of glory or victory to the Spaniard'—and which command would have been obeyed but for the interference of the remainder of the mutilated crew— presents a view of perhaps the most astonishing naval conflict ever delineated. It is written with great clearness and vigour, and breathes a fervid spirit of loyalty and patriotism in its indignant reprobation of the conduct of Spain for her bloody and injurious designs, purposed and practiced against Christian princes, over all of 'whom she seeks unlawful and ungodly rule and empery.'

This article appeared originally in *Exercise Exchange* 9 (Apr. 1962), 20–21. Reprinted by permission of *Exercise Exchange,* Clarion University, Clarion, Pennsylvania 16214.

A NOTE ON NOTE CARDS AND NOTE-TAKING

Irwin Hashimoto

The more I teach writing and work with both successful faculty and student researchers, the more I am convinced that doing research is very much an individual process: what works well for one researcher often does not work well for another. Nowhere, in fact, is this more apparent than in the systems people use to collect information for their research projects. On my campus, researchers use a wide variety of methods and systems, ranging from making out note cards to writing in notebooks to scratching ideas on loose sheets of yellow paper to photocopying to sorting information in computer files. Yet curiously enough, although research paper textbooks acknowledge at least a few of these systems, they all advocate the use of note cards as the preferred system—in most cases the only system—students ought to use. This advice is narrow-minded and wrongheaded and ought to be modified to take into account individual differences in both researchers and their subject matter.

The actual system of using note cards is well known and generally well stated in textbooks. Students begin by copying their information (in paraphrase, summary, or direct quotation) on $3'' \times 5''$, $4'' \times 6''$, or $5'' \times 8''$ cards. They are generally cautioned to follow certain procedures. Someplace on the card, for instance, they should record title of source, author, and page number. They should also label each card according to subtopic. (Although these subtopics are often planned in advance in an outline, students can make them up as they do their reading.) Sometimes students are told to write on only one side of a card and to take notes in ink. Finally, perhaps most importantly, students are told to write only one idea on each card because cards with more than one idea do not sort well.

I have no doubt that the main reason that this note card system is advocated by all current research paper texts is teacher comfort. Of all systems of note-taking, the note card system is best for teachers. Teachers can spend a couple of class periods going over note card form so that when students turn in their notes, each set will be 4" × 6" and square on the corners. Because each card contains only one idea, teachers can use the number of cards students turn in as an index of student ideas and, hence, diligence. Teachers can also use note cards to discourage plagiarism. If a student is going to plagiarize, chances are he or she won't want to go through the grind of collecting decent note cards first. Finally, teachers can emphasize a logical and orderly research process which, if followed exactly in an ideal world, will lead inevitably to a logical, well-documented product.

While such a system is certainly a useful one for teachers, textbook writers have much difficulty justifying to students their choice of a note card system over other note-taking systems. Edward Bailey, Jr., Philip Powell, and Jack Shuttleworth, for instance, emphasize that taking notes on cards forces students to become "actively involved" and helps them to remember small details.[1] Marsha Cummins and Carole Slade suggest that taking notes on cards is "the best means of learning and organizing other people's ideas for yourself."[2] But there is no reason to believe that taking notes on cards is any more active than taking notes in notebooks or on loose sheets of paper. Indeed, students who take voluminous notes in their notebooks and take notes on their notes or students who write voluminous comments in the margins of photocopies may, in fact, be engaging in a much more active, discriminating process than those who simply record information on cards and stack them in decks.

Stephen Weidenborner and Domenick Caruso suggest that the limited size of note cards encourages students to be concise and economical in their note-taking.[3] But I do not see why cards force students to be concise and economical. Indeed, some authors, such as Audrey Roth, suggest just the opposite:

> If you are ever in doubt about whether to record information or
> to ignore it, better write it down. Should you discover later that
> you have more information than you need, you can cut down
> the quantity. But once you begin writing your paper and
> discover you are short of material, you face a problem that is
> difficult to overcome.[4]

And I would think that faced with a choice of being economical and precise (Weidenborner and Caruso) or overly complete (Roth), students will often opt for abundance—abundance in both size and quantity of notes. I recall that the last time I seriously tried a note card system, I had to staple two and three cards together, but I still got plenty of information on my cards.

Ellen Strenski and Madge Manfred suggest that note cards can help keep students from turning in papers that look like one long string of quotations or paraphrases.[5] But I don't see how *any* note-taking system can stop students from stringing quotations and paraphrases together if they have never learned how to write papers or how to use evidence to support their generalizations.

William Coyle suggests that "like most professional scholars, college students generally find that material can be recorded most efficiently on cards."[6] But, again, I see no reason to believe such a statement. In fact, in a recent survey of faculty members at the university where I teach, only 20 percent of the faculty reported that they regularly used note cards for their scholarly research, whereas 43 percent reported that they regularly used loose sheets of paper to take notes for their professional writing, and 28 percent reported that they regularly used notebooks of different sizes and shapes.[7] Furthermore, as a director of a university writing center, I see many students who are working on research papers, but in over five years—except for composition students—I have yet to see one note card in the hands of a student writing a research paper.

Finally, writers of research paper texts almost invariably emphasize the *flexibility* of note cards. With one note on a card, students can mix cards up, deal them out into little heaps, flip them up one at a time across the top of their desks. In one of the more interesting statements of this belief, Coyle writes:

> Notes taken in a notebook are frozen in a single order and are difficult to organize. You will find yourself following one source too closely or overlooking important points. Many a student in desperation has taken shears and clipped notebook pages into slips so that they could be arranged in sequence. The height, or depth, of inefficiency is to take notes in a bound notebook and write on both sides of the page. Even shears are of no avail in this dilemma, except for *hara-kiri.*[8]

For some reason, Coyle as well as James Lester[9] and Joyce Inglish and Joan Jackson[10] and Anthony Winkler and Jo Ray McCuen[11] and every other writer of research paper texts on my shelf considers this shuffle-ability as an asset, although I am not sure why.

One drawback in shuffling cards is that once students have shuffled their cards, they have difficulty reconstructing individual authors' ideas and arguments without going back to original sources. In some cases, students must stack their cards by author and source and then order each stack to reconstruct an author's argument. Another difficulty is that in order to shuffle stacks of cards, students must have clear labels or categories for their cards, but categorizing and labeling are difficult tasks. The chairman of our Anthropology Department remarked to me the other day that note-taking on cards was particularly difficult for him because in order to take organized notes, he had to make choices of categories of information he would take notes on and that very often categories that at one time seemed relevant or clear-cut lost relevance and precision as he gained more and more control over his subject matter. Consequently, sorting his cards became a major, difficult undertaking because the labels he initially used often did not help him gain later control over the information in his cards.

Although as we have seen there are a few inadequate reasons for prescribing for students a note card system for taking notes, there are several other persuasive reasons for *not* using note cards. First, on the practical side, note cards can be a messy system. One researcher I talked to in history pointed out that note cards are all right for small projects, but he could easily get buried in note cards. At one idea per card, it would be possible for him to use up a couple of hundred cards on one good source. At that rate, with ten good sources, it might be possible to generate over a thousand cards—each of which would have to be labeled and organized into useful categories. Furthermore, one thousand note cards at three-fourths of an inch per hundred amounts to a stack seven and one-half inches high weighing about three pounds. To try to shuffle through such a stack to find one idea (one card), even with clear categories, might be an entire afternoon's project.

Second, although writers stress that students should take short, concise notes and that these notes should be taken only after students have thoroughly read an article or chapter, understanding is not always a one-shot step in some kind of linear research process. Many researchers return to important texts over and over again—each time bringing new awarenesses that affect the meanings they get out of these texts. Consequently, notes taken at one time may not be useful upon rereading. Short, concise notes may even be *less* useful because in order to reread efficiently, readers often need a great deal of context and large chunks or original text. A very successful researcher in Russian history down the hall from me uses note cards but only as a *second* step in a research system that is far from economical:

> I type voluminous notes—a habit that probably developed because so many of the sources I use are hard to get and I will probably never see them again. If a typewriter is not available, I use the bound notebooks. Notecards only come in during the final stages—when I have a pretty good idea what I am going to write and can set up particular sub-topics. I can go back through my original notes and type the material I know I am going to use onto note cards, topically arranged, so that when I write, I work from the note cards, not the original notes.[12]

Another historian in the same department has a related system. He uses full sheets to transcribe or paste up primary sources and documents and uses half sheets to collect information from secondary sources. He claims that such a system allows him to keep track of different kinds of information that he can refer to over and over again as he writes his papers.

Third, the note card system does not store well. Other systems of note-taking—for instance, hardcover notebooks—have a permanence note cards cannot approach. Such notebooks can be filled up, indexed, and put on bookshelves for future reference. Note cards get stuffed in drawers where the rubber bands holding them together eventually get brittle and fall off.

Fourth, and most important, there are many cases where the note card system is not the only viable system students can use. Students who like to take notes and store them for rereading may find a spiral notebook with dividers and index more practical than a note card system. Students who find they need to put more than one idea on a page or find they do not need to shuffle their notes and deal them out into stacks may feel more comfortable and be more efficient taking notes on loose sheets of paper and either filing them in manila folders or storing them in loose-leaf or three-ring notebooks under various subject headings. (Such notebooks also often have pockets which students can use to store odd-shaped notes or miscellaneous handouts.) Students who discover that their papers hinge on three or four seminal articles may find they will do much better if they photocopy those articles and make clear notes in the margins of their copies. And students who find they are careless or who find they cannot trust their handwriting or typing may find they can be much more precise researchers if they photocopy everything in sight, put their photocopies in folders, and carefully index their folders for future reference.

Indeed, what I want to suggest as a conclusion is that teachers of research paper writing cannot simply prescribe one all-purpose note-taking system for their students. There *is* no such system. In order to write this paper, if I accept the advice of research paper texts, I should begin with a little stack of note cards, shuffled and organized, and a clean desk top—with no stacks of papers, no open textbooks, no loose notes hanging off the corner of the desk. But things aren't that efficient. As I write this paper, I have a stack of comments written by faculty in response to a note-taking questionnaire, fourteen research paper textbooks (with markers in their pages and comments in their margins), two dittoed sheets given to me by a history teacher describing the "scientific method" and the "artistic" method of research in history, and a short stack of notes (loose sheets of various sizes) that I have made periodically over the last five or six days. And as I think back on the work of my colleagues (one of whom has not seen the top of his desk clear of loose papers in over five years), I am convinced that we cannot adequately deal with note-taking skills or any other research skills unless we help students to recognize not ideal systems but systems that researchers actually use—different systems and different methods each with advantages and disadvantages, each appropriate for different projects, different subject matters, and different writers.

NOTES

1. Edward P. Bailey, Jr., Philip A. Powell, and Jack M. Shuttleworth, *Writing Research Papers: A Practical Guide* (New York: Holt, Rinehart and Winston, 1981), 52.
2. Marsha H. Cummins and Carole Slade, *Writing the Research Paper: A Guide and Sourcebook* (Boston: Houghton Mifflin, 1979), 56.
3. Stephen Weidenborner and Domenick Caruso, *Writing Research Papers: A Guide to the Process* (New York: St. Martin's Press, 1982), 73.
4. Audrey J. Roth, *The Research Paper: Process, Form, and Content*, 4th ed. (Belmont, Calif.: Wadsworth, 1982), 93.
5. Ellen Strenski and Madge Manfred, *The Research Paper Workbook* (New York: Longman, 1981), 135.
6. William Coyle, *Research Papers*, 5th ed. (Indianapolis: Bobbs-Merrill, 1980), 58.
7. These figures are based on questionnaires returned by 77 percent of the faculty at Idaho State University, spring semester, 1982.
8. Coyle, 58.
9. James D. Lester, *Writing Research Papers: A Complete Guide*, 3rd ed. (Glenview, Ill.: Scott, Foresman, 1980), 42.
10. Joyce Inglish and Joan E. Jackson, *Research and Composition: A Guide for the Beginning Researcher* (Englewood Cliffs, N.J.: Prentice-Hall, 1977), 34.
11. Anthony C. Winkler and Jo Ray McCuen, *Writing the Research Paper: A Handbook* (New York: Harcourt Brace Jovanovich, 1979), 83.
12. Personal correspondence.

A FOLLOW-UP THEME ON THE RESEARCH PAPER

Elmer F. Suderman

Author's Comment:

The following exercise takes advantage of the students' acquaintance with a considerable body of material with which they have worked extensively, usually for at least three weeks. Thus they have at their command, or should have, specific and concrete material rather than the vague impressions they too frequently rely upon. If they have opinions, they need not now remain unsupported.

The exercise can be used in a number of ways. I have used it for an in-class theme, but it should work as well or even better for an out-of-class theme. It could, in fact, be given to the students before or while they are working on the research paper to alert them to important goals of a research project. The questions are extensive enough that they could serve for two or more papers after the research paper has been completed. Indeed, question 2 alone would be sufficient for a single paper, as would a combination of questions 3 and 4. One advantage of assigning more than one follow-up paper on the research theme is the obvious one that such a procedure requires that the research paper be completed early enough that both teacher and students have a better opportunity to evaluate the work.

Two final comments: This paper often reveals with startling clarity which students have borrowed another's research paper or have depended too heavily upon their sources without reflecting on the material. Students who have done their homework thoroughly often write better on the follow-up than they did on the term paper itself.

Exercise:

Analyze your experience in writing the research paper. Avoid the vague and general statements that would apply to any term paper. For example, any student begins by choosing a subject and going to the library to consult the standard bibliographies. Consider what distinguished your experience from others rather than what it had in common with others. Be critical of your experience. While you will not be able to discuss all of the following questions, they should serve as a guide in writing the paper. Since you will want to develop a controlling idea so that your paper will be unified and coherent, you may wish to emphasize only a few of these points, but the controlling idea should subsume as many of the questions as possible.

1. What unique resources did you use to collect your bibliography?
2. What steps did you take to limit your paper so that it became tractable? Examine the success you had in limiting your paper.
3. How did you arrive at a thesis? What theses did you discard before you finally settled on the final choice?
4. Did you overcome any specific problems in outlining the paper? How did the thesis affect the principle of division you used in the organizational pattern? Did you reject any other principles of division? Why?
5. To what extent were you able to cover and master the subject you chose? What obstacles interfered with your mastery of the topic?
6. Was your choice of subject a wise one? Were you satisfied with your topic or would you now choose a different one?
7. After you had completed the first draft of the paper, what specific steps did you take to rewrite it? Did you substantially reorganize the paper after you had written the rough draft? In what ways?
8. If you find conflicting or contradictory views on your topic, how did you evaluate the conflicting statements?
9. How would you rewrite the paper now if you had the opportunity? [Here again is a topic that would do for a single theme. One could well ask the students to rewrite the theme,

eliminating or simplifying the footnotes, using a different principle of organization or a different point of view.]

10. If you were asked to spend the next three weeks continuing the research on your topic, how would you proceed?

This article was originally published in *Exercise Exchange* 13 (Mar. 1966), 19–21. Reprinted with permission.

BIBLIOGRAPHY: MODEL COURSES, UNITS, AND APPROACHES TO SPECIFIC PROBLEMS

Baskett, Sam S, "*1984* and the Term Reports," *College English* 18 (Nov. 1956), 99–101. Discusses the positive effect reading and discussing Orwell's *1984* had upon the quality of students' research papers. Attributes the freshness of the research to modeling of significant questions about *1984* during preceding class discussions.

Bjaaland, Patricia C., and Arthur Lederman. "The Detection of Plagiarism," *Educational Forum* 37 (Jan. 1973), 201–206. Categorizes and thoroughly analyzes signals of plagiarism, including such seemingly innocuous items as changes in title, unusually neat and well-typed manuscripts, and long bibliographies. Suggests countermeasures.

Bleifuss, William W. "Introducing the Research Paper Through Literature," *College English* 14 (Apr. 1953), 401–403. Suggests that if it is analyzed not only literarily but also for its social comment, literature may be used to help a student decide on a topic which lends itself to a short research paper.

Brenner, Catherine A. "Teaching the Research to ESL Students in American Colleges and Universities," M.A. thesis, School for International Training, 1989 (ERIC ED 311714). Outlines challenges to ESL students and offers a collaborative approach to six steps in the development and writing of research papers.

Cook, Robert I., and Paul McElhiney. "The Audiovisual Term Report." *Audio Visual Instruction* 12 (Sept. 1967), 697–698. Discusses introduction of the assignment, selection of the topic, investigation of the field, permission to photograph, organization of the materials, and presentation hints in this proposal of a plagiarism-avoiding slide presentation as an alternative to the traditional research paper.

Culbertson, Barbara. "Media Report Versus Written Report," *Educational Technology* 11 (Oct. 1971), 62. Suggests that teachers utilize available visual and auditory technology for student presentations of research, instead of insisting on the traditional written term paper.

Davis, William E., and George F. Estey. "Research and Writing by Student Groups—Difficult but Rewarding," *College Composition and Communication* 28 (May 1977), 204–206. Describes changes in Boston University's interdisciplinary fifty-page group-written sophomore research paper, its strengths and weaknesses.

England, Kenneth M. "The Use of Literature in the Freshman Research Paper," *College English* 18 (Apr. 1957), 367–368. Argues for the *literary* research paper, requiring that students' library papers cover recurring themes in four novels by a given novelist.

Fuchs, Gaynell M. "Mona Lisa Writes a Letter: An Alternative to the Research Paper" (ERIC ED 282194). Students research to assume the identity of a woman in an art work to look at the idea of feminine beauty through time and space.

Gibb, Carson. "Reporting and Exposition," *English Journal* 60 (Feb. 1971), 251–254, 259. Differentiates among reporting primary sources, reporting secondary sources, and exposition.

Grasso, Mary Ellen. "The Research Paper: Life Centered," *College English* 40 (Sept. 1978), 83–89. For the first month of the semester Grasso begins her community college classes with her own "trivia" presentations. These evolve into student participation and a "life-centered" research paper which she maintains answers all objections raised to the research paper.

Hipple, Theodore W. "Politics and English: Presidential Election Offers Unusual Classroom Experience," *Clearing House* 47 (Sept. 1972), 12–14. Describes a research assignment to cover some phase of the (then) upcoming presidential election, from its introductory interest-the-student phase through the finished product.

Kerr, Elizabeth M. "The Research Paper as a Class Enterprise," *College English* 13 (Jan. 1952), 204–208. By involving all class members in researching different topics of the same general subject, class interest was generated, teacher load was decreased, each student gained a great scope of the research subject, and the quality of research improved.

Laban, Lawrence F. "One Model for Teaching Research Skills," *Exercise Exchange* 21 (Spring 1977), 16–19. A staged program to resolve the form-versus-content problem: 1) evaluation of a book the student reacted strongly to; 2) comparison of two articles on the same subject by different authors; 3) comparison of two points of view in four or five articles; 4) the full research project. First three steps build skills in paraphrasing, summarizing, evaluating, collecting, and synthesizing evidence.

Larmouth, Donald Wilford. "Life Around Us: Design for a Community Research Component in English Composition Courses," *College Composition and Communication* 23 (Dec. 1972), 383–389. Advocates student research in current community problems as a means of enlivening the teaching of research skills and allowing students to contribute their solutions to current community concerns.

Lawson, Anita S. "Teaching Research as a Reading Skill" (ERIC ED 175033). Emphasis may be placed as much on reading-comprehension skills as writing skills by requiring students to research corroboration for statements made in textbooks.

Malloch, A. E. "A Dialogue on Plagiarism," *College English* 38 (Oct. 1975), 165–174. Objects to plagiarism "because it is a form of lie, and [therefore] violates the compact that is built into all speech, [and] amounts to a rejection of the very basis of academic instruction, the compact of discourse between students and instructor." Therefore, plagiarists should be considered as having withdrawn from the course.

Marshall, Colleen. "A System for Teaching College Freshmen to Write a Research Paper," *College English* 40 (Sept. 1978), 87–89; comment by Martha A. Fischer. Counters the disappointments of teaching research papers by a sequential approach: teaching basic reading skills, selection of universal topics—family, work, education—and posing the thesis as a question in very personal terms. Students then answer this question in an undocumented opinion paper, revise it, list the implicit questions and findings, and, finally, research and write up their findings. Fischer suggests that "the stimulation of other views" in small groups during Marshall's latter steps will help solve logical problems and encourage openness to opposing ideas.

Morrill, A. Reed. "Evaluating Term Papers," *Improving College and University Teaching* 14 (Summer 1966), 181–182. Improves students' performance by distributing a detailed, easily comprehended evaluation scale early in the semester.

Murray, Michael. "A Term Paper Alternative," *Clearing House* 45 (Mar. 1971), 447–448. Claims to maintain a "high involvement level" in a long research assignment by pairing novels and plays by theme, style, or characters and limiting each student's practice in documentation and analysis to one of the pairs.

Parrish, Beryl Margaret. "The Study of Trade Names: A Research Project," *Exercise Exchange* 7 (Dec. 1959), 5–6. Allows freshman composition students to discover the "living, growing" aspect of language by requiring them to go to both primary and secondary sources in the historical development of trade names.

Proctor, Betty Jane. "The Freshman Research Paper: A Comparative Approach to Biography," *Exercise Exchange* 24 (Fall 1979), 1, 14–15. Attacks the problem of critical reading deficiencies as well as the wide-focus term paper by having students compare two biographies of the same person. This comparison becomes the raw material of a five- to seven-page paper searching for "the truth about a single incident in the historical figure's life."

Ralph, Ruth S. "The First Six Weeks Research Paper Scheme," *Teaching English in the Two-Year College* 4 (Fall 1977), 33–36. Introduces a once-a-week, three-hour class to freshman English with an armful of magazines. Reading in these magazines initiates a five-page research paper over the next six weeks. Thus the major hurdle of the course has been surmounted early in the semester when the students have plenty of enthusiasm.

Rodrigues, Raymond J. "Informal Research in the Methods Class: Toward Independent Investigators and Teachers," *English Education* 10 (Feb. 1979), 163–170. Demonstrates an informal research project which has student teachers research contemporary word usage.

Saalbach, Robert Palmer. "Critical Thinking and the Problem of Plagiarism," *College Composition and Communication* 21 (Feb. 1970), 45–47. Students plagiarize because of uncritical immaturity. Teachers should encourage maturity by assigning controversial subjects with which students may agree or disagree on the basis of their own experience.

Samuels, Marilyn Schauer. "A Mini-Course in the Research Paper," *College English* 38 (Oct. 1976), 189–193. Enthusiastically outlines CCNY's videotaped between-session mini-course in the research paper, intended to meet the needs of poorly prepared college students while easing the demands on students and teachers of freshman composition.

Soll, Lila. "Writing an Original Research Paper Involves an Ability to Perform" (ERIC ED 140331). Written for teachers in Open Admissions schools. Delineates two assignments to build rapidly analysis, interpretation, synthesis, abstraction, and organization skills.

Steinmetz, Lee. "The Freshman Research Paper: A Classroom Approach," *College English* 21 (Oct. 1959), 24–26. Suggests teachers can help with much of the groundwork for a literary analysis research paper by assigning four novels by the same author, then requiring four short papers on subjects from the novels using traditional patterns of development.

Stewart, Marian F. "The First Footnote Paper," *College English* 14 (Apr. 1953), 403–405. Leads up to a major research paper by offering helpful comments on writing a "thousand-word footnote paper" analyzing discrepancies between reviews of a popular novel.

Suderman, Elmer F. "A Term Paper on New Words," *Exercise Exchange,* 16 (Summer/Fall 1969), 15–16; reprinted in Littleton Long, ed., *Writing Exercises from Exercise Exchange* (Urbana, Ill.: NCTE, 1976), 132–134. Term paper project in which new words are cited and analyzed by each student according to the words' origins, methods of creation, and quality contributed to the American language.

Swales, John. "Utilizing the Literatures in Teaching the Research Paper," *TESOL Quarterly* 21 (Mar. 1987), 41–68. Teaching of research English in groups based on sociology of science, citation analysis, technical writing, and English for academic purposes.

Taylor, Louis. "Experiment in Freshman Research Writing," *College English* 18 (Apr. 1957), 368–369. Discusses positive aspects of organizing students into committees, each committee headed by a student advisor, for the purpose of assisting each student in writing a creditable research paper.

"Term Paper Companies and the Constitution," *Duke Law Journal* (Jan. 1973), 1273–1317. Complete coverage of the legal issues, concluding that the First Amendment stricture against "prior restraint" rules out legislation against term paper companies. Best remedy may be academic reaction: formal codifying and announcing of sanctions against term paper plagiarists.

Thilsted, Wanda M. "An Interdisciplinary Report Writing Course," *Technical Writing Teacher* 2 (Spring 1975), 1–3. Attempts to motivate students in report writing by combining disciplines, the major subject instructors advising students in their subject choice and source work and the English faculty advising the students in writing.

Waltman, John L. "Plagiarism: (II) Preventing It in Formal Research Reports," *ABCA Bulletin* 43 (June 1980), 37–38. Suggests such "unobtrusive safeguards" against plagiarism as strict control of topics, formal research proposal, requiring recent periodical sources, collecting research materials, including drafts, and an unannounced in-class description of the paper.

Wells, David M. "A Program for the Freshman Research Paper," *College Composition and Communication* 28 (Oct. 1977), 383–384. Describes a strictly supervised teacher-assigned, teacher-directed literary topic two-week 900- to 1,000-word research paper. Follows a time schedule precisely and finishes with an unusual evaluation procedure in the library.

Whittaker, Della A. "From Term Paper to Brochure," *Teaching English in the Two-Year College* 59 (Fall 1978), 45–46. Technical writing students use the time after turning in term papers to produce brochures on their term paper topics.

ABOUT THE EDITOR

James E. Ford (B.A., Brigham Young University; M.A., San Francisco State University; Ph.D., The University of Chicago) is Associate Professor of English at the University of Nebraska–Lincoln. In addition to courses in the history and theory of criticism, he has taught research methods and research writing on the undergraduate and graduate levels. His several articles on research paper instruction in such journals as *College English* and *College Composition and Communication* include the first comprehensive bibliography on the subject, and he organized the first session on research paper instruction at an MLA convention. He has conducted workshops on research paper instruction for teachers and librarians based on the research strategy model which is reprinted in this volume and which forms the basis for a research paper general education requirement at the nation's largest private university, Brigham Young.